The Poem in the Story

The Poem in the Story

Music, Poetry, and Narrative

Harold Scheub

The University of Wisconsin Press

The University of Wisconsin Press
1930 Monroe Street
Madison, Wisconsin 53711

www.wisc.edu/wisconsinpress/

3 Henrietta Street
London WC2E 8LU, England

1 3 5 4 2

Printed in the United States of America

The photographs on pages xvi and 96 reproduced courtesy of Special Collections,
University of Cape Town Libraries, University of Cape Town, South Africa

Library of Congress Cataloging-in-Publication Data
Scheub, Harold.
The poem in the story : music, poetry, and narrative / Harold Scheub.
pp. cm.
Includes bibliographical references and index.
ISBN 0-299-18210-X (cloth : alk. paper)
ISBN 0-299-18214-2 (paper : alk. paper)
1. Tales—South Africa—History and criticism. 2. Oral tradition—South Africa.
3. Folk music, African. 4. Folk poetry, African.
I. Title.
GR359 .S337 2002
398.2'0968—dc21 2002004454

Though we can never recover the myth as it stood in the mind of its creator, we can re-create it in our own minds.

—Frederick Clarke Prescott, *Poetry and Myth*

There is never an end to stories.

—Nongenile Masithathu Zenani, a Xhosa storyteller, November 17, 1975

Contents

Illustrations

Preface

The storyteller never forgets the music.

Many of us, when we tell stories, when we hear stories, look for lessons—obvious and simple Aesop's fable–type morals. But stories are not preachments, didacticisms. They are moral, but they are not morals.[1] It is only nervous observers who give the stories such foolish contexts. What they are is music, song, dance. The moral, or message, or meaning of a story is not what is so obviously basking on its surface. Too often, when we think of story, we want to convert the story to what we think is history; we want to flatten it out, to see only its linear surface, and we miss the curvature of the story. We become hopelessly snarled in the linearity of the story, and in the process we lose the true meaning. Then we go about tagging everything in the story as if we were identifying the parts of a cadaver. By the time we are finished, the story is indeed a cadaver. We have exhaustively identified everything; we have explored the parts. In the process, we have destroyed the story. Stories are much more complex, much more vital. Lessons, morals, and meanings are deeply entwined in human emotions, which is where meaning can be found, as well as wisdom and catharsis.

"And now for a story . . . ": Time collapses, and we are in the presence of history; it is a time of masks. Reality, the present, is here, but with these explosive, emotional images giving it a context. This is the storyteller's art: to mask the past, making it mysterious and seemingly inaccessible. But it is inaccessible only to our present intellect: it is always available to our hearts, our emotions. Story provides a space for real-life experiences. It gives those experiences a sense of theater. But that alone does not provide release, catharsis, and consummation. The narratives of past events never occur in isolation. The stories we tell of present events occur within a wider context. There is always the sense of the familiar about stories, the sense that we have been there before. That recognition, that resonance that we experience when we hear stories is the poem in the story, the ancient past forming, shaping, commenting upon our real-life experiences. Story is a contextualization of our lives into the wider world and into the past. When we tell stories, we are always living the present by reliving the past: that is the way we make sense of our world. The experience of storytelling is precisely that juncture of present and past, when the two come into emotional union. That does not mean that the experience, the story, of the present is thereby assuaged, life wiped clean. Rather, storytelling provides context, not closure. This is our rekindling, our purgation. Two stories—an experience from the present, and a fragment from the past—merge into metaphor, and are borne on the wings of the hearts of the teller and the hearer. The past has never been frozen in time. It has always been a restless repository of images, the flotsam and jetsam of human existence brought to life in contemporary times by storytellers who have designs of their own. So it is that history is always revisionist history. Story does not provide an index to the past in the sense that the past can be perfectly reconstructed as it happened—as Ryunosuke Akutagawa reveals in his story, "In a Grove."[2] So story is not history. It is, rather, restorative, reforming, reshaping, a way of seeing and feeling. Faulkner said, "The poet's voice need not merely be the record of man, it can be one of the props, the pillars to help him endure and prevail."[3]

Fact and fiction meet at the boundaries, in the liminal area, the betwixt and between, which is where transformations always occur. That is the area of ambiguity, where coalescence occurs, where fiction becomes truth and fact is endowed with meaning. Story begins where ambiguity, irony, metaphor—in that order—join forces. This is where history, autobiography, reality merge with fantasy, fiction, fabrication. That is the area of irony, the area where living metaphor occurs, as fact and fiction come into analogical alignment, an orientation that is constructed not of words, but of feelings—those of the audience, those of the storyteller. The storyteller works the very feelings of the audience into metaphor, into story, into meaning. At the blurred edges where the one comes into contact with the other, all becomes ambiguous, and then the real has an ironic relationship with the fictional world. The result, metaphor, occurs as story develops, and so our real experience is given a new form. That is how our real-life experience is given meaning, given context. It is the story's curvature that seduces an audience. Through the ambiguity and irony that are at the heart of all good stories, we become an active part of metaphor, and this occurs whether we are sitting around a hearth fire or before the glowing screen of the internet. Above all, what story must do is make us a part of it. Its power is what the story does to us emotionally through its music. Music is the meaning of the story. It is when the storyteller touches the heart of the story, touches his heart, touches the hearts

Storyteller

of the audience that story comes to life and does its work. It is when metaphor is defined as a living activity involving the emotions of the storyteller and those of the members of the audience—when the audience becomes an active part of metaphor—that story comes to life and has its effect. All is theater, all is irony, all is truth.

At the heart of the story is a device that evokes emotion. If the story lacks that inner spark, it is not really a story, and has no power. That device enables the real and the fantasy, present and past, to come into union. This musical center of the story is its mythic origin, a shard of myth that invests every effective story with its meaning. We attach our story to the big story, the mythic story. There is an aura in story that has its genesis in the ancient myths that give our lives their ultimate meaning. The myths—ancient, distant, even long forgotten—emerge in holographic ways; they are shining particles, potent remnants that continue to order, organize, shape, and form our experiences. Our stories take their shape from the origin myths; they take their meanings from primal acts, from the earliest shaping of the world. We never escape those myths; the stories that we tell today, fiction or truth, occur within the context of the myths. Do we literally believe in the myths? As a storyteller once told me, stories, myths, are not true, they are a way of getting at truth.

Arriving for a storytelling performance

An American television producer contemplated his success. "The formula is simple," he wrote, "and it's reduced to four words every kid in the world knows: Tell me a story. It's that easy."[4] Well, maybe not quite that easy. Speaking of one petitioner appearing before South Africa's Truth Commission, a supplicator who failed in his quest, an observer wrote, "It was a pity—and an irony—that George Dube, the victim in question, failed to seize the dramatic moment afforded by the present occasion. The man simply couldn't tell a story."[5]

Storytellers would agree with Sallustius, the fourth century Neoplatonist writer, who observed, "these things never happened, but always are."[6] We who talk about stories will fret and strut our hour upon the stage, then be heard no more. But the stories—they will live on. Some of them, those that touch us in our deepest places, they will live on forever. Story is the way we remember. "Time," Henry David Thoreau wrote, "is but the stream I go a-fishing in. I drink at it; but while I drink I see the sandy bottom and detect how shallow it is. Its thin current slides away, but eternity remains. I would drink deeper; fish in the sky, whose bottom is pebbly with stars."[7]

The storyteller knows that eternity, the storyteller fishes in that sky.

At the Heart of Every Story Is a Poem . . .

THIS IS THE STORY . . .

Díä!kwąin, a San storyteller, relates the story of |nųĭn|kúï-tęn, a magician and rainmaker who had the ability to transform himself into a lion.[8] When he did so, however, he would go about only at night because he was afraid that people would shoot at him and cause him to kill someone in self-defense. Once while on such a magical expedition, moving about as a lion, he killed the ox of an Afrikaner. The Afrikaner raised a commando against him, and |nųĭn|kúï-tęn was shot. He told Díä!kwąin's father, χāä-ttĭn̈, that he was about to die, but that he first wanted to teach him the secrets of his magic. "At another time Father must sing the songs which he had taught Father, then Father must sing about him." And so χāä-ttĭn̈ did sing the songs, one of them a lament, sorrowful because "the string is broken," the "ringing sound in the sky" was no longer heard by the singer as it had been heard when the magician was still alive. The string had been broken, said Díä!kwąin, because "that string was what he used to hear, when |nųĭn|kúï-tęn had called forth the Rain-bull. That was why things were not like they had formerly been."[9]

. . . AND THIS IS THE POEM IN THE STORY . . .

People were those who
Broke for me the string.
Therefore,
The place became like this to me,
On account of it,
Because the string was that which broke for me.
Therefore,
The place does not feel to me,
As the place used to feel to me,
On account of it.
For,

Día!kwąin

The place feels as if it stood open before me,
Because the string has broken for me.
Therefore,
The place does not feel pleasant to me,
On account of it.[10]

Pages from a Journal

A DANCE AND A TRANSFORMATION

Teenagers are preparing for one of the signal transformations in their lives, the puberty ritual. As they prepare for this chapter in their life stories, they organize their feelings of anticipation and dawning identities with song—the poem in their story.[11]

August 15, 1967

It is one o'clock in the afternoon, in front of the shop belonging to Patrick Magadla in Jengca, Tsolo District, the Transkei, in South Africa.[12] The shop is situated in the valley between mountain ranges, a magnificent area. A number of Mpondomise children and teenagers engage in a spirited dance and song; dancing accompanies the *amaqaba* song.[13] The participants, about thirty of them, stand in an irregular line, the boys together, the girls together. The boys kneel during one section of the song, beating the ground with the sticks that they carry. The boys move in a circle (they finally get a large truck tire and move around that), the girls standing to one side, dancing in place, often clapping. At times, one or more girls will step from the group and execute a few dance steps, then rejoin the group. The boys carry sticks, waving them in the air. One of the boys is the leader of the boys, and a girl takes the leadership of the girls. During the songs that follow, the boys make heavy breathy sounds as they move in a circle, brandishing their sticks, and the girls make deep, throaty bass sounds. The boys, most of them, wear white capes; the girls are in red capes, wearing numerous leg and arm bracelets. The audience consists of about fifteen men, ten women, and a number of children who are not participating in the singing—all are Mpondomise.

They dance in an asymmetric line that weaves among a number of large discarded tires. There is a brief introductory song, sung purely by the girls, about a movement away from home. Then the clapping starts, a pulsating and very rapid beat that continues throughout the performance. The boys continue making their deep, sensuous breathing sound, and the girls counterpoint this with their melodic and very, very deep, throaty sound. From time to time, a member of the audience will musically counterpoint this: "Ho! Ho! Ho!" All the while, the teenagers dance—a love song almost wholly composed of sounds made by the human voices.

Mpondomise dancers

July 15, 1975

Earlier today I attended a dance of traditional doctors. The doctors dance in a circle in the center of a rondavel, spectators sitting around the walls—a single file circle of doctors, moving, singing together. Then they stop, and one of the doctors makes various comments and observations, while the others say, *"Camagu!"* and *"Chos'!"* after each such comment.[14] Then the circular dancing goes on again, until once more it is interrupted by one of the doctors-dancers with a series of observations.

The Poem in the Story

Prelude

> The aesthetic attitude is that of feeling embodied in "form."
> —Bernard Bosanquet, *Three Lectures on Aesthetic*[15]

Storytelling involves more than a linear movement from conflict to resolution. It does include that linear movement—necessarily, for there can be no story without it. But what makes a story artistically engaging and emotionally evocative is the poem in the story. Every story has such a poem: at its heart, a metaphorical center that is alive and compelling. In the end, it is not the explicit shallow maxim that is the significant and memorable aspect of story: meaning is more complex, more lyrical. All parts of the story rhythmically move the members of the audience—whether that audience be responding to an oral or a literary narrative—to that molten nave where the emotions evoked by the images that have been craftily, guilefully devised by the storyteller are arranged, organized, and worked into vessels of form. It is those formal experiences, alive with contained emotions of members of the audience, that are the reason audiences keep coming back to story.

Dance is a part of storytelling, music is the essence of storytelling: it is not possible to divorce stories and their tellers from dances and their dancers, from music and its musicians. There is a melodic line in storytelling that is memorable, suspenseful, and that effectively claims the attention of the members of the audience. But there is something more, another kind of rhythm, a pulse that subverts the melodic line, incorporating it as it simultaneously fragments it, then reorganizing it into a more intricate set of sounds composed of words, but going beyond the lexical, denotative content of those words. It touches an audience not in the intellect but the imagination. It is forged of emotions that take thought and recreate it into a textured experience, the weave shaped by words, yes, but more importantly composed of the feelings evoked by those words and of the images that they cast.

Story is composed of words, of images, of feelings, of rhythm: all of these conspire to create the metaphorical yeastiness that is the poem in the story.

This, then, is the argument . . .

Images are the raw material of the story. They are drawn from two sources, the contemporary world which produces realistic images, and the ancient tradition from which fantasy mythic images are taken. The storyteller brings these two kinds of imagery into relationship during a story performance. They have the effect of evoking emotions from members of the audience, feelings of familiarity from the contemporary images and a wide range of emotions from the ancient tradition.

When the storyteller, using rhythmical patterning, unites these two kinds of imagery, metaphor is created. This is the music of the story. Complexities are discovered in the two lines that stream through the performance. One of those is the surface narrative, the melodic line, the ordering of the contemporary and mythic images in a linear cause and effect movement to a resolution. The other is the rhythm of the story, the complex patterning that has the effect of subverting the melodic line without obscuring it, and thereby leading the story, and the audience, into new layers of experience.

The meaning or message becomes more intricate than the obvious surface homilies revealed by the melodic line, as the storyteller moves the audience into a more profound experience of the linkage between their contemporary lives and the worlds of the ancient tradition. There is a transformation; characters move through transitional experiences on the linear surface, a kind of rite of passage, as the audience simultaneously engages in the transformation emotionally.

Storytelling is ritual. The ultimate meaning of the story is essentially emotional, as the varied feelings of the members of the audience are worked into new forms that, for the duration of the performance, have the added effect of welding the audience into a unity. The story becomes a ritualistic experience, the objective of which is to move the members of the audience into that metaphorical center, into the poem in the story.

POSHOLI'S STORY

Posholi (c. 1795–1868) was a brother of the Sotho king, Moshoeshoe (c. 1786–1870), a leader who struggled against the Afrikaners and against other African peoples, especially the Thembu.[16] In 1820, Moshoeshoe settled at the foot of Botha-Bothe Mountain at a time when Shaka, the ambitious leader of the Zulu, was expanding his kingdom. Fleeing the might of Shaka in 1822, the Hlubi of Mpangazitha and the Ngwane of Matiwane moved into the land of the Sotho. In 1824, Moshoeshoe and his followers had to seek refuge on a mountain called Thaba Bosiu,[17] which became for them a natural fortress. Because of refugee incursions, the land of the Sotho was thrown into upheaval. The Hlubi and Ngwane also fought between themselves. From this chaos, the Sotho nation arose under the leadership of Moshoeshoe. In 1829, Moshoeshoe regularly conducted cattle raids against the Thembu people who lived below the Drakensberg Mountains. Now, there were two Sotho groups vying for hegemony—Moshoeshoe's Sotho at Thaba Bosiu and Sekonyela's Tlokoa at Marabeng. When Sekonyela's Tlokoa laid siege to the mountain, the four entrances to Thaba Bosiu were defended by Moshoeshoe, his father, and his brothers, Makhabane and Posholi.

Struggles with Chief None

One of the first references to Posholi occurs in 1824. That year, Moshoeshoe and his followers, the Mokoteli, overpowered an enemy, Chief None of the Mantsane people. In an effort to establish better relations between the two peoples, Moshoeshoe released None for a payment of seventeen head of cattle. In October of that year, Moshoeshoe's people grew sorghum along the eastern slopes of Thaba Bosiu. When Moshoeshoe visited the fields, he also visited None and his councilors; they became friends. By the end of that year, however, they were adversaries once again because of this incident: One night, Chief None was visiting Moshoeshoe on Thaba Bosiu. Seephephe, who was the father of Moshoeshoe's senior wife, Mamohato, collapsed after eating some sorghum bread and died. After None departed the next day, Posholi came to visit his brother, Moshoeshoe. Posholi insisted that he knew why Seephephe had died—the sorghum bread that he had eaten had been poisoned by None. Posholi then castigated Moshoeshoe for agreeing to None's release, demanding to know why he did not have him killed. But Moshoeshoe disagreed with Posholi, insisting that None was his friend. A short time later, Posholi and his followers moved into None's community and set fire to some of his kraals, forcing None and his subjects to flee into the hills. Moshoeshoe watched the rout and, fearing that None's people would be destroyed, demanded that Posholi end the fighting. He was

Map of southern Africa

angry with his brother and decided that he must be punished. But when Posholi returned a week later, Moshoeshoe's anger had subsided. He did not punish him, although he was urged to do so by the elders. Posholi, when he learned that Moshoeshoe had been angry, made fun of him, delighting his warriors. In years to come, he would continue to make light of Moshoeshoe's mild manners, and this would get him into difficult situations.

Disagreements with Moshoeshoe

During one of the struggles between Moshoeshoe's Mokoteli and Matiwane's Ngwane at Thaba Bosiu, the latter were pushed back when the Mokoteli sent boulders down on them as they moved up the mountain. Then the Mokoteli moved down the slopes and destroyed the remaining Ngwane who had survived that onslaught. Aided by Posholi and Makhabane, Moshoeshoe and the Mokoteli army sent the Ngwane into retreat. When Sekonyela assaulted Thaba Bosiu, he and his Tlokoa followers were overcome, but barely. Moshoeshoe was urged not to lead raids into neighboring territory himself, instead to allow Posholi and others to do that. Moshoeshoe was frequently generous to newcomers to Thaba Bosiu, and Posholi and Makhabane criticized him when he sent them livestock to keep them from settling on Thaba Bosiu land. Behind Moshoeshoe's back, the two rounded up seven hundred head of cattle he had presented to one such group; they were reprimanded for that. But Posholi insisted that he, a son of Makhachane, was entitled to overrule a policy of Moshoeshoe if it was clear that it harmed the people. Moshoeshoe angrily threatened Posholi with death, and one newcomer insisted that Posholi be executed at once. But Moshoeshoe reconsidered and said no, that Thaba Bosiu was a place of peace. Posholi was fined instead. The newcomer angrily left; he and his followers joined a band of Koranna, who invaded Thaba Bosiu.

War against Afrikaners

The wars continued: Mzilikazi's Ndebele attacked Thaba Bosiu in 1831; Moshoeshoe's brother, Makhabane, was killed during a battle with the Thembu in 1835. There were also skirmishes with the Kora people during this time.

From 1836 to 1848, there was relative peace as the Sotho, uprooted during the *lifaqane* (the widespread turmoil triggered by the persistent efforts of Shaka to expand his kingdom), accepted Moshoeshoe as their leader. In 1833, French missionaries arrived in the area, and some Sotho converted to Christianity. Also, the white Afrikaners, moving north from the Cape, were intruding regularly and steadily on the land of Moshoeshoe.

The British considered Moshoeshoe an honorable man. In January 1846, Captain H. D. Warden of the Cape Mounted Rifles became "British Resident among the Native Tribes to the North East of the Colony," and he moved to a site that would become Bloemfontein. The hope was that somehow a peace could be brokered between the Sotho and the Afrikaners.

But there was concern about troublemakers like Posholi, who was considered a brigand unfaithful to his own king, Moshoeshoe. In 1846, Posholi was living with his followers at Thaba Tseu, but he was frequently at Thaba Bosiu, stirring up trouble and making demands of Moshoeshoe. He had considerable influence over Moshoeshoe and the councilors.

Posholi decided in February 1846 to move his people from Thaba Tseu to Bolokoe (called Vechtkop by the Afrikaners). Those on Thaba Bosiu were relieved to see him go. They fortified Thaba Tseu. Strangers were attracted to Posholi and recognized him as their leader. They followed his orders with zeal, going with him on cattle raids, even killing for him at times. Only Posholi decided how the plunder was to be dispersed and who was to be punished for cowardice. In the meantime, at the end of that month, Moshoeshoe sent three hundred of his followers to occupy a stretch of territory, but they were routed by Sekonyela and his followers. Warden concluded that the Sotho could remain in that new territory.

In March, the War of the Axe commenced between the Xhosa and the British, and Moshoeshoe, to order to maintain good relations with the British, ordered the Xhosa to leave his territory. Four months later, when the Xhosa finally departed, they took thousands of Sotho cattle with them. Many Xhosa were killed as a result. But there were hundreds of refugees from Cape Colony pouring into the area, and Xhosa cattle herds moved into Afrikaner and Sotho lands. In one night, Posholi lost one-fourth of his cattle. Moshoeshoe had given the refugees sanctuary in his territory in return for which he received much of the weaponry that the Xhosa had looted from the British, and Warden became convinced that Moshoeshoe had deceived him.

In 1847, Posholi and his followers at Bolokoe launched numerous stock raids, but the Afrikaners and the British held Moshoeshoe responsible for the thefts, though he was innocent. In 1848, Harry Smith annexed much of the territory between the Orange River, the Vaal River, and the Drakensberg Mountains, which became known as the Orange River Sovereignty. At the same time, the followers of Sekonyela and Moshoeshoe continued to struggle against each other. The British drew a line between the Sotho and the Afrikaners, the Warden Line (after Major H. D. Warden, the British Resident at Bloemfontein), a line that favored the Afrikaners, and then the Sotho were at war with the British as well.

In 1849, when Warden demanded that Moshoeshoe come to Bloemfontein to discuss a new Afrikaner–Sotho border, Moshoeshoe refused to go; he nevertheless signed the map, though it cut off many Sotho farms and Posholi's fortress as well. But the line would not contain the peoples living in the area. At the beginning of 1850, various fights broke out among them, with fields destroyed and farms looted. Posholi lead a commando at night and raided Afrikaner farms in Transorange, taking away thousands of cattle and sheep. Sekonyela also raided African and Afrikaner farms. Posholi warned an ailing Moshoeshoe that the border drawn on Warden's map must be challenged; otherwise, he and others would continue to invade Afrikaner farms. Warden was convinced that the Sotho were preparing for war, but he was ordered by Harry Smith, the governor and high commissioner at the Cape, not to involve the British in a war. Instead, he should wait for the missionary Eugene Casalis's return from abroad and let him talk with Moshoeshoe. But Moshoeshoe told Casalis in December that he could not prevent these activities of his forceful chiefs. In 1851, the struggle between Sotho and Afrikaner reached such proportions that Warden called a meeting of all leaders of the Sovereignty to avert an all-out war. In 1851, the Sotho were triumphant at Viervoet, and the following year Moshoeshoe's followers kept a British cadre at bay. But relations between Sotho and Afrikaner did improve, and even more so in 1852 when the Warden border was no longer recognized and Warden had been removed from office. Posholi's territory would be restored to the land of the Sotho. The Sotho overwhelmed the Kora and Sekonyela's Tlokoa in 1853. Finally, in 1854, the British left the Orange River Sovereignty. The Afrikaners organized themselves into an independent nation, the Orange Free State, and the Sotho were left alone.

Death

Posholi was a contender, often in conflict with Afrikaners and Thembu, and also with followers of members of his own family, his brothers Moshoeshoe and Makhabane. For protection, he and his followers built a community in the mountain fastness at Bolokoe. The Afrikaners, always seeking land and regularly encroaching on that of the Sotho, became his enemy; Posholi and his followers conducted routine cattle raids into Afrikaner territory. In 1858, they pursued him, but he outmaneuvered them, taking their cattle and forcing them to surrender.

When the British withdrew, the rooted animosities between Sotho and Afrikaner continued to fester. The Warden Line was declared to be unfair to the Sotho, but the Afrikaners resolved to maintain it. Cattle raiding of Afrikaners by Moshoeshoe's followers continued, and in 1858, the Afrikaners declared war, invading the land of the Sotho, who then moved into Afrikaner farmland, continuing to raid the cattle. In 1865, the Afrikaners again declared war, and the Sotho were defeated and forced to repair to Thaba Bosiu. In 1866, Moshoeshoe was forced to come to terms with the Afrikaners, and the Treaty of Thaba Bosiu gave much arable land to the Afrikaners. But the Sotho refused to give up the territories, and the fighting resumed. Again, the Sotho were defeated. This time, in 1867, Posholi was killed.

POSHOLI'S POEM

Tlali, sootho ea 'MaMakhabane,
Tlali, sootho ea metsi, sokoloha
U boele litopong tsa maobane.
Tlali ho otla e pheo-lephatšoa,
E pheo-lesoeu ha e ke e otla,
E lese Mofephe a qete mohlaba,
E sale e mo otla lehoatateng,
Mohale ea koana Kapa oa loa,
H'a hlola a batla matšoele-tšoele.
Matšoele ke oona moriri oa hae.
Khomo e tolotsana e ka khak' a Linala;
Khomo ea RaMothele e khoalipana,
E tolotsana e ka khak'a Linala.
Khomo e tšoara mofehlo kaofela,
Ea tšoara khosing, ha Makhaola.
Lumela, ntoa, letena-batho,
E tenneng Molulela le Lehana!
Tau ea Bolokoe le Marajaneng,
Tau ea Bolokoe, nala li ntšo,
Nala li ntšo ke mali a Bathepu!
Tau ke ena e konetse mafahla,
Athe e konetse Maluke le Selete.[18]

Lightning, African of 'MaMakhabane,[19]
Lightning, African of the water, turn back,
Return to the dead of yesterday.
Lightning who strikes with wings white and black,
The one with white wings does not usually strike,
It permits Mofephe to destroy the land,[20]
And afterwards strikes him on the plain.

The hero from the Cape is fighting,
He does not spend time seeking myriads of people,
As many as the hairs on his head.
Cow black with white spots like the guinea-fowl armed
with claws;
Cow of RaMothele black with white spots,
Which is black with white spots like the guinea-fowl
armed with claws,
Cow that seizes all the buttermilk,
Which seized it at the chief's place, at Makhawula's.[21]
Greetings, war, which exhausts people,
It exhausted Molulela and Lehana![22]
Lion of Bolokoe and Marajaneng,[23]
Lion of Bolokoe, claws that are black,
Claws that are black with the blood of the Thembu,
Here is the lion that has hidden its twins:
It has hidden Maluke and Selete.[24]

THE POEM IN THE STORY

> In order to write poetry, one must have some kind of language system, or *prosody*—a theory of poetry *composition* or *an organizing principle*—within the bounds of which one can build the *structure* of the poem.
> —Lewis Turco, *The Books of Forms*

In the Sotho poem about Posholi, the poet enumerates various images in the second half of the poem: "Cow," "Greetings, war," "Lion." Though initially it may appear to be a mere medley of vaguely connected images, the poem is tightly constructed. The key to the poem is in the opening images:

Lightning, African of 'MaMakhabane,
Lightning, African of the water, turn back,
Return to the dead of yesterday.
Lightning who strikes with wings white and black,

The lightning obviously refers to Posholi's military might, and the poet is urging him to renew the attack on his adversaries. He develops the imagery of the lightning, suggestive of Posholi's cunning tactics on the battlefield:

> The one with white wings does not usually strike,
> It permits Mofephe to destroy the land,
> And afterwards strikes him on the plain.

One of Posholi's regiments, "the one with white wings," allows Mofephe, who had turned against his former chief, to have a lead, then destroys him. The poet then sums up this set of lightning images:

> The hero from the Cape is fighting,
> He does not spend time seeking myriads of people,

He needs no additional forces, he is strong enough. Into the context of this imagery of successful violence, the poet introduces three more images: the cow, war, and the lion. Each of the images further develops that of the opening set about lightning, adding to it and giving it deeper dimension. First, the cow:

> Cow of RaMothele [Posholi] black with white spots,
> Which is black with white spots like the guinea-fowl armed with claws,

"Claws" may seem problematic here, but it will be instrumental in tying the imagery of the cow to the lion later in the poem.

> Cow that seizes all the buttermilk,
> Which seized it at the chief's place, at Makhawula's.

The cow is Posholi. Posholi, or RaMothele, likened to a cow, is a cow with a unique strength, handsome (guinea-fowl), and strong (claws), two sides of the bovine image (linked to the earlier two-sided image, "with wings white and black"). The poet, as always, gives a specific example: Posholi's defeat of the Mpondomise, with the aid of the Bhaca chief, Makhawula.

The poet has to this point been speaking of violence—lightning, which has violence built into it, and the cow, which does not, but which the poet now invests with violence as he openly states his theme:

> Greetings, war, which exhausts people,
> It exhausted Molulela and Lehana!

The poet remembers two of those defeated by Posholi in war. In the final images Posholi is a lion:

> Lion of Bolokoe and Marajaneng,
> Lion of Bolokoe, claws that are black,
> Claws that are black with the blood of the Thembu,
> Here is the lion that has hidden its twins:
> It has hidden Maluke and Selete.

It is this image of "claws," clearly associated with the lion, that when linked to the cow unites the two opposed images, making them one. That unity reveals the essence of the poem—the dualism of this complex Posohli. The whole narrative history of Posholi is not included here, but the poem provides a deft if brief picture of his storied might. The lion imagery in the final five lines is explicit enough—Bolokoe and Marajaneng are places where Posholi had held sway, and he engaged the Thembu in bloody attacks. He protected in the process the future rights of his sons, Maluke and Selete. But it is the parallel images of cow and lion that render the portrait of Posholi rich and imaginative. Damane and Saunders argue that "it is often impossible to see any connecting link between one stanza and the next,"[25] but the internal image linkages here are clear. Cow and lion are drawn together into an unlikely unity, and so the poem illuminates the story. At the same time, a certain sound will dominate in a line, then give way to another that will dominate in a succeeding line, with a suggestion of this imbedded in the preceding line. This also provides internal linkages.

The grid in this brief poem is created by the imagery. It is a grid composed of (a) lightning (b) warrior (c) cow (d) war, and (e) lion. What makes these images a grid is not their lexical parallels, but rather their thematic, metaphorical similarities, each referring to violence in battle. The unifying element across this grid is the movement of Posholi, who slowly takes on these images of violence, his character becoming more and more warlike as the poem develops. The image of Posholi is the sum of the various separate images: it is the unspoken character of Posholi that moves across this network of images. The poem is placed at the nexus of history and biography: it combines the two, and moves history and biography into the realm of music. Posholi's life is first fragmented, then joined to the poet's sense of history, which is also fragmented. What unifies the two linear stories is the poem, its mythic images and, above all, its rhythm. The story has no meaning, no emotional content, no life until the poem is placed at its center. Then Posholi becomes a part of metaphor: of lighting, of lion, of cow.

A Page from a Journal

Journal Entry—June 5, 1975

Storytellers do not usually use props, but the performer may pick up a nearby piece of grass or a stick, and pretend that it is an object or a person in the narrative, then proceed to treat this stick or grass as if it were indeed that object or person.

—TENSION—The tension in both verbal and nonverbal elements is between precise, literal representation and symbolic representation.

—SYMBOLIC REPRESENTATON—Does it develop into nonrepresentational actions? Is there a movement from natural or realistic representation to symbolic representation thence to abstract representation? Or, are natural and symbolic actions connected to each other, but not abstract? There are two categories: representational gesture and body movement and words (including the symbolic), and nonrepresentational or abstract gesture and body movement (rhythm, other supplementary forms).

—There is a hierarchical movement: representational, symbol, abstraction (cf., visual art).

—The result: mime, body movement, and gesture that reflect, give representational dimension to, the spoken word. Symbol results as body movement, telescoped, becomes symbolized, loses its mimetic content, and now contains within itself meaning not readily attainable from observing or experiencing the external form of the gesture or body movement. Abstract, nonrepresentational movement is very common; it exists apart from representational actions and symbol, but interrelates with representational actions and symbol—repetition, emphasis, body movement and gesture in harmony with the rhythm of the spoken word. Representational actions and symbol reflect the *content* of the spoken word. Abstractions to some extent echo the *form* and *sound* and *rhythm* of the spoken word, an external *form* of the spoken word, but they do more than that, of course.

—There are the spoken word, complementary gestures and body movements, and there is also the *rhythm* of the words, the *sounds* of the words, the *poetry* of the words, their verbal *form* not related intimately to *meaning*. There is also the rhythm of the *body*, a nonverbal *form* not related intimately to the purely mimetic aspects of gesture and body movement in performance. There are times when the body is at rest; only *words* are communicated. And there are times when the verbal aspects of the performance are stilled; only the body is in motion, communicating. Or the body and voice are active simultaneously.

The Oral Artist's Script

> Insights of all kinds are welcome; but no wisdom will substitute for an instinct for action and pattern, and a perhaps savage wish to hold, through your voice, another soul in thrall.
> —John Updike, interviewed in *Writers at Work*

"Kwathi ke kaloku ngantsomi. . . ." "And now for a story. . . ." The storyteller pronounces these familiar formulaic words, and moves her audience into the bounteous riches of the cultural past, into a world charged with fantasy and festooned with delights and the bijoux of the storyteller's art. But in the process, members of the audience never leave the tangible, perceptible world: the storyteller moves them into antiquity, scrupulously making the connections between past and present, and in that magical nexus shapes their experience of the present.

Story occurs within the mesmerizing, unreal realm of performance—it is a world unto itself, with its own set of laws. Patterning involves the repetition of fantasy images and their satellite contemporary images. It involves the aesthetics of performance: the body of the performer, the music of her voice, and the complex relationship between her and her audience. The storyteller breaks through the force of the linear movement of the story to move the audience to deeper and more complex experiences. She does this to a great extent by juxtaposing unlike images, then revealing, with the full emotional participation of the members of the audience, the connections between them that render them analogous. In this way are past and present blended: ideas are thereby generated, forming our conception of the world that we inhabit.

Performance gives the images their context, and gives the members of the audience a ritual experience that bridges past and present, shaping their contemporary lives. A performer of oral narratives utilizes the materials of her culture much as a painter uses color. The audience must therefore not mistake the cultural elements found in such narratives for direct reflections of the culture itself. There are few one-to-one relationships between the events in the performances and the artist's society. It is this poetic truth that South African storytellers underscored for me again and again in discussions regarding their stories. If the narrative tradition does mirror nature, it does so only in intricate, aesthetically perceived forms, which ultimately have the same effect on an audience as visual art, dance, and music do.

Performance is the ritualistic organizing of mythic images: the audience is ceremonially moved into the center of the story, to the poem in the story. This ritual is composed of and accompanied by the music of the story, the melodic line and the rhythmic undercurrent of that line, with meaning as the result. This combination of music, mythic image, contemporary image, and ritual results in metaphor. The poetics of storytelling involves all of these, but most especially metaphor and the music that constructs it as the poem at the center of the story. So meaning in story is essentially a complex combination of varied feelings elicited by words and images, which are then worked into form. It is the formal containment of the emotional experiences of the members of the audience that generates the meaning, or message, of the story. In the poetics of storytelling, the story begins with a mythic image; that image is organized in linear form with other more contemporary images. The combination of mythic image and other imagery is worked into a melodic line or theme that may be combined with other themes occurring within the context of other images that reflect upon, reinforce, and otherwise color the theme or themes. When there is more than one theme, they are contrapuntal. The poetics of storytelling deals with meaning, with emotion, form, repetition, and myth. It has to do with music and the consequent metaphor; and with performer and audience, with ritual and performance.

This is the oral artist's script. His materials include ancient images, his body and voice, his imagination, and an audience. Within a broad thematic framework, he is free to deal with the images as he chooses, and he is praised by the audience for the originality with which he weaves them. Little is memorized, so the artist must depend on his imagination and on the controlled cooperation of the members of the audience to develop the skeletal mythic image that he has drawn from a repertory of remembered images inherited from a venerable artistic tradition.

The development of the linear plot is not always the most important achievement in a performance. The performers are storytellers, intellectuals as well as artists, a role that has been defined for them for generations. They are craftsmen who can use the narrative surface as a tool to be utilized to state a theme, to create an argument, or to elicit some emotional or intellectual response from the audience. The image that is externalized has never before been produced in just that fashion, and will never again be created that way. The narrative surface can be manipulated by the artist, and made to project a certain idea at one time, a special emotion when it is produced the next time, a solution to a problem plaguing the society the next, as well as communication of the artist's own preoccupation. But most important are the emotions called forth by the mythic images and then made rhythmical. This plotting of images is really the special language of all humans: communication happens not through words but by images created with the assistance of nonverbal as well as verbal techniques.

In the creation, combination, and manipulation of images, ideas, values, arguments, and the affirmation of social institutions will emerge. These are stated and developed in a manner that is logical and rational within the context of the oral traditions. The linear narrative plots are constructed of mythic images, that part of the special language of the tradition that is transmitted through the generations. These easily remembered mythic images contain implicitly the conflict and resolution that will become evident only when the artist develops them in a performance, giving the mythic image life with his words, with his body, with the rhythm of the language. As the artist urges the images forward in a linear development, underlying structures simultaneously guide the imaginations of the members of the audience in a circular fashion, so that the surface narrative becomes a means of commenting upon itself. It is through this commentary that metaphor emerges. What critics often dismiss as a simple fascination with a world of fantasy is really a metaphorical language, sophisticated and useful, that is transmitted through the ages.

As the performer projects the remembered mythic image, he is constantly in need of the assistance of the audience, and if he is a talented and confident artist, he makes use of the many potentially disruptive tensions that exist between him and the members of the audience. That audience has the same repertory of mythic images as the artist, and it therefore fills in gaps left by a performer who, in his concentration on some special aspect of the image, may neglect other aspects, perhaps even leaving out certain parts of the narrative. This is not an aesthetic problem as far as the audience is concerned. Artistic proportion is a concern of members of storytelling societies, but this typically goes beyond the linear plot itself: members of the audience become involved in the complex logic and interweaving of the imaged language itself. What initially appears a simple matter of verbal equivalence is actually a unique metaphorical language.

This relationship between artist and audience becomes further complicated when one considers its nonverbal quality. The performer expects that the members of the audience will physically and vocally assist him in the development of his images. It is necessary to the success of his production that he wholly involve the audience in the work of art, and to do so he utilizes several devices. These devices are used most obviously to externalize the images, to clarify the plotting of those, and to take it to its climax. The participation of the audience in these verbal and nonverbal aspects of production assists in this process. But at the same time that the audience, always under the control of the artist, is helping to create and sustain the images, it is simultaneously being integrated into the images. The audience is a part of the work of art in two ways: it helps to build the images, and it is emotionally caught up in the images. The linear plot is the most apparent of these narrative devices. The conflict develops and slowly moves toward a resolution; with a deft alteration of mythic images, the artist can change it to suit his own designs. The opening images of the performance are often filled with realistic details drawn from the immediate environment of the audience as the artist seeks to make the transition into his world of metaphor as smooth as possible. The demand for realism goes beyond this, of course. In fact the entire performance is realistic, the fantastic and magical elements being the metaphorical extensions of reality. The artist will exploit the rhythmic possibilities of the language, with its sounds constantly ready to dissolve in song. He will move his body, arms, face, and shoulders rhythmically; at times he is dancing in place, all that rhythmic movement ready to dissolve into pure dance. These musical characteristics of the performance have their own beauty, but they are also used to bring the members of the audience into a fuller participation in the developing images. They move their bodies in harmony with that of the performer; they clap, sing, express their approval, and are in physical and emotional accord with the artist and his creation. The audience knows the hackneyed plots, for its members have witnessed their production countless times. But there is a freshness about the work that is not evident on the surface. Moreover, the artistic delight in the performance goes deep, and the rhythms set in motion by the performer sustain images that are very complex.

The society is somehow affirmed every time the mythic images are elicited with serious intent and the members of the audience are wholly caught up in that narrative. They are totally involved in the images being paralleled metaphorically in the performance. At the moment of creation, the entire society is woven into the artistic image. The audience learns not by means of analytical investigation, but by emotional involvement in the artistic logic of the imagistic structures that the artist is manipulating. All of the aesthetic tensions in the production, the repeated images, the surface plot, the song, the dance, are calculated to attract and involve the audience in the developing image. The entire aesthetic system has developed as an integral part of this compelling system of communication and communion, existing both for mnemonic and communicative purposes. Form and content are indivisible, for the aesthetic allows for no separation; to attempt to isolate one from the other is to miss the point of the performance. During the production, the members of the audience are immersed in their culture as it is ideally visualized by the artist-philosopher, involved in its structure, and emotionally caught up in its values and aspirations. The externalized image brings the members of the community together, ties them rhythmically into the developing performance, imbues them with the ideals of the society in an aesthetic system that is never openly didactic. It allows no direct moralizing and preaching, but instead communicates values by means of a language of images.

When he reaches the climax of one mythic image, the performer may choose to incorporate yet another into the production, one that may not have any apparent connection with the previous image. Through his artistic genius, he introduces it into the production, skillfully linking it to the image that is being created, and giving the whole an illusion of unity. He can bring as many such mythic images into the performance as he chooses, using a complex mental cuing and scanning process to call up from his repertory those images that can be made relevant to the developing work of art. There are many mythic images in his repertory, and the possible combinations are endless.

The mythic image is repeated a number of times in the development of a performance, and in its repetition the linear image plotting is steadily moved from conflict to resolution with allied and supporting details connecting the repeated images. These repeated images move characters and events forward toward resolution, but an alteration must usually occur in that repetition if the resolution is to be attained. In the final repetition of the mythic image, a slight change may take place, the perfect pattern of repeated images with the mythic image at their center is broken, and it is in that change that the images are brought to resolution.

A Page from a Journal

August 12, 1967

The royal residence of King Diliz' lintaba Mditshwa at Tsolo consists of a series of low, rondavel-style structures, some furnished in traditional Xhosa style, some in contemporary European style, including guests houses, storage structures, arranged before a large open space dotted on its outer reaches by kraals for cattle, goats, and sheep. When the poet Mdukiswa Tyabashe arrives at the royal residence on a warm morning in 1967, he is dressed in a dark suit and carries a cane. Over one hundred people are already present, others are arriving—guests, councilors, hangers-on, all in a holiday mood because the king will that day preside over celebrations attendant on the emergence of a group of young women from a period of confinement, initiation, education that marks their transition, their rite of passage, from childhood to adulthood. The house of confinement is not far from the royal residence, and the king and his retinue ride horses to the event, his subjects following on foot. One of the kraals is now a mass of blood-red carcasses, sixteen oxen freshly slaughtered for the feast for the occasion, the flesh now being expertly carved by a small army of butchers. Racing oxen, being prepared for the ox race competitions, which will be a part of the coming out festivities, are draped in colorful cloths, their horns decorated as well. Women wear traditional Xhosa attire, and men are garbed in customary togas. The brilliance of cotton capes dyed with red ochre is everywhere seen. This is the backdrop for the poet's performance.

THE POEM AND THE STORY

The Poetics of Storytelling

> Feeling is the nub of all structures expressed in drama; in fact, feeling lies at the core of all mental operations and external acts.
> —Richard Courtney, *Drama and Feeling*

"And now for a story. . . ." The opening formula is pronounced, and the audience realizes that an enchanting fusion of the two worlds is about to transpire, that time is about to be arrested, history is to be experienced. At the explosive center of the storyteller's art can be found our deepest hopes and dreams, the quintessence of the society. Here also lurk our hates and nightmares, the underside of the human condition. These venerable images, never forgotten, routinely recalled with their compressed emotional potential, are meticulously arranged by storytellers in such a way that they organize and shape images from the contemporary world. The storyteller deals essentially with the heart, with our emotions. Nongenile Masithathu Zenani, a Xhosa storyteller, told me, "The art of composing imaginative narratives is something that was undertaken by the first people—long ago, during the time of the ancestors. When those of us in my generation awakened to earliest consciousness, we were born into a tradition that was already flourishing. . . . Members of every generation," she said, "have grown up under the influence of these narratives."

There never was a story without a poem. It is in the nature of storytelling that the narrative is constructed around a poetic interior. Within that interior is the engine of the story, that which animates and motivates, that which keeps the narrative in motion, that which provides the rhythmical flow of the story, that which elicits, controls, and thereby shapes the emotions of the audience into metaphor—the poetic center of the story.

A Zulu child who is learning to tell stories becomes caught up in and enamored of the patterns of storytelling; she initially ignores the linear construction of the story. This learning process is instructive, revealing that the essential initial emphasis of a maturing storyteller is not the story, the plotting of images in a conflict-resolution activity. Rather, it is the fragmentation of the story, the patterns, the rhythm. The youthful storyteller begins not with the linear narrative, but with the poem, and builds the narrative around it.

The storyteller instinctively knows where the force of the story lies, that force which will do two essential things: summon emotions from a willingly submissive audience, and weave those emotions into the poem that is at the core of the story. In the fashioning of the poem can be found the same emphasis on rhythm, on patterning of imagery, on the artful combining of mythic imagery with contemporary images.

There never was a story without a poem, and there never was a poem without a story. The poem that seems to exist outside of the story is itself composed of fragments of the story, reworked, realigned, reconstructed, but the story is there nonetheless, even if as a shadow.

The Poem

> The body is poetry's door; the sounds of words—throbbing in legs and arms—let us into the house.
> —Donald Hall, *Poetry: The Unsayable Said*

The poem is the key. But it is not the naked poem. The poem never exists without a story, nor can a story stand without a poem.

To be sure, we must know the nature of the naked poem if we are to appreciate the pivotal role it plays in the construction and experience of a story. The naked poem has its own attractions, is an art form itself.[26] To comprehend the true nature of story, it is imperative that one be aware of the composition of poetry, integral as at is to the composition of story.

Poetry is in the very temper of story, in its melodic and rhythmic influence on the organization and shaping of images. The nature of imagery is, therefore, also of crucial significance, since images are the building blocks of stories.

The raw material is emotion, that of the performer and, most signally, that of the audience. The images are not so much repositories of emotion as evokers of emotion. But it is not enough for a storyteller merely to elicit emotions: to do that alone would be aesthetically perilous and irresponsible. The images have two functions: to move the story and to move the audience—the first in a cause and effect manner, the second in an emotionally resonant way. Primary, or mythic, images must do both. Other subordinate images will cement, detail, and support these central images. There is a second repertory of images that is contemporary in nature and emotionally evocative, but not as deeply so as the mythic images. Both are crucial, for the ancient mythic images will work their way with the contemporary.

Three things are happening here: one is historical (the contemporary images shaped by myth), the second is narrative (the linear movement of images from conflict to resolution), and the third is aesthetic (the shaping of the released emotions into form). To make a narrative work, the melodic line is crucial, for it is the logic of storytelling. To make the story into art, rhythm is vital, for it is the message.

This ordering of imagery into form, this shaping of emotions into form: that is the poem in the story.

The Poetics of Storytelling

The Music in the Story

> The real substratum of myth is not a substratum of thought but of feeling.
> —Ernst Cassirer, *An Essay on Man*

THE POEM IN THE STORY

The king's official bard takes the history of the people and fabricates it by building its images, ancient and contemporary, around the song that, through its ordering of the historical images, reveals the poet's truth about the story.

It is a day on which the symbols of the Xhosa past openly and brilliantly compete with those of the present. The king, Diliz' Iintaba, appears, dressed in a white suit, and, as he emerges, the throng raises arms and salutes him thunderously. During the tumult of the greeting, the king busies himself with his wife and councilors, seeming to ignore the mighty salutation. Then, the salute still in progress, the poet, Mdukiswa Tyabashe, who has been lost in the crowd conversing with some elderly men, slowly comes into view. As he walks to the center of the vast courtyard, the crowd, still shouting greetings to the king, slowly and respectfully makes way for the bard with anticipation, clearing the space, their shouts subdued somewhat as the court poet approaches with dignity the center of the space. "Shu! Shu! Shu!" he shouts, his voice thundering above the roar of the crowd. "Diliz' Iintaba! Diliz' Iintaba!" The roar decreases to a murmur. "Shu!" the poet cries, "Shu! Shu!" Suddenly, all is quiet. Those carving the carcasses of the oxen that have been slaughtered for the occasion also fall silent. The king, in an exaggerated way ignoring the bard, continues to speak in whispers to his advisers. Tyabashe stops walking now: "Shu! Shu!" The crowd softly arranges itself as though choreographed. Tyabashe faces the king. "Diliz' Iintaba!" he roars. Holding the head of the cane in his right fist, its point to the ground, he salutes the king. The king stands solemnly in the shade of a small veranda of one of his houses, now speaking quietly and calmly to his wife. "I have been hurt by an old sore!" cries the poet. A number of people in the crowd respond. Slowly, they move out of their disorganized state and into ranks, forming a half arc behind the poet, a human amphitheater. Far beyond, the king now takes his brother, also a Mpondomise leader, and goes with him and a councilor to chairs; they sit at one end of the space.

When Mdukiswa Tyabashe appears in the court of King Diliz' Iintaba Mditshwa of the Mpondomise and begins, with an awesome protean voice and graphic use of his body, to evoke the muscular images of the Mpondomise past and to hurl them with acerbic wit and sarcasm against the flaccid flickerings of the present, he is the center of a theatrical event, a tense performance that is also a political event. He is not so much regulating behavior—he realizes that a poet does not have that power—as he is railing against contemporary affairs with stinging ridicule through comparison and metaphor. Sitting before him, mutely accepting the rain of criticism, is that king himself, diminished symbol of the once substantial power that, as Tyabashe has often lamented in his poetic oral histories, once stretched from the Mzimkhulu to the Umthatha rivers, from the Drakensberg Mountains to the limits of the Mpondo nation.[27] That glory is now gone, and what remains is a shriveled and impotent principality in thrall to racist Pretoria. Tyabashe is a realist; he accepts the Xhosa shift to the west. What he regrets is the broken way in which the move has been accomplished.

An earlier king was more suitable to Mdukiswa Tyabashe. When he was the poet of the Mpondomise king, Lutshoto, Tyabashe started out one day from his home near St. Cuthbert's Mission in the Transkei in South Africa, and walked up the road towards the village of Tsolo. As he left his home, he started to proclaim the praises of the king and walked for some considerable distance, never once repeating any of the images that he was evoking. Finally, the story goes, the automobile of the king met him, and the king, seeing Tyabashe, called for a horse for his bard. All this time without pause Tyabashe continued to chant the praises of his king. Still speaking eloquently, he mounted the horse, and then led the king's entourage back to the mission station, not once

Mdukiswa Tyabashe

interrupting the flow of images and rhythm. Only when they arrived at the mission did this extraordinary poet stop singing.[28]

Oral poems evoke, express, explore, and mold feeling. History and narrative are among the materials that foster this process. The poem is in one sense a dramatization of history; it is also an externalization of narrative, a revelation of idea. Underlying the poem is history, culture, and the narrative moment. But if the narrative of history is present, it is evident only in fragments; it is submerged, its contours apparent through inference. It is a vague and muffled undertow. The unspoken ligaments of history do act as added support for the holding of diverse images in form. With the rhythm of the poem, the patterns being established by rhythm and image, and the polarities generated by the images, historical narrative has a role, albeit shadowy, to play in the experience of form. But it is the least important of these for purposes of structure. Its more important function is as one of a series of discontinuous images that are given shape and a unique unity by the poem. The movement of oral poetry is within polar fields, which, more significantly than historical narrative, help to link the varied and seemingly unrelated images. Through the control and organization of these images in performance, the poet guides the audience to meaning by enabling its members to experience their relationships. In the oral tradition, the connection between images is not always apparent; rather, it is felt.

The poet speaks not for a king, not for a person, but for tradition. The king is praised or blamed to the extent that he represents that tradition, to the extent that the tradition is revealed through him and his actions and his office. The poet does not praise the king, he is not a praise-poet, these are not praise-poems; rather, he is an upholder of tradition, and the king's place is the office that is responsible symbolically for sustaining the tradition.[29] The poet assesses the success or failure of the king to uphold the responsibilities of his office; the tradition is the important thing, not the person. The poet may direct the poetic tradition to personal praise, for whatever his reason—of himself, of his cattle, of kings. But the tradition is as usefully served when the images are of the past, and the present is measured by that stick.

The audience is emotionally caught up in the performance, as its own well-being is at stake. The emotions of the members of the audience are knitted into the images being performed, and so tensions are temporarily tightened and resolved. This is the effect of the performance, the tightening and releasing and redistribution of tensions through form, the tying in of current uncertainties with the permanence, enlightenment, and seeming ideal perfection of the past. The past is necessarily golden in the poems: it conjures up certain strong positive supportive emotions. It is a very selective world that the poet creates—which is in the nature of poetry. It is a world that achieves perfection both in its positive and negative aspects. That is, its negative images are results of the quest for perfection. A metaphorical dualism is the key. The connection is with the dream world of the imagination, with which the place names, battles, and people of history are connected. That is a central effect of the unrealistic, even fantastic, imagery. It is the fantasy and myth of the past that give the scattering of historical data a framework, an understandable and interpretable context, a context emanating from a tradition shared by all members of the performance. The summoning of imagery and emotions from that tradition provides a stirring connective context, and gives meaning to the welter of present-day images. This is also the ultimate effect of the performance—to make possible the connection between the two worlds. This effect is made more dramatic by the very physical presence of elements of the present: the chief or king, for example, members of his retinue, and his subjects.

Poetic performances are characterized by a unique use of language that, while it does not deviate in any major distorting way from nonpoetic usage, nevertheless pushes normal usage to its limits. Delivery is always rhythmical, the images declaimed with force, almost sung at times, chanted, and frequently uttered at a rapid pace, but never to the point that meaning is lost. All occurs within a theatrical context. Images comprise the material organized by the delivery and manipulation of the language. The images concentrate heavily on the past, but the themes are often intensely contemporary, building on, measured against, and refracting the historical past. In the poetry, the bard evokes an image, which immediately calls forth its echo—more than an echo, it elaborates on or expands the original image. The poem slowly gives form to the vague but insistent whisperings of the past, touching deeply remembered and experienced chords, calling them up, linking them through the form of the poem, rhythm, to the present.

Traditions, the handing down of information, beliefs, and customs by word of mouth or by example from one generation to another without written instruction, are what give our lives their roots. Without traditions, we would be rudderless, without direction. Traditions tie us to our forebears, to ancient beliefs, to our social ideals and our customs: traditions assure us that we are not alone, that our lives have meaning. Poets and storytellers use familiar images that provide connections between our contemporary experiences and our past. Poems and stories regularly bring us into communion with the past, with the beliefs and behavior of our parents and their ancestors. These art forms, poetry and stories, are one of the institutions that bridge our present experiences and our historical past. Societies have developed many means of establishing conduits to their pasts. These are all a part of our traditions, the network of remembrances that teach us, shape us, inform us, and link us to antiquity. The symbols produced by the artist provide linkages to our past, assuring us that our lives have context and meaning. Poets and storytellers make a community of us, enabling us to experience ourselves at our best, and at our worst. The poetry and stories are an art form that richly remembers and celebrates our finest impulses, as it recalls and commemorates our cruelest proclivities. For better or for worse, poets and storytellers forget nothing; they scrutinize our history, they plumb the most ancient depths of our human experience. They remind us that we continue to be motivated by emotions as deep as humanity itself. It is profoundly true that, as far as our emotional lives and histories are concerned, there is nothing new under the sun: our traditions regularly remind us of this. Susanne Langer writes, "The reason why literature is a standard academic pursuit lies in the very fact that one can treat it as something else than art."[30] But it is nothing if it is not art.

The poet uses tradition to comment on the present: Tyabashe addresses the king directly.[31] He is

The one
Who topples mountains,[32]
Cold, lofty mountains,
The Drakensberg Mountains,
The Nomkholokhotha Mountains:
He splinters them!

But the poet knows that this is the way it was, not the way it is. The tone of his voice is shaded with sarcasm, his body slumps slightly away from the king. The poet is not talking to the king at all, he is really addressing the crowd. And he returns to his opening lines, establishing his rhythm, but now he expands it. In present time now, standing before the monarch, the poet laments,

This old wound,
A new torment
Has been inflicted by Diliz' Iintaba,
Perpetrated by Diliz' Iintaba!

What is that "old wound"? Tyabashe is reminded of the past, and as he is so reminded, his bowed body slowly straightens, life comes to his voice, a ring of joy,

It was splendid to see Gqirana
Stalking astride the Malephe and Mjika Rivers

A different rhythm has now grown out of the original one, and he plays with it, with the images that are composed by it:

He was so tall
He touched the heavens.
And he was beautiful,
This forebear of Diliz' Iintaba:
He was beautiful

Because he lived up to
The standards set by Ngubenani!

The poet rhythmically catalogues the great heroes of the past, the giants who bestrode the waters of the region, who in their greatness touched the very clouds. His body flows with the rich images, his voice caressing them; they are cradled in the rhythmical pattern. To emphasize this central concern, he breaks the regular rhythm:

I have said it again!
I have said it again!
I have said that

And the poet reverts to the characteristic rhythm of the poem:

The heroes of Jengca have class.
The children at Xhwangu's place
Are distinguished

They were the great ones, the noble warriors of the past. But when he turns his attention to the modern generation, his body and voice sag, slip into the alternate rhythm, the subdued mood, and at these points the poet addresses the present king more directly, arguing that

Rambatotshile's people,
Falase's people:

are weak; they do not represent tradition the way it was upheld in the past,

They do not compare
To this child of Matshiliba.
He fought against growing old,
He contested age.

The poet reverts to the earlier pattern, again touched with pride. *He* loved life,

He clung with his legs
To the milk-skin,

He drank ravenously
From the calabash.

Then Tyabashe brings the images vehemently together, violently revealing the contrast, his body steely erect, his right hand angrily, regularly pumping the cane, pounding it into the earth, his voice raspy now with frustration and defeat:

Zebangweni was startled:
He considered himself
The great one of his home.
. . . .
We know that the real successor
Surpasses this little fellow

Now referring directly to the sitting king,

Even in the sound that he makes!

Caught in the rhythm, still angry, Tyabashe pursues the contrast:

He is the child of Makhamba
Who was exposed at Mabilokazi's place:

The poet ends,

It was said that he was a puny thing;
A feeble thing!

Tyabashe uses the Mpondomise past, the history of the Mpondomise, to decry the slide of his people to their current unhappy state. He apparently praises Diliz' Iintaba by placing him within a historical context, but so strongly positive is the historical characterization, and so weak the present circumstances, that a profoundly negative appraisal results.

Rhythm can be established, and patterns; these are sounds, nonverbal aspects of performance. The rhythms have their own aesthetic function, a function having to do with feeling—the poet's own or those of the members of the audience. Interwoven with these feelings given form by sound are the historical and fantastic images of the poem, which call forth their own emotions, more particular, more discursive: historical victories, defeats, routings, comparisons, sadness, tragedy, triumph, joy. The nonverbal rhythms create a form of the image-evoked emotions, giving those experiences regularity, imposing a regular flow on those images.

"The purpose of analysis," argued the poet John Ciardi, "is not to destroy beauty but to identify its sources. There is no such thing as a beautiful object without characteristics."[33] At the heart of the story is poem, "the gathering up of imagined sound into utterance."[34] At the core of poem is metaphor; half of that metaphor is as old as time itself, and half of that metaphor is as fresh as today. What unites the two halves of metaphor and makes them the same is rhythm; rhythm is performance that makes the audience, through its emotions (which the two images of metaphor elicit, the rhythm binding these emotions into form), a part of performance.[35] Mythic images elicit emotional responses from members of the audience.

Again, this is of significance: Rhythm, patterning, other forms of ordering shape these responses into a common response, a vessel composed of emotions woven through with the melodic themes of the story, so that the images, historical and artistic, become a part of an emotional experience. Rhythm, music, ritual, metaphor, and, most consequentially, the emotions: these are the materials of the storyteller.

Repetition, the rhythm of storytelling, is the principal activity of the performer and it has to do with the placing of a song at the core of a story, then building the images around that core. As those images, both realistic and fantasy, build around the core, they reveal, through their repetition, the rhythms, the patterns of performance, the meaning of the experience. And meaning is very complex. It has little to do with didactic morality and much to do with music, with repetition, with poetry, with the metaphorical heart of the story. Freud wrote, "repetition, the re-experiencing of something identical, is clearly itself a source of pleasure."[36] Repetition is a slow, ponderous flow, wavelike. It is a return to the preceding image, and a growing out of that image, a development from that image, a slow blossoming of a set of images that develops from a single image. That is the key. The poet begins with a febrile, fertile, seminal image, and this is repeated, as he slowly develops it, working images from images. The work of the poet is also the work of the storyteller. It is the voice of the poet: "That voice I hear every day," writes the poet, Eavan Boland, "which is my own voice, which is emerging from the deepest origins of my self," which is never practiced, rehearsed, or made artificial by self-consciousness, "has begun to invade my lyric sense of the poem."[37]

But repetition by itself is not enough: "Novelty is always the condition of enjoyment."[38]

Repetition must not be allowed to dull the experience of the story. Music and emotion, the two cardinal ingredients of a story, assure that this will not happen: "Music is a tonal analogue of emotive life."[39] It is the poem—music that elicits and then forms emotions—that is at the heart of storytelling.[40] While the music may have varied effects on members of the audience, it is up to the storyteller to work these reactions into the form of the story.[41] Franz Boas wrote, "Artistic enjoyment is based essentially upon the reaction of our minds to form."[42] But, argues John Blacking, "the forms are produced by human minds, whose working habits are, I believe, a synthesis of given, universal systems of operation and acquired, cultural patterns of expression."[43] The experience of story is more than catharsis: we become one with history.

Story involves the unleashing of a considerable power. Fantasy and reality are aspects of story, with interactions and interconnections. The story is framed; its beginnings and endings are put into the frame. There is the rhythm of the story, and there is the melodic narrative of the story. The audience is moved to the center. Transformation and transition are at the heart of narration; they evoke metaphor, a poetic process, the poem in the story. The mystical content of the story is myth. With the stirring mythic image at the center, a complex message is forged. Its meaning can be understood only by participating in the performance. Interacting, interlocking patterns trap us in the rich and varied language of storytelling. "For what is 'reality' except as it is presented through language?"[44] But the most obvious ingredient of stories is also the most misleading: words. Words are a beginning, but only a beginning, of the architecture of stories.

Pages from a Journal

The evening of June 4, 1975

Other kinds of gesture:
—The body at rest—explore this. Gesturing does not occur at all times. At times, the body is at rest. What causes gesture and body movement to be reanimated? Is there something in the verbal elements? The music of the verbal? The rhythmic patterning of narrative?
—Rhetorical gestures—Are these supplementary? How are they linked to miming and other forms of gesture?
—That gesture followed not by words but by gesture: the storyteller sets it up with an introductory word (*uthi,* for example, in Xhosa), and this is followed by a gesture rather than a word. Strictly complementary?
—Body's movement rhythmically in time with song.
—Gestures: Are they like words? Do they have a grammar? A vocabulary? Do specific gestures have a syntax as well as a context? To what extent is that syntax or context verbal? Nonverbal? A mixture of each?
—THE RANGE OF GESTURES Gestures range from exact reproduction of reality (mime) (verbal: ideophones) to symbolic representation (verbal: all other words). The latter acts as a kind of syntax (or context? both?) for the other. Does it convey "meaning" as symbolic words do? How does gesture become symbol?

January 31, 1976

Action: action in the narrative, the physical movements of the characters in the story; action of the body of the performer: gestures and body movements. These latter harmonize with the former (in mime) and also provide a rhythmic grid (a shaping device) for the realization of the mimed actions.

February 3, 1976

Gestures: (digit 105[45]) the performer shows how deep water is with a long piece of straw; (107) *yenjenje,* hands folded, pointed downward; (114) feels about on the ground with right hand; (121) hands and fingers quaking; (148–9) claws my leg with her left hand (before the song); (152) right hand up to indicate fire, then hand down but the fire image has now been established, and she looks at it as she narrates and sings; (158) hands circle just below elbows, ankles; (169–70) refers to bundle of thatch; (171) rubs hands together as if grinding; (171–2) left forefinger in mouth to illustrate smoking, draws on finger; (188–9) "walking" with hands, a kind of pumping motion; (190–1) hands held, palm of left hand and back of right hand; (196) acts as if washing hands; (199) right hand moving emphatically, forefinger pointing; (206) demonstrates on left forefinger; (209) grasps and hits right leg; (213) *engaka,* points to bottom of right forefinger; (214) *senjenje,* moves right forefinger about; *le ndawo,* right shin; (219) refers to right shin; (226) *enjenje,* right thumb, forefinger, and index finger shaped like a claw; (234) throws with both hands; (358–9) *njenje,* hands held together, palms towards her; (397) *yathi,* both hands palms up, as if getting under something; (398) *yathi,* left hand flapping in air; this is repeated then (399) left hand slowly descends; (400) *eli chibi lenjenje,* two forefingers and index fingers form diamond shape; (403) *njenje,* right hand up in front of body, palm away from body; (416) uses left forefinger to illustrate; (417), repeats dgt. 400; (419–20) repeats dgt. 397, except only left hand goes "under"; (420–1) *apha,* left hand runs along left thigh; (422) "water" to armpit; left hand up, quivers; (430) repeats dgt. 419; left hand then goes up in the air again, waves, then descends at dgt. 431; repeats the entire process (397, 419, 430) a number of times, with almost identical gestures; (438) hits the ground with small stick, claps, then again hits the ground with small stick; (445) *njenje,* left hands floats around (she is now reclining on her right side); (452) *xhimfi,* left hand flaps about; (452–3) *rhm! rhm!* left hand rubs against right; (457) *njenje,* two hands as in dgt. 190, but with forefingers up and out, hands moving; (458–9) *gaqa,* etc., hands as if creeping; (459–60) as in dgt. 190; (461) *balandela,* as in dgt. 190; (462) as in dgt. 400; (463) *ngaphezulu,* left hand two feet from the ground; (463) *yathi,* left hand dives into the ground; (463–4) left hand in the air, descends in starts, fingers up; (464–5) left hand rises in starts; (474) left hand, as in dgt. 430; (479) *eli chibi,* draws circle on the ground; *itshona apha,* drops right forefinger into circle; (480–1) *esithi,* hands rising, one inch apart, fingers up; (483) *imile inkungu,* hands above head, as if in prayer; (485) *yenjenje,* hands raised, forefingers up, about three feet apart; turns in another direction with the same gesture, then yet another direction; then, at dgt. 487, another direction; much demonstrating with hands, touching each other, parts of her body; (492) *kule ndawo . . . apha,* right thigh; demonstrating, illustrating, pointing, miming, drawing, sketching, measuring, hands playing roles of characters going into the water, hands are the water too, shows depth of water with straw, etc.; hands gracefully sketch contours of the action, then the action itself. . . . Certain words become a kind of refrain, repeated dramatically at various parts of the narrative; note that when she begins a new image sequence, she moves into it slowly, rather matter of factly, not much body action (shaping, mainly), slower, less demonstrative, as she builds the initial images and reveals the repetition structure to the audience; these established, things pick up, and there is much drama and body movement.

February 11, 1976

Ancient mythic images and contemporary realistic images are brought together here. But images are also found at the point where dream-time and reality blur and merge. There are dream and dream symbolism in oral narratives also. Disguise, illusions, tables turned, things not what they seemed, the strong made weak, deformities, inability to speak or deformed speech: Why?

The Poetics of Storytelling

A Catalogue of Poetic Images

Poetry is not the thing said but a way of saying it.
—A. E. Housman, *The Name and Nature of Poetry*

THE SONG OF THE WOMEN BECOMES THE POEM IN THE STORY

As newly initiated young men, their puberty ritual at an end, return to their homes after some weeks of isolation in the mountains, they can hear the song of the women, in the distance, vibrating through the hills, a song that takes the fragments of the youths' brief histories and gives them form.

At the end of a circumcision ceremony and subsequent six-month seclusion, a group of freshly initiated young men one morning wash the symbolic white clay from their bodies in the cold water of a stream.[46] Each is given a large kaross by his father, and each is subsequently praised. A slow procession home to the village then begins, the young men not looking back as their fathers set fire to the circumcision lodge that contains the artifacts of the initiates' childhood—clothes, toys, teenage ephemera. The structure goes up in flames as the chain of youth formally snakes its way up the valley wall and into the village where scores of relatives and friends will salute and welcome them. Along the way, they hear the words of the song sung by the women of their community, and, when they arrive at home, the poets sing their praises in traditional poems.[47]

The poet "celebrates victories of the nation," Archie Mafeje suggested in an essay on Xhosa oral poetry, and "sings songs of praise, chants the laws and customs of the nation, he recites the genealogies of the royal families."[48]

A. C. Jordan noted that the subject of the poetry "may be a nation, a tribe, a clan, a person, an animal, or a lifeless object."[49] Writing on oral poetry in *The Critic,* G. P. Lestrade commented, "All special occasions are instrumental in causing the production of some new praise-poem—of the chief of the tribe, or of some other great man."[50] Edison M. Bokako considered the Tswana oral heroic poem "a story of endeavor, of resistance overcome, of something accomplished. In it an individual was glorified, a momentous occasion recalled, or the achievement of victory celebrated."[51] Every Zulu boy, observed B. W. Vilakazi, "was expected to know something of these praises and to recite the most important ones, dealing first of all with his own ancestors and persons of importance still living."[52] R. C. A. Samuelson recalled that Zulu poets "select the most brilliant incidents in the career of their Chief or in the history of the nation and people for their songs and ballads."[53]

In 1835, Andrew Smith observed the creation of Tswana *mabôkô,* or heroic poems,[54] and commented that the Tswana, "When they perform any feats of what they consider importance or prowess, compose a history of the circumstance," then recite these "on various occasions, either when alone or in company with their fellows."[55] Boys undergoing initiation rites preceding the creation of an age-set learned to compose such poetry. In 1857, David Livingstone, the missionary, wrote that each of the boys "is expected to compose an oration in praise of himself, . . . and to be able to repeat it with sufficient fluency."[56] Composition of heroic poetry formed a part of their routine in the third and final month of the rites. "They were gathered every evening round the camp fire," wrote Isaac Schapera, "and took turns in reciting their compositions." The men responsible for their education offered suggestions when the poems were weak. At the end of the ceremony marking the close of the rites, the boys returned to their homes with their fathers, "where, to the applause of the people assembled to welcome them back, . . . 'they praised their names,' i.e., each in turn recited his composition."[57]

The seemingly discontinuous image is the basis of the oral poem. Images can be historical, realistic, contemporary, mythic, or fantastic. The poet's repertory consists of numerous such images, and he builds his poetic patterns around images that contain considerable emotional capacity. Implied in poetry is a story, a story sometimes heavily detailed, other times merely sketched and hinted at. But the two do not exist without each other: the poem always has a story, and the story cannot exist without a poem at its core. Oral poetry is a complex interplay of vivid images, more than mere accumulation, but the complexity begins with the solitary image.

The poet's repertory of images is broad and varied. Images, for example, describe people:

> Powerful warrior who covered himself with branches,
> On the great tract of the cattle of Nxaba;
> And when he arose he devoured the children of Nxaba,[58]

and animals:

> Great cow of the steep path, red one,[59]

and the poet will link these images to other characters:

> He will barter with which royal person?
> He will barter with Mbangambi son of Vuma at the Mashobeni kraal[60]

to natural occurrences:

> Sun that came out bright,[61]

to plants:

> Noxious herb that inflames the bowels,
> medicine that's bitter when eaten,
> the buffalo-thorn is bitter,[62]

and to wild animals:

> Crocodile, raise clouds of dust on the land,[63]

to natural objects:

> Black pool,
> In which leopards sleep, and lions![64]

and sometimes to fantastic creatures:

> Wide-mouthed beetle
> Which daily swallows herds of men.[65]

In fact, the hero often has a special relationship with nature:

> He is Dela, he troubles the heaven with wind,
> The one of above: still longing for above;
> The one of below: still longing for below.
> The one who wakes up late has seen nothing
> Because he has not seen the python uncoil.[66]

and with fantasy:

> Curved iron piece of the Europeans,
> Snaring the fabulous water-spirits.[67]

The poem may contain miniature inventories of the community. Tools, for example, are mentioned:

> I'm a two-pointed awl of the Masonya,
> that pricks both cloak and sewer;[68]

and cultural activities:

> He presents his tribute to the king,
> A drove of his white-spotted cattle.[69]

Images depict the strength of the hero:

> He is a wild-cat, muscular dog of Qonce,[70]

in various ways:

> He is Farter-on-a-stone-until-it-breaks.[71]

He performs wonders:

> He who twists the skin of the buffalo into reins,[72]

and, while creative,

> The wild animal with long placentas,[73]

he is also destructive:

The continuous downpour,
A thing like the great rain that killed cattle.[74]

He is violent:

The thing with horns with drops of blood,[75]

he is peaceful:

He is Mgungu the yellow dancing ox,
The white dancing ox and the yellow;
The white one with red patches.[76]

Yet it is a fragile peace that can turn to violence:

The one who dances in debris,
The one who dances with a gun,
He wants to shoot the people of the dance.[77]

He is ambiguous:

He is Tree-I-am-dry-yet-I-am-green,[78]

again:

He likes food that he can steal without seeming a thief,[79]

and again:

He is the dark tortoise that is beaten but does not die.[80]

Like all heroes, he faces the unknown:

He is Sutlani who has black horns,
He turns the tuft of grass, a lurking animal inside,[81]

and:

Where the bees sleep we do not know,
We hear the roaring of the forests.[82]

Leaders are reminded of the source of their authority:

> The chief is a chief when he is strong,[83]

and:

> a chief is a chief through the chief's wife.[84]

And the audience is frequently reminded of bleak states of affairs:

> The heroes are finished at kwaNgqika,
> They have been finished by the nation of whites
> From across the sea.
> He is the seized heart, the one of Gxabhana,
> The hero who remains at kwaNgqika.[85]

Relations between the races and between oppressor and oppressed are major themes in the poetic imagery:

> He is Nohamile, a thing with a saddle-back for the Europeans to sit on,[86]

and:

> He is Mandoli, not allowed among the Europeans,
> He will be seized the year he is seen.[87]

Animals are also praised:

> It is the yellow leopard with the spots,
> The yellow leopard of the cliffs,
> It is the leopard of the broad cheeks,
> Yellow leopard of the broad face, I-do-not-fear,
> The black and white one, I-get-into-a-small-tree,
> I tear off the eyebrows,
> Clawer I am, I dig in my claws,
> My adversaries I leave behind,
> Saying: This was not one leopard, there were ten.[88]

A vulture is the subject of a poem:

Big black vulture, the decrepit one,
When it perched the tree bent down.[89]

Inanimate objects are praised—the bicycle, for example:

Horse of the Europeans, feet of tire,
Iron horse, swayer from side to side.[90]

And the train:

I am the black centipede, the rusher with a black nose,
Drinker of water even in the fountains of the witches.[91]

In poetry, images are removed from their normal primarily historical contexts—their linear, sequential temporal and spatial settings—and are worked into myth. As time and space are collapsed into myth, it becomes an artistic experience. These images evoke emotions, for they are selected at least partially for their ability to arouse emotional responses in the members of an audience. Such images, made discontinuous, are worked into new configurations with the historical temporal and spatial elements a significant but not decisive echo.

These two stages of poetic activity, the rendering discontinuous and the reshaping of the imagery, were explained to me by southern African oral poets. Their poetry by its nature, they argued, supports tradition, cultural ideals. But they insisted on the second stage, the reshaping, as their crucial aesthetic activity: they were not simply describing tradition.

Reordering occurs after images have been shorn of normal contexts by means of a process of reshaping, by patterning the discontinuous images, by giving them an artistic and poetic, rather than historical, context. Patterning of images provides the texture of the poem. This texturing is the felt experience of the reconfiguring process. It also provides a grid, the chief formalizing element, which, like the separate images and rhythmic molds that form it, is emotionally evocative. Patterning takes many forms, moving between the extremes of precise lexical patterning and thematic parallelism, and ultimately to metaphor. When images of reality are initially severed from their temporal, linear contexts and given poetic form, they are no longer history. They are, rather, myth: real time and space collapsed into poetic patterns. The transformation of history into myth occurs by means of a poetic process.

The image, the crucial building material of the poem, is an action

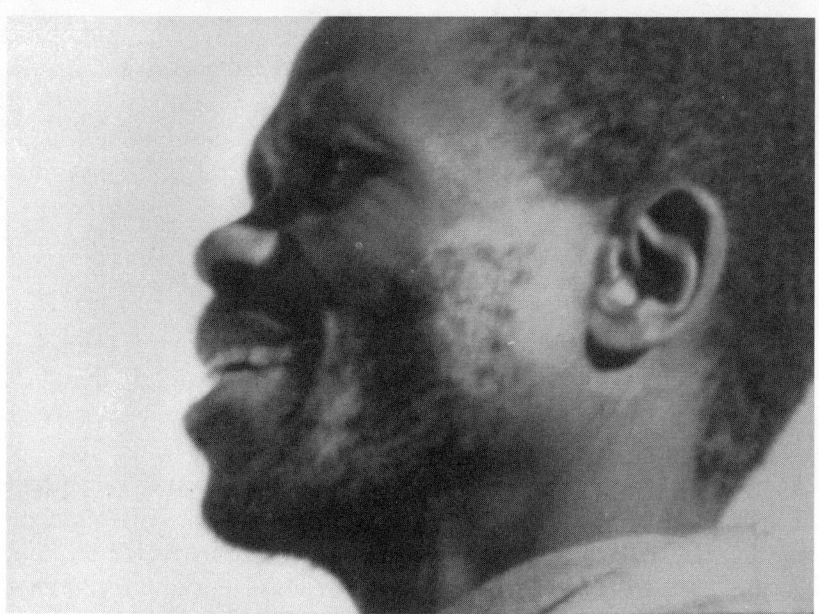

Ashton Ngcama

contained within a metrical, rhythmical line, complete unto itself, that has only a peripheral relationship to time and space within the poem. Yet it wholly owes its existence to and echoes the temporal and spatial contexts outside the poem. The audience, aware of the latter, is emotionally caught up in the activities of the former. The line is the primary reconfiguring device: it patterns and reorganizes the image, the discontinuous minimal or basic unit. Texture is the relationship between the lines.

Although the images are taken by and large from historical contexts, the poetic images are unhistorical rather than historical, in a linear sense. But the poems substitute one kind of linearity—poetic, which subverts the linear, transforming it into the cyclical, the essential tool for metaphor, the basic meaning device of poetry—for another—historical. The experience of the poem is poetic rather than historical, cyclical rather than linear, paradigmatic rather than syntactic, repetitive rather than causal. Yet there *is* a linear and causal movement or pulse in the poem, albeit developed on poetic terms. Through characteristic patterning of the poem and its resultant circularity, the poem moves into an argument or metaphorical mode. This argument or metaphorical mode is based on a historical underpinning, but its expression is myth.

The repeated combination of image and line—line containing

imagery—creates a texture: this texture also operates as the grid of the poem, the necessary metronomic unit, a rhythmical poetic grid, against which the poet slowly reveals a theme. Through the consequent reshaping of the imagery into new forms, and because of the resulting emotional involvement and composition of the audience, the poet slowly imbues that audience with theme.

It is not photographically detailed portraits of historical characters that the poet seeks to create. He wants to reveal a certain attitude toward his subjects, so that they often become distorted, one-sided, even caricatures because of the selection and alignment of images. The poet has a certain feeling about a character, and proceeds to limn that feeling. He is selective, and because of that his character frequently seems warped. He may, for example, provide so many details about a character's warlike abilities as to make other perhaps equally significant aspects of his nature wither into irrelevance. By selectivity, arrangement, and patterning, the poet may praise a character or damn him, make unpleasant suggestions about him or elevate him into myth, knot him into a symbol and through juxtaposition compare what he is made to stand for with a later or earlier age. The poet is not striving for an objective appraisal of history; he is providing an interpretation of a character, a feeling about a character, and in the process he reveals something about that character in history. But the appraisal is achieved through feeling.

It is the function of the poet, then, to excise images from the linear continuity of story, of history. Through repetition, these images are worked into patterns, becoming a metrical grid that is predictable, and creates satisfying anticipation in the experience of the members of the audience. As the poet creates a grid of the images, by the arrangement of the images in rhythmic form, the images, wrenched from their former contexts, are placed in new, stimulating, regular, echoic patterns, and are given new environments and forms. The images thus brought into novel contact with one another are reshaped into new, metaphorical forms. But this is done always carefully, never chaotically, always against a grid that holds the images safely, allowing the new arrangements and environments to occur without a loss of regularity. They are not linear, but wholly new forms, working the previously sequential images into new cyclical configurations. The audience has always had certain emotional relationships with these images: in their linear form, in real life, in other stories and poems. The poet, calling these emotions into being by merely uttering them, now creates the grid by means of them, thus releasing new emotion, a neatly balanced symmetrical texture of emotions from many diverse sources, into a single textured experience that becomes the new theme of the old familiar images, the new message.

So it is that the poet creates the poem in the story.

Pages from a Journal

February 12, 1975

The expansible mythic image and patterning: expectancy in storytelling. A pattern is established, the audience learns or experiences the pattern, then expects, anticipates its continued repetition. What is the psychology of this? There is no doubt that the audience finds it aesthetically pleasant during the period when exact repetition of images is being experienced: expectation fulfilled. But the fact is that the audience's satisfaction with the regular repetition is intensified when an alteration in the pattern occurs. It is something of a storytelling shock, aesthetically pleasant when the rhythm and associated attitude of expectancy, familiarity, "lulled into half-sleep / By the lapping of water"[92] are broken, and the alteration of the image organization occurs. It is at junctures between rhythmic expectation and rhythmic dislocation that the mingling of emotional responses is clearest, more on the surface than at other times in the storytelling process—it is a momentarily confused mingling of diverse emotions, as the narrator seizes these dispersing feelings and expertly works them back into form, as she moves the audience into a new rhythmical expectation, a new set of patterns, and so there is once again the pleasant mesmeric somniloquy . . . until again, there is the jostle of disjuncture, and the members of the audience are moved into a new phase of the story, a satisfying inventive layering of their emotional responses.

January 23, 1976

The narrative with a beginning and an end: the rites of passage in stories dealing with the beginning and end of the body, and with the socialization of the body. Stories also deal with lives, full lives, of people. But the relationship between body and narrative is all-important. It is the temporality of the body that gives rise to the temporal narrative.

—Transformations: How do they work? Getting from one body movement or series of body movements to another. Dance is the key here: Storytelling is essentially dance, in a wondrously focused and controlled way.

—There are various definable gesture types—mime, emphasis, punctuation, shaping. But these are seldom encountered in isolation. It is always a complex network (and overlapping of simultaneous networks) of gestures, a mesh within which the verbal elements are externalized and their structures (messages) revealed. There is indeed a tension between complementary and supplementary gestures and body movements, but it is very complex. Is complementary/supplementary a useful categorization? There are links, as the types blend one into the other—graceful, dancelike links.

—The combination of body and structure (are they the same?) reveals message.

The Poetics of Storytelling

A Range of Rhythmic Patterns

> Readers who enjoy this small poem don't think about its balances and variations; we *feel* them, the way we feel a musical theme that returns slightly altered: expectation fulfilled and denied.
> —Donald Hall, *Poetry: The Unsayable Said*

THE POEM AT THE HEART OF HUMAN CRISES

The poet makes sense of his world, of the issues and details, the events and experiences that ripple and rumble through the community. It is his work, his poem placed unerringly at the heart of people's lives, that organizes the uncertain strands, that shapes the jumbled threads of those stories, giving them, in turn, meaning and form.

S. E. K. Mqhayi, a Xhosa writer who attempted to transpose oral heroic poetry to written form, describes the power of the oral poet in his imagined account of a Xhosa trial in the novel, *Ityala Lamawele* (*The Case of the Twins*). The trial ends when sentence has been passed by Hintsa, the Gcaleka king. But the people are confused; they mill about, vaguely dissatisfied. The oral bard, Dumisani, is disturbed by this reaction to the king's judgement, and he admonishes the people:

> *Hoyina! Hoyina! Hoyina!*
> Go home, you people, the case is at an end.
> Go home, people, the discussion is over.
> So says Fearful-eyes,
> So says the greatest of Gcaleka,
> Who is the horns of an old cow
> Not sleeping along the difficult way.

Dumisani reminds the people,

In olden days when mountains appeared,
One person was placed as ruler of us all.
It was said this was a person of royal blood,
It was said this was the child of the nation,
It was said this person must be submitted to by all,
And he in turn must submit to God
Whence law and custom emanate,
And when the king is wrong it will not be good:
Trouble and confusion will result.

There is a great silence when the poet begins, his voice purposely kept low, not strident, his tone in sympathy with people's hearts made tender by the day's events. So elegant is his poem, so forceful its images, that men weep, women do not attend to their cooking and the food burns. Some who have been smoking burn their pipe stems. No one among them moves, some unknowingly stand naked, others pull their garments too tightly around their bodies and tear them.[93]

The basis of the poem is the image that, with other images, is worked into a network of sounds and stresses to become a part of a regular, predictable pattern. The rhythmic patterning of the poem takes a number of forms: the patterning of the sounds of the poem, its music; the sound of the poet's voice, the manipulation of stresses and silences. The recurrence of images throughout the poem resolves itself into pattern, from simple and obvious arrangements to highly complex relationships.

In its simplest form, pure verbal repetition with little or no deviation creates pattern, as in this except from a "Shaka" poem:

Oth' esadl' ezinye wadl' ezinye,
Wath' esadl' ezinye wadl' ezinye;
Oth' esadl' ezinye wadl' ezinye,
Wath' esadl' ezinye wadl' ezinye;
Oth' esadl' ezinye wadl' ezinye,
Wath' esadl' ezinye wadl' ezinye.

He who while defeating some defeated others,
And as he defeated others he defeated some more;
He who while defeating some defeated others,
And as he defeated others he defeated some more;

He who while defeating some defeated others,
And as he defeated others he defeated some more.[94]

This simple pattern has variations:

Inyon' edl' ezinye!
Yath' isadl' ezinye, yadl' ezinye.

Bird that defeats others,
As it defeated others it defeated some more.[95]

Other variations are possible:

Wadl' uNomahlanjana, ezalwa nguZwide, emaPheleni;
Wadl' uMphepha, ezalwa nguZwid', emaPheleni;
Wadl' uDayingubo, ezalwa nguZwid', emaPheleni;
Wadl' uNombengula, ezalwa nguZwid', emaPheleni;
Wadl' uMntimona, ezalwa uGaqa, emaPheleni;
Wadl' uMpondo-phumela-kwezind', emaPheleni;
Wadl' uNdengezimashumi, emaPheleni.

He defeated Nomahlanjana, born of Zwide of the Phela;
He defeated Mphepha, born of Zwide of the Phela;
He defeated Dayingubo, born of Zwide of the Phela;
He defeated Nombengula, born of Zwide of the Phela;
He defeated Mntimona, born of Gaqa of the Phela;
He defeated Mpondo-phumela-kwezinde of the Phela;
He defeated Ndengezimashumi of the Phela.[96]

Genealogical data, names of people and places, battles, conquests, along with historical and cultural fragments, will form patterns. To accommodate such data, the poet includes simple formulas, altering each repetition only to supply a different name. Again, from the poem to Shaka:

uGasane kade *lubagasela;*
Lugalsel' uPhungashe wakwaButhelezi;
Lwagasel' uSondaba woMthanda ehlez' ebandla;
Lwagasel' uMacingwan' eNgonyameni;
Lwagasel' uNxaba kaMbhekane;

Lwagasel' uGambush' emaMpondweni;
Lwagasel' uFaku, emaMpondweni.

Stalker: for long *he has attacked* them;
He attacked Phungashe of the Buthelezi;
He attacked Sondaba of Mthanda as he sat in the assembly;
He attacked Macingwane at Ngonyameni;
He attacked Nxaba son of Mbhekane;
He attacked Gambushe in Mpondoland;
He attacked Faku in Mpondoland.[97]

A formula is established: He attacked ______ of/at ______, and the poet repeats the formula, adding appropriate names and places, and, at times, comments (for example, *ehlez' ebandla,* as he sat in the assembly). The possibilities of the formula are apparent also in a Sotho poem created for Letsie I:

O tšaba ha e le leqheku Mosiea,
O tšaba ka hae lipohomela,
Llo *o tšaba* sa motšeo oa ntlo,
O tšaba sa mor'a Tlhabeli, Letuka.

He is afraid, since he is an old man, Siea,
He is afraid of the wailing of his home,
He is afraid of the crying within the house,
He is afraid of that of Letuka, son of Tlhabeli.[98]

In a Xhosa poem, the poet begins with the image of an elephant. Then with the size and might of the creature in mind, he develops a formula:

Ndlovu edla eXonxa,
Izingele ime ngoZidabane.
Nkosi *engango*Sarhili *kwezakwa*Gcaleka,
*Engango*Ncaphayi *kwezakwa*Bhaca,
*Engango*Ndamasi *kwezakwa*Faku,
*Engango*Tshaka *kwezakwa*Zulu,
*Engango*Mbhandine *kwezakwa*Swazi,
*Engango*Sobhuza kaNdungunya *kwezakwa*Sotshangana,
Engango Bhungane *kwezama*Hlubi,
*Engango*Mzilikazi *kwezama*Ndebele,

*Engango*Dweba *kwezama*Zizi,
*Engango*Mshweshwe *kwezabe*Suthu,
*Engango*Napoleon *kwezabe*Mlungwini,
Ndikufanisa noNgubengcuka *kwezako*wenu.
Kude kulo ma.

Elephant that eats at Xonxa,
It hunts and stops at Zidabane.
Chief *as big as* Sarhili *among those* [regiments] *of* Gcaleka,
As big as Ncaphayi *among those of* Bhaca,
As big as Ndamasi *among those of* Faku,
As big as Shaka *among those of* the Zulu,
As big as Mbhandine *among those of* Swati,
As big as Sobhuza son of Ndungunya *among those of* Sotshangana,
As big as Bhungane *among those of* the Hlubi,
As big as Mzilikazi *among those of* the Ndebele,
As big as Dweba *among those of* the Zizi,
As big as Moshweshwe *among those of* the Sotho,
As big as Napoleon *among those of* the whites,
I liken you to Ngubengcuka *among those of* your home.
It is far from Mother's place.[99]

Many things can be done poetically with such patterning, from the straightforward repetition of formulas:

Ibicongo elimzimba buthaka;
*Obe*mzimba muhle, nangendlal' enkulu.
*Obe*buso, *bungenandawo yokusolwa;*
*Obe*mehlo, *engenandawo yokusolwa;*
*Obe*mlomo, *ongenandawo yokusolwa;*
*Obe*zandla, *zingenandawo yokusolwa;*
*Obe*zitho, *zingenandawo yokusolwa;*
*Obe*siphundu, *singenandawo yokusolwa.*

Tree with a frail body;
Whose body was beautiful even in the great famine.
Whose face *was faultless;*
Whose eyes *were faultless;*
Whose mouth *was faultless;*

Whose hands *were faultless;*
Whose feet *were faultless;*
Whose limbs *were faultless.*[100]

to playing with words and names, as in this example, in which the proper name, Mananga, is deliberately paralleled with *lumananga,* lily:

uHlumayo *lumananga,* uDlungwane,
uHlumayo *lumananga,* lunkone;
uMananga ubehamba kwaJiyampondo.

Sprouting *lily,* violent one,
Sprouting *lily,* white-spotted one;
Mananga was walking at Jiyampondo.[101]

The basis for such wordplay is the image, and its effect depends on the manipulation of identical words into patterns.

Theme, meaning, message—it is achieved by the paralleling of images. The poet establishes a predictable rhythm in his line, so that the succeeding lines are somehow measured against that archetypal line. The audience is thus led either to experience a parallel that would not otherwise be felt were it not for the paradigmatic form established in earlier lines, or an alteration of that expected parallel. These are two basic effects of the texture of the poem, and from the tensions created between them is born the experience that is theme.

Underlying the poem is unspoken history, the story from which the images are selected and made discontinuous. But the making discontinuous of the image does not mean that the historical context, the historical linear movement, the story, is forgotten. In fact, there is the unspoken historical context and the spoken poetic context. It is the tension and relationship between these two that creates myth, the ultimate effect of the poem. Myth is not history, it is not poetry; it is necessarily a combination of the two. Poetry is not history, but it partakes of and depends on historical linear plotting and continuity. A major source of its images is the story of history. History is not poetry, but it contributes vitally to poetry. These images are given poetic form, and the result is myth: an emotional experience, grounded in and dependent upon history, but building on the historical base an emotional experience that is not history but is poetry.

Historical image becomes allied with nonhistorical imagery (a king becomes a labyrinthine sea, a leader becomes a viper, a ruler becomes the bite of a dog) and becomes generalized, excised from history, moved to another plane of experience that has its own laws and pulses and logic. Historical imagery allied with poetic images and the force of metaphor is the first step in the reordering process.

Essential to the success of the oral poem is the patterning of the images into music. The images are ordered in two ways. Associated with musical patterning—the voice of the past, its cadences, its tone and pitch, and the body of the poet—is the verbal organization of the imagery; images of a certain type will interweave with other types of imagery establishing a sensory texture in the poem. This measured recurrence of image types, violence of war and homely images in the "Shaka" poem, for example, will create patterns. Genealogies and genealogical fragments, names of people, names of places and events—historical and cultural materials—will form their own patterns. They may not necessarily be chronologically ordered; there may be another poetic purpose underlying the organization of facts, events, and places.

Images are first evoked: "You are a beetle with mouth widely spread: / You daily devour herds of men."[102] Emotions are educed by individual images, culled from the audience's past and present experiences of reality and the art tradition. Such imagery, the choice of which is limited by the historical and cultural world of the audience, manipulates the audience within this unique poetic performance. Images call forth specific responses, but feeling becomes progressively denser as more and varied emotions are tapped by the images. Within a few lines, for example, the poet may elicit emotions of violence and emotions of peace:

> The child of the chief knows the clouds:
> When he goes to war the mist would close down:
> The mist has closed down on the snowy mountains,
> On the mountains where the winds are raging:
> There is wind, there is snow, mighty warriors,
> There is wind, there is snow in the mountains:
> Some would be fond of their pillows and stay.[103]

The images trap within themselves the emotions that they call forth. These images are locked into a metrical scheme. It is crucial that a pattern of image organization be discernible by members of the audience early in the poem. In oral poetry, the key pattern is in the relationship of sound between and among lines rather than within the line. The poet provides his audience with sufficient material to enable its members to conceptualize a rhythm-design for the poem, a model experienced perhaps only in their minds, establishing an ideal context, a paradigm, for comprehending and managing the actually produced lines.

The line in certain oral poems includes the following general characteristics: there is an initial explosion of sound and energy by the poet, occurring at and signaling the beginning of the line; there is a down-drift in the line thereafter, as the syllables resolve themselves into a chanted, patterlike form; there are attempts to reverse the down-drift along the way, within the line, to establish a tension, contributing to the incidence of prominence against the regular beat, or metrical grid, of the poem, and create the characteristic rhythm of the poem; the down-drift is momentarily arrested at the end of the line, typically with a brief—usually one syllable—rising tone often accompanied by a minor reinforcing explosion, usually followed by a reversion to down-drift, a final glide, a distinct falling tone in most cases. More rarely, it is a rising glide. But rising or falling, it marks the end of a line or a transition to another, a definite alteration in the patterned tone of the poet's voice as the line comes to an end.[104]

A line is, therefore, defined as the evocation of an image or images characterized by an explosion of sound at or near the image cluster's commencement, followed by a generally regularly intoned chant, moving down, ending with a rising or falling glide with a possible secondary sound explosion. The intervening regular chant is expansible in the sense that it can be expanded or contracted to accommodate a greater or lesser number of syllables without interfering in any appreciable way with the character of the line.

The poet establishes a recognizable, predictable rhythm, and then proceeds to manipulate the pattern he has created. The essential design of the line is never altered, but it may give way to other patterns and interweave with other patterns. In any case, all such individual patterns become a part of the poem's overall scheme. In addition, short exclamatory lines are frequently interspersed with longer lines.

By purposeful oversimplification and some slight exaggeration, a typical line of oral poetry might be described as follows:

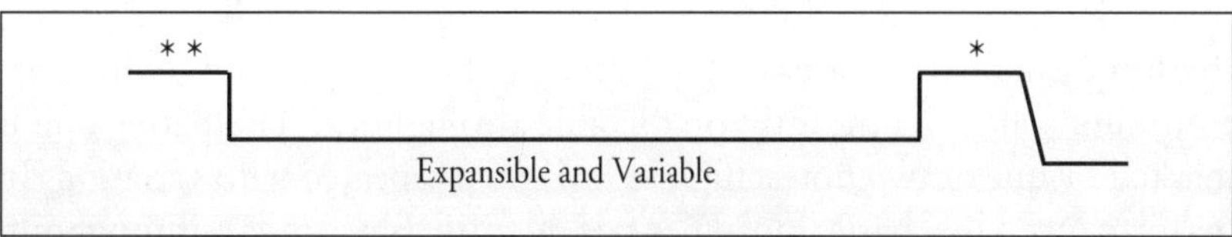

Figure 1

The poet characteristically begins a line on a high note with a major explosion of sound (**), this resolving itself into the expansible low-noted chant. The end of the line is signaled by the breaking of the regular chant with a rise of tone, and a glide usually to the dominant lower tone, often with a minor explosion of sound (*). That is the typical line. The break in the regular chant of the line is a sign of the its approaching end, or an indication of imminent transition. It may or may not be followed by a pause or breath. It is not pause or breath that signals the completion of the line. Rather, it is the character of the line, the regular patterning of a group of sounds, an explosion, for example, on a high note. There might be a down-drift with a series of expansible regular low notes, which are variable and which rise to a high note with a possible second explosion, followed by a final downward glide to a low note.

Within the expansible part of the line may be a combination of low and high notes creating its own subsidiary pattern, but more frequently a single tone level predominates in that part of the line. It is a modulated tone, but there will often be a certain amount of musical variation within the line. The beginning of the next line is marked by a fresh explosion, but it may actually occur two or even three syllables into the line. Rather than a single characteristic, then, it is the entire line that establishes its character. Lexical repetition, of course, also assists in the definition of the beginning and end of a line.[105]

Heightened tone syllables are more prominent than the low-toned. Long syllables are more prominent than the short. The penultimate syllable of a word or word-group or sentence usually exceeds the preceding lengthened syllables in prominence. Because of fast declamation, the penultimate syllable in certain lines is of lesser duration and prominence than in others. These two peaks balance, the fact of the first peak being lesser than the second knitting the two segments into a single verse.

A pattern of sounds is created, an arrangement of beats, stresses, and pauses—building and then rapidly falling off. A basic rhythm is established, then repeated, developing into the poem's identifiable rhythmic grid, or character. Within this pattern, many syllables may occur, chanted in various patter arrangements, but these only expand the basic rhythmic pattern, they do not alter it. Certain sounds will give unique rhythmic character to a basic line, varying the patter sounds, which are continuous and significantly predictable throughout. The patter line is marked by one or two notes, high or low, then repeated with variation. In performance, the basic movement is identifiably similar throughout. Small deviations may begin to alter the pattern, variations on sound themes leading ultimately to new patterns. A basic pattern may also be interrupted without this gradual movement by a new pattern, breaking abruptly with the basic pattern; and there may or may not be a return to the basic pattern. A new pattern will have been established, growing out of and having much of the character of the previous or original one.

The poet's voice is also an instrument. Sound in itself is significant. It provides one of the categories of patterning in poetic performance, and it attracts the audience as it limns the object of the poem, binding them as one. It ties all to social rhythms, for the poet's rhymes are those of his poetic and linguistic tradition.

With the development of the imaged argument, the explosion occurs, then moves along and modulates. Another explosion opens a new set of images that complements the first, and so on. From time to time, this regular movement of an argument requires further energy to keep the line alive, and so brief, often hortative exclamations occur, to which the members of the audience respond vocally and physically. The poem is a series of major and minor explosions with succeeding images connected to those explosions that are punctuated from time to time with the terse exclamations, always eruptive, dramatic, serving as emotional buttresses for the regular movement of the argument; these form the grid against which the argument moves. There is a curious lacing of the first part of the longer lines and the sententious explosive segments, interconnected by sound alone.

These emotional spires, with the regular metrical beat of the spoken images, transport members of the audience. The combination of stress and explosion begins to form a textured pattern against which the images are experienced. The images themselves evoke emotions, but these emotions are of a different sort—more specific, particularized—than the explosive, metrical sounds, which are nonverbal, abstract, mixing with the movement of the poet's body, and forming the abstract grid against which the images are developed, but also trapping the emotions of the members of the audience in a nonverbal, nonintellectual way. They respond to the rhythmical beat and the sounds with their emotions, and this irresistibly provides an aesthetic context for the experiencing of the images, which are also geared to call forth emotions. But here we are on a cognitive level, here we are dealing with the images of history, for example, of places and people known, of creatures, personifications; and this more conscious evocation of emotions becomes inextricably entangled in a most complex way with the regular nonverbal abstracted activities caused by sound and body. Neither of these two processes is a mere background or metronome; each is vital to the experiencing of the poem, to its ultimate meaning. "Meaning," of course, in a complex sense that includes—indeed, is dominated by—feeling. That is why performance context is so critical to an analysis of oral poetry.

The poet sets up a metrical grid against which he will work, and he develops that grid through repetition. But he also takes liberties with it, plays with it, distorts it, but never diminishes its essential outlines, its basic character; he always returns to that. It is his context, his sound and nonverbal touchstone; it determines the meaning of the poem, it is the very structure within which he works. It is the form of the poem, a form composed only of the poet's voice, his words having sound as well as meaning. It is the sound that is the crucial part of the performance. The poet has a reservoir of sound, and he exploits it, diminishes it, refreshes it, distorts it, but he does not exhaust it until the end of the line. He establishes a rhythm, then follows it, obeying its pulses, subtly ordering it, altering it, methodically shaping metrical patterns from it. But each pattern slowly and subtly grows out of the preceding one.

Here is another possible development of the line in oral poetry. The poet establishes a definite regular rhythm, a metrical beat, and then he slowly alters one part of this, one important stress, and so creates a new metrical beat, a new rhythm, and then he alters a part of that, having repeated it a number of times. So the poem reveals its developing form, moving from rhythm A to rhythm X, and A and X are very different indeed. But the intervening rhythms have been slowly altered, and A and B are recognizably similar, as are B and C, and C and D; but now A begins to show definite signs of being different from D, greater still from E, from F, from G, and so on. That is, rhythms A and B are not perceptibly different, but as we move further away from rhythm A, change becomes more identifiable as it becomes more and more distant from original rhythms. Yet, a close study of the rhythms of the poem will show the relationship between A and F, between A and X. At the same time, early lines will contain within them certain possible patterns that will later be developed into full patterns.

As noted, the rhythm is established by explosions of sound, with a gradual diminishing of the explosive energy as the line winds down and moves towards its close. There is some kind of terminal activity on the penultimate syllable before the usually dying final syllable of the line. The emotions of the poet and audience are thus contained within the limits of the line and the context that the poet has been establishing. He may move the entire poem to a point where he uses verbal sounds—a long cry, for example—to move it to a high pitch, followed by another gradual downward movement.

It is not an argument that moves from point A to point B to point C. Rather, it is a transition, a move from one state to another by means of various devices and techniques, tools, and management of images. It is repetitive: the same thing is repeated a number of times, but with each repetition there is friction, some irregularity. Yet the repetition remains sufficiently similar and identifiable that the structure of the work remains intact. But it is fluid, always changing. Within the context of repetition, a gradual transition is occurring, patterns give way to other patterns, argument is being advanced—this, both in terms of imagery and of sound, image and rhythm. The repetition keeps the structure intact: it *is* the structure. The irregularity allows for the transition, a necessary transition, to take place and, therefore, for the argument to occur—that is, the argument is the move from state A to state B. But state B is always prefigured in state A. The transition from the one to the other is the argument. It is not so much a movement from state A to state B as it is an examination of state A through a dynamic process. State B is not removed from state A, it is an explanation of state A in imagistic terms, a development of state A in terms of both image and sound. We move not so much in a rational way in these works of art as into the statement of a position, then through a series of transformations, transitions, and repetitions—these repetitions with slight variations so that movement is possible—that examine and develop that position. Following the statement of the problem, repetitions one and two and three and four and five restate the problem; they remain much the same when viewed against their immediate neighbors. But with gradual changes those changes become more marked if we view repetitions one and five, for example, in their relationship to each other. These changes represent not so much the thread of an argument as the transition from one state to another. The transition must not be so rapid or abrupt as to lose the form of the work—chaos and a loss of comprehension would result. Repetition assures that the form remains stable. And with stable form, the rhythm of the performance assures audience allurement and involvement. Within this context, changes occur, transitions take place; the transition is an examination and at the same time a restatement of the first set of images. Our perception of state A has changed because of our experience of state B. But more: state B is composed of state A plus new imagistic and emotional material. Further, state B is a part of, an anticipation of, state C. All three states retain the same form, but alterations acceptable within that form, so that the character of the form is not lost, are occurring. Some of the images and cadences are purely emotionally evocative. Others remain constant. The distinction is drawn, and the relations and tensions between the two are established.

Lines have character. It is not the syllables in a line that are important, but the character of the line in terms of sound. The regular beat of the line, obeying the normal stress of the language, is dramatically altered. Notes are stressed or downplayed abnormally, but never to the extent that normal rhythms are distorted. The line thus achieves its own character, a melody unique. The poet plays with this novel rhythm that he has established. The poet, in other words, establishes his own music within a tradition and the realities of his language; his work makes sense only within the context of the language and the tradition that he knows and that the audience knows. Without the tradition and linguistic realities, it makes no sense. Deviation and friction mean nothing if the norm is not known, felt, and intimately experienced, as he simultaneously puts words to the music. He is aided by the music inherent in the language, the linguistic tradition that passes on certain speech patterns, the artistic tradition that passes on certain aesthetic patterns, and his own experience and imagination—and various combinations of these.

The length of the line can change, as long as the character of the line does not change, at least in any respect that makes it impossible to discern that basic rhythmic character, to recognize a predictable organization of sounds. Tension is in the down-drift; there are efforts to pull the line up, as inevitably as it moves downward, as energy is dispelled and the movement is a winding down. "Down" is the natural model. But "up" is the goal. Normal tones are manipulated. Each line is a series of explosions, generally separated by breaks, the explosion decreasing in volume as silences and exhaustion of energy move towards the final downward movement. The regular stresses of the words are a pull towards the normal cadences of the language. But these are heightened; they are dramatically altered, notes are stressed or muted abnormally; poetry creates tensions in sound when the poet plays with and even distorts the normal language sounds. Or the usual beats are overstressed, overemphasized. The line thus achieves its own character; the bard creates his own music as he simultaneously puts words to it. The tension in the down-drift of the line is confirmed by the final distinctive glides; there are efforts to pull the line up, but inevitably it moves to finality.

These are the mechanics of some of the poetic devices employed by poets to elicit emotions from members of audiences, to develop anticipation, to sustain that expectation, and then, within that context, to take apparent liberties with established rhythmical patterns. The words dance within these rhythms at the same time that they form them, so that in the end it is not entirely clear which, word or rhythm, has the greater impact on the audience. When the poem appears in the story, it has the effect of weaving its rhythmic tentacles into all parts of the narrative, so that the narrative and the poem become one.

A Page from a Journal

June 3, 1975

Two general types of body movement: supplementary and complementary.
—SUPPLEMENTARY: Masithathu Zenani creates images with her hands and her body. Clapping is used to a certain extent. These gestures are in addition to those gestures that reflect the verbal aspects of the performance. They are generally graceful and aesthetically attractive. These become the contexts for the complementary gestures. More than that, they provide the shaping of the external form of the story.
—COMPLEMENTARY: These are graceful movements that reflect the verbal aspects of the performance. The body and hands reveal graphically and vividly what the words convey. They give dimension and body to the words.
—There are subcategories of these types, and these might be said generally to bridge the two larger categories:
—Itemizing things, mainly with the fingers: one hand takes the fingers, holding a finger while a point is made; then the next finger is grasped while point number two is being made, etc. The gesture is noncomplementary in form, but functionally it is complementary. This is a gesture that thus bridges the two general types.
—Emphasis: Again, the hands accompany the words, and the gestures are in that sense complementary. But they are not complementary in form. They are hence both complementary and supplementary. Emphasis takes varying forms: the index finger is pounded into the palm of the other hand; a clapping motion is made with the open hand (the sound of one hand clapping); the hand or finger is pounded on the knee; a finger chops the air, etc.
—Repetition: A use of gesture and body movement that is frequently very dramatic. Clapping may be involved here. Repetition is sometimes complementary; more often, it is supplementary. Again, it bridges the two types. Such gestures cannot be separated from the verbal elements, yet they are not used specifically to create images. Repetition accompanies and supplements the verbal aspects of performance. Thus, walking is suggested by fisting the hand, thumb out, then moving the fist, etc. Regular movements of the body can suggest various activities and things. It is repetition verbally that frequently gives rise to nonverbal repetition.
—The full performance is a rich combination of such gestures and body movements. The performer may also merely play with something idly to keep

her hands busy when she is not gesturing. This is the range: there is movement of the body from pure movement (that is, not related to the verbal aspects) to movement that complements and reflects words strictly, with all the combinations in between. Masithathu Zenani picks up a stick, as a complementary gesture, then keeps the stick when the verbal image has passed, and it now becomes a supplementary gesture. Commonly, there is movement of the gesture from complementary to supplementary, from supplementary to complementary, and back again. The gestures and body movements of Masithathu Zenani are muted at times, often becoming more frequent as the narrative becomes more and more dramatic. Gestures and body movements are more frequent at crises, during chases, and at other dramatic high points.

The Poetics of Storytelling
Poetic Organization

Je persiste à penser que le poème n'est accompli que s'il se fait chant, parole et musique en même temps.
—Léopold Sédar Senghor, "Comme les lamantins vont boire a la source"

THE UNERRING MOVE TO THE POEM IN THE STORY

Young people participating in a ritual unerringly move to the poem in the story, when, in their dancing and singing, they envelop the transition that they are experiencing in a poetry that is traditional, connecting their current activities and their transition to the history of the people even as they move into a new state of being.

It is August 12, 1967, and from 10 A.M. to 5 P.M. an *intonjane* celebration among Xhosa residents of Tshiqo is occurring—girls having moved through their puberty rituals, moving to womanhood.[106] The place is the homestead of a man who is celebrating the completion of the puberty ritual of his daughter and seven of her age mates. The occasion is one of the final steps in the *intonjane* ceremony—the young women are still in the *intonjane* lodge during this celebration, but will be emerging in two or three days. Eight cows are slaughtered, one for each of the *intonjane* women; this is done by the relatives of those women, in the cattle kraal of the man who is organizing the celebration. In the morning, the other women are not yet dressed in their celebration garb—they sit about, talking and drinking, and there is some singing and dancing. But these are not the official song and dance of the *intonjane* ritual.

The carcasses of the cattle are cut up, the meat distributed first to the relatives (with the first cuts going to the *intonjane* women in the lodge), and then to members of the community. The names of various locations are called out by the man who is organizing the party, and those residents go to the kraal to get meat, which is cooked, served, and eaten. In the afternoon, the women are dressed in dazzling clothing, with beads and red and blue capes. The mothers of the *intonjane* women are anointed with white ochre and they wear traditional garments made of animal skins. Now the official dancing and singing begins. The women are arranged in a circle, and move counter clockwise. The men watch, drinking and walking about. Cattle are draped in white sheets and chased through the crowd by boys and young men. Men strike their shields with sticks, and the cattle are rushed hurriedly through the group. The people stand on both sides, and they ritually strike the cows with sticks. Then the cows are rounded up, again one for each of the *intonjane* women, and they are herded in very close formation (surrounded tightly by the men and boys) to the lodge (this is, some observers comment, symbolic of the importance of cattle in the approaching marriages of the *intonjane* women; they should not run off and marry anyone, but should undergo the proper *lobola* ceremonies).[107] While the women continue to dance, the young men and the boys go to another part of the area to have stick competitions. There, the young men and boys (none of the competitors has yet been circumcised) arrange themselves on two sides, and one emerges from each group at a time to stick-fight with a member from the other. The sticks are held, one as a shield (with a blanket wrapped about the hand) and one as a fighting weapon. Whistling and singing accompany the competition, and a victory song is sung by the winning side. There are area competitions: boys from one area compete with those of another. Men and elders stand along the sidelines to make certain that this does not erupt into a serious fight, but there is no sympathy for the vanquished boy: this is a part of his growing up. The celebration ends at sundown.[108]

In a San song in which the poet, ||kábbo, laments the loss of his tobacco pouch, the pure repetition depends for its dirgelike effect on the music of the poet's voice:

|χùru é,
|χùru é ų,
|χùru kaň |ké ų.

|χùru é
|χùru é ų,
|χùru kaň |ké ų.

Tobacco-hunger is that which is here,
Tobacco-hunger is that which is here,
Tobacco-hunger is here.
Tobacco-hunger is that which is here,
Tobacco-hunger is that which is here,
Tobacco-hunger is here.[109]

Such repetition is not the only form of patterning available to the oral poet, nor is it necessarily the most common. But whether patterning is lexically identical or thematically parallel, the principle underlying its management and arrangement is the same. In June, 1880, the San poet, !nańni, recreated a song he had heard his father, ɘá-llné, sing:

Young moon!
Oh! Young moon!
Oh! Oh!
Young moon!
Young moon! Speak to me!
Oh! Oh!
Young moon!
Speak to me of something!
Oh! Oh!
When the sun rises,
You must speak to me,
That I may eat something.
You must speak to me
About a little thing,
That I may eat.
Oh! Oh!
Young moon.[110]

There are three sets of patterned images in this poem: (1) "Young moon!" (2) "Speak to me!" and (3) "That I may eat." There is a slow, crescendoing unfolding of images, as the poet retraces his imagery, reinforcing it, before moving to a new image or to a development of the already evoked imagery. The poet uses the regularly patterned "Young moon!" image to establish a grid across which the incrementally developed imagery moves. "Young moon!" gives way to a new image that contains the old but includes the new: "Young moon! Speak to me!" followed by "Speak to me of something" and "You must speak to me." These are developments of the "Speak to me" image. This new "Speak to me" material, worked into the "Young moon" grid, now itself becomes a grid, or a part of a grid, a reinforcing device giving form to the poem and holding the new and yet unassimilated material in form. "Speak to me," only an isolated image held in form by the "Young moon" image in the first part of the poem, becomes the grid for the second part of the poem, growing out of the repeated "Speak to me" lines of the first part. The new material, "That I may eat," now becomes a part of the grid in the same way, by means of its own patterning. Thus, "Young moon!" becomes "Young moon! Speak to me!" which in turn becomes "You must speak to me," and finally, "You must speak to me / About a little thing." This is linked to another developing image, also being worked into the grid: "That I may eat something" and "That I may eat." The strong patterning of "Young moon!" and "Speak to me!" and "That I may eat" makes it possible for the two lexically unlike and unpatterned lines, "When the sun rises" and "About a little thing," to exist poetically though they have no formulaic correspondences. They will also be fitted into the rhythmical measure of the poem. This final unpatterned touch, "When the sun rises," adds urgency to the poet's prayer to the young moon and his request—"Tell me of something" so that "When the sun rises," "I may eat something." The regular patterning of imagery gradually works into its grid additional threads, some patterned, some not, but always—as here, in the final two lines—the poet returns to the original pattern, tying the new strands into that.

At the opening of this book can be found the story told by Díä!kwą̄in about |nų̆in|kúï-tęn, the magician and rainmaker who could transform himself into a lion:[111]

|k'ĕ kăṅ ddóä ē,
|kąṅn kwā kā |nūïṅ
Hé tíkęn ē,
Tĭ |nĕ úä kkā,
Ī,
Ŏ |nūïṅ ā ddóä |kwā kā.
Hé tíkęn ē,
Tí-g |nĕ)áuki ttăṅ-ă kkā,

Tí kă ssĭṅ |kwēï ttā kkā,
Tí kă ssĭṅ |kwēï ttā kkā,
Ī.
Tā,
Tĭ |kŭ-g |nē ttă bbōkęn |khéyă kā,
Ô |nūïṅ ā |kwā kkā.
Hĕ tíkęn ē,
Tí)aúkĭ |nĕ ttă ≠hăṅnwă kkā,
Ī.

People were those who
Broke for me the string.
Therefore,
The place became like this to me,
On account of it,
Because the string was that which broke for me.
Therefore,
The place does not feel to me,
As the place used to feel to me,
On account of it.
For,
The place feels as if it stood open before me,
Because the string has broken for me.
Therefore,
The place does not feel pleasant to me,
On account of it.[112]

The poet starts with a fecund image, and that is repeated as he carefully develops it, working new images from it, repeating it with variation. He develops a companion image, peeling a new image from the juxtaposition. The first two lines, "People were those who / Broke for me the string," establish the problem; the poet Díä!kwąin then explores lyrically what this has meant for him, formulating his basic image set three times, incrementally revealing his feeling with each repetition:

1. Therefore,
The place became like this to me,
On account of it, . . .
2. Therefore,
The place does not feel to me,

PATTERNING IN POETRY		
"The Song of the Springbok Mothers" performed in June, 1879, by |háń≠kaśs'ō:	A Tswana poem, the subject of which is Isang (1884–1941), 2nd son of Lentswe, chief of the Kgatla (1875–1941)	A poem in praise of Shaka, by Nombhonjo Zungu, a Zulu poet, performed in 1973
A-a hn! O! Springbok child! Sleep for me! A-a hn! O! Springbok child! Sleep for me! Á-áhn̉, Wái-ʘpųă wwĕ ʘpųoin̉ya kĭ. Á-áhn̉, Wái-ʘpųă wwĕ, ʘpųoin̉ya kĭ.	He surpassed the son of Motswasele, Legwale, He surpassed Kgope, the hill Kwenaland, He surpassed Makanke and surpassed Modipe; He's as big as Matone's hill, He's as big as Matlhore, the Wise One, He's as big as Matlhore and Sefikile; He's the hill of Kgeste Segolo's, He's the hill of RaBailekae's people, He's the hill of Tshwabi Seoka's. . . .	Hero who surpasses other heroes! Swallow that disappears in the clouds, Others disappearing into the heavens! Son of Menzi! Viper of Ndaba! Erect, ready to strike! It strikes the shields of men! Father of the cock! Why did it disappear over the mountain? It annihilated men! That is Shaka, Son of Senzangakhona, Of whom it is said, Hail! You are an elephant!

Figure 2

As the place used to feel to me
On account of it. . . .
3. The place feels as if it stood open before me,
. . . .
Therefore,
The place does not feel pleasant to me,
On account of it.

The poet is expressing his feeling, what it meant to him when the "People . . . / Broke for me the string." In the first exploration of this unhappy event, he explains that the place had become "like this" for him. In the next set of images, he explains "like this" somewhat further: "The place does not feel" as it used to feel to him. And finally, he develops this with another image: "The place feels as if it stood open before me / . . . / The place does not feel pleasant to me." The sense of loss, of hollowness and alienation, is the objective here, not the actual history of the event.[113]

The relationship between a San song and a Tswana poem seems fairly obvious, but a Zulu poem by Nombhonjo Zungu seems not to follow the compositional patterns set by the San and Tswana poems (see figure 2).[114] The "Shaka" poem by Zungu is a lyric poem like the other two, but repetition in it is not immediately discernible. The lexical repetition in Zungu's poem, of the lines, "Swallow that disappears in the clouds, / Others disappearing into the heavens," has its obvious counterpart in the San poems ("Oh! Springbok child!" and "Oh! Young moon" and "the string . . . broke for me") and the Tswana formulas ("He surpassed ______," "He's as big as ______," and "He's the hill of ______"). In the San lullaby, the repeated singing of the song, with minute variations in the poet's repeated musical renderings, establishes a mood of calm—in the story from which the song comes, the storyteller notes, "The springbok mothers sang (soothing the children)." The quieting effect of the San poem is paralleled by the building effect of the Tswana—the cataloguing of Isang's moments of strength, conquests, and protectiveness helps to create a sense through lexical repetition of a praiseworthy leader. In the "Shaka" poem by Zungu, in the place of repetition, the poet supplies apparently different imagery, but swallow, viper, cock, elephant, each with its stated or implied extension ("Viper . . . / Erect, ready to strike," for example) in some way affirms, reinforces, or extends the sense of the opening line, "Hero who surpasses other heroes." Each subsequent image repeats that opening line in the same way that each repetition of the San and Tswana images intensifies a mood or feeling. From the point of view of feeling and the construction of the poems, there is a parallel function of the lines:

Oh! Springbok child! Sleep for me!	. . . He's as big as Matlhore and Sefikile. . .	Viper of Ndaba! Erect, ready to strike!

Figure 3

The movement towards complexity is already seen in the shift from the San poem to the formulaic predictability of the Tswana poem, and is most readily seen in the shift to the thematic parallelism of the Zulu poem.

While identical repetition provides the form of the San poem and formulas hold variation in form in the Tswana, the Zulu poem is dependent on sound rhythms and thematic parallels for its more complex form. The differences in the lexical variations are as follows: in the first poem, the repetitions are identical; in the second, they begin to deviate, but remain recognizably related lexically. The principal, however, of segments that relate to each other thematically as well as lexically is carried to the third example in which thematic similarity has wholly replaced lexical similarity. Many poems will include all three of these categories, the second being the most active, shunting the audience back and forth between lexical and thematic correspondences, simultaneously providing for the smooth, thematic linkages which override all others. This is poetic texture.

In many poems, thematic parallelism is a major device, unifying the poem. In a Sotho poem, for example, Jonathane Molapo's martial abilities are compared with violent natural images: "Whirlwind of the troops of Lejaha."[115] Into this unifying, steadying matrix, the poet will place images that have more flexible valences, which adapt themselves readily to whatever image environment they happen to be in: "Down-horned cow confronts Agitator," for example, and "Buffalo of the Mphaphathi family." These lines take on the coloration of the dominant images around them and add to the illusion of unity. Images are "dominant" because they form a set and unify the diverse parts of the poem. The violent natural images dominate the Sotho poem and act as the unifying element, with comparisons with violent animals—not a part of the main thematic movement of the poem—juxtaposed and, both sets dealing with combat, supporting the dominant set:

Rhinoceros of the Teketoa of Leribe,
Down-horned cow confronts Agitator,
Whirlwind of the troops of Lejaha.
Whirlwind threw people down,
People seized by a torrent of spears,
A summer downpour, a tempest,
Hail with granite stones;
Always causing people to perish,
Leading them to the Maloti, in the East!
Youth of the Buffalo, Pursuer,
The Pursuer chopped people into pieces,
The Fierce-starer chopped them into groups,
Buffalo of the Mphaphathi family.

Sharp-horned Buffalo gored,
It gored with its javelin-like horns,
Rhinoceros of the boy of the Takers.
The heaven struck at the chief's place,
It struck, raising the ashes!
Take out the child, Mother of summer,
The Teketoa and Fierce-starers are causing war,
They are burning this little village.[116]

The nature imagery dominates the first half of the poem, and then is complemented by images about goring buffalo, the chopping pursuer, and the fierce-starer. But the strength of the natural imagery reasserts itself in the end ("The heaven struck . . ."), and the almost unrelieved imagery of violence is touched with the tragic meaning of the destruction in the line, "They are burning this little village."

In a segment from a "Shaka" poem, the Zulu leader is followed as he travels restlessly, relentlessly, to two of his father's councilors, Ndima and Mgovu, to the top of Bhuzane Mountain, towards Nomagaga and his people against whom Shaka plans a surprise attack. When the attack is thwarted by the rising sun (announced by a cock), he goes on to the Thukela River where he confronts Khungwayo and the Ngobizembe warriors. Finally, he moves along a ridge, passing among the bones of the Tayi who died of cold when fleeing Shaka for protection from Macingwane at Ngonyameni:

He who passed through to Ndima and Mgovu,
And the pregnant women bore their young easily;
The second crop they left cut short,
The seed they left at the abandoned kraals.
He who passed to the top of Bhuzane,
He encountered a file of rhebok,
He passed by Mcombo as the cattle went home.
He whose way they sought from Dunjwa,
But they should have sought it from Mbozane;
He who had first gone to Nomagaga,
A cock arrived and prevented him.
He who is an approaching storm—preserve the children,
Only the older will flee for themselves,
Dunjwa along the sky has crushed.
He who went and built temporary shelters on the Thukela,

Where there was snared in a trap a lion,
He came with Khungwayo and Ngobizembe.
He who moved lazily along a long ridge;
He passed among the bones
Of the Tayi people,
Who became cold while going to Macingwane at
    Ngonyameni.[117]

Along with this restless martial movement, which in this segment does establish a loose narrative web, the poet creates a harvest of images unified by the fact that they depict the results of Shaka's depredations: the destruction of the young and crops, the abandonment of kraals, and, as frequently appears in Zulu war poetry, images of the hearth and home juxtaposed with those of violence. In this segment, the images of violence are forthright for the most part, factual and historical, with two metaphorical reinforcing images of war: Shaka is compared to an approaching storm, and he snares a lion on the Thukela, that is, he overcomes Khungwayo. These images of war move through images of the heart—a dual grid composed of images of war and images of hearth, not without irony by mere juxtaposition. But they are images of destruction: the devastation of the young, of crops, abandoned kraals, the cock that prevents the assault, the children who must be preserved from his onslaught, the bones of fleeing people dead of exposure on the plain. The segment is in six parts, and indicates the manner in which the poem as a whole is constructed.

The figure of Shaka is constructed by means of images showing the results of his deeds. The poet, Mtshongweni, treats the actions of a king, but the king himself is characterized by images showing his impact on the common man. The poet addresses himself to king and subject. It is true that "The second crop they left cut short" seems unrelated to "He passed among the bones / Of the Tayi people," but all images in this segment are really the same thing. Whether they refer to actual history, historical narrative, or to metaphor, the fragments are unified by their relentless replication of the violence and damage wrought by Shaka. The poet sketches in the images of the peaceful countryside: crops, kraals, buck, cattle, women, and children. It is the contrast that creates the view of Shaka, and the crushing effects of war on these homely images. It is, then, a theme, a thematic parity, a thematic paralleling that holds the images together, and, with the rhythm of performance, that holds them in form. These "He who ______" sections are not separate one from the other; the "He who ______" pattern is one of the unifying devices of the sections. But it is not necessarily a narrative. The

"He who ______" patterning simply brings together a number of Shaka marches, not necessarily ordered chronologically. They are not so much meant to recreate history as to create a certain Shaka—a restless and plundering Shaka. The restless Shaka may be seen as narrative, the plundering Shaka as nonnarrative.

Organization of poetry is determined by the bard's artistic needs. These dictate the image choices that he makes and the historical events that he will explore, images and events that will be recontextualized during the poetic moment. The audience always has a historical linearity in its memory even as it participates in the breaking of that linearity while the poet creates a lineal *poetic* order that is fixed by the surface image organization and, more importantly, by the rhythmical patterning that has the effect of redisposing those surface images. It is a bard's brand of sorcery that enables him to undertake such reshaping without actually disturbing the outer order of the images. It is in his choice of historical and mythic imagery and in his linear and rhythmic ordering of that imagery that the poet imposes his own imprimatur on history, creating illusions that make the poetry at once aesthetically attractive, mysterious, and informing.

Pages from a Journal

A USEFUL SYMBOL OF CHANGE

During the Xhosa marriage rite of passage, an interesting character sometimes appears—the *unozakuzaku,* or master of ceremonies.[118] Why is this clownish character significant, and what does he tell us about the ritual? The *unozakuzaku* exists in real-life representations of the marriage ritual, symbolizing the betwixt and between stage of the transformational rite. He blurs real life and the fantasy world of the oral narrative tradition: in fact, he seems to step out of the fantasy world of story into the real world, a poetic figure who comes to embody the changes being experienced by the bride as she moves from one state of being to another.

July 20 and October 15, 1975

The *unozakuzaku* (always a man): like the artist, he moves things, people, beasts about, making the movements of the rites run smoothly and rhythmically. The *unozakuzaku* is the director, a perfect symbol for movement in narrative, paralleling the role of the artist as the mover of people and events in the story. Both in real life and in the narratives, the *unozakuzaku* becomes the prime mover, an artistic device, revealing in his own demeanor the transformation occurring within the bride: she has lost one identity, is in the process of procuring another, and in this transitional stage, her uncertainties are reflected in the ambivalent activities of this erstwhile respected member of the community, the *unozakuzaku,* now behaving in this harlequinesque way. Story and reality here come into nervous tension.

A Bride's Remembrance

The leader of our group was that older man of the two men in the group. He was leading us now. Behind him in the [wedding] procession was a young married woman, and after her came a girl. Another girl followed her, and then I [the bride] came along. Yet another girl came after me, and she was followed by another young married woman. That was the composition of our procession, with the master of ceremonies in the front, carrying a stick. He walked along in front of us, clearing the way of bad things, kicking dried cow dung out of the way, clearing the path so that we would not stumble. . . . So it was then, we walked until we came to the kraal [at the house of marriage] . . . We were now uncovered by the master of ceremonies."[119]

The Poetics of Storytelling

Feeling and Its Containment

In former times, people played the lute
together with the drum for dancing.
Today I can only play the lute for my storytelling.
I am a young man,
my lute is beautiful,
because of my lute I have planted no plants,
because of my lute I now have nothing to eat,
because of my lute I now have nothing to eat.
—Hans Himmelheber, *Aura Poku*[120]

A HUMAN MIRROR, A HUMAN METAPHOR

The human body, in its relationship with other human bodies, can become a metaphor, and, in the process, can also become the poem in the story.

On the 23rd and 24th of August, 1972, Manyawusa Sodidi, about 60 years old, participated in an extraordinary storytelling performance.[121] A large audience was in attendance during her performances in Lubaleko Location, Mount Ayliff District, the Transkei. With her was a younger woman, Manto Matshezi, about 35 years old. Sodidi was the storyteller, and her stories were her customary lengthy, detailed, dramatically produced works. But something striking was happening, something that delighted the members of the audience and clearly drew them more forcefully into the story, worked them more effectively into the webbing sinews of the narrative. Manto Matshezi became literally the poem in the story. She did not speak throughout the presentation, but hers was just as commanding a performance as that of Sodidi. Sitting directly behind and slightly to the side of Sodidi, Matshezi began by nonverbally mirroring everything that Sodidi was doing—duplicating her body movements, miming the activities of the story being told. But then, once she had established herself as the nonspeaking replication of Sodidi's story, Matshezi's deportment began to alter, slightly at first, then more decisively, as her body became a nonverbal commentary on the words and actions of the performer. They were joined as one at the beginning, because of Matshezi's magisterial linkage of her body to the body and words of Sodidi. Once she had achieved that connection, once her body and that of the teller were perceived as one, then the two bodies began to separate, Matshezi continually coming back to the regularity, the rhythmic sameness of the bodies, but she also deviated from this, establishing new rhythms, her own rhythms, and these were then meshed with those of Sodidi. And so it was that Matshezi became the poem in the story, and so it was that metaphor was created, as she became the embodiment of the emotional experiences of the members of the audience.[122]

Mdukiswa Tyabashe exploited the tension of the event, created it, using the object—the king, for example, who is frequently only a mask for larger themes—and manipulating the emotional involvement of the members of the audience. Poets in the nineteenth and early twentieth centuries would often wear masks, animal parts over their heads, diminishing their own personalities, heightening the theatrical aura, and making contact with the past. Both Tyabashe and Ashton Ngcama of the Transkei in South Africa were angry poets, their lines raging, their images in the past but their concerns in the present, the past the rhythmic measure of the present, their villains the tepid, toadying leaders of the present. The contemporary political realities were keyed into the poems. The villains were not so much the whites in South Africa as those Africans who had been cowed or otherwise won over by the whites, these blacks who had forsaken their hallowed, brave traditions. In present time (the poems were created in the years before the Transkei was granted its dubious independence), there are no great kings and chiefs. Today, the leaders are being forced by the exigencies and realities of the present to relinquish traditional power, to deal with Pretoria, to give up authority first to the whites and then to the extensions of the whites, the puppet black rulers. Thus, the poets, who are nothing if not the upholders of tradition, must inevitably criticize the kings and chiefs. The kings and chiefs are in an unenviable position. The king

Manto Matshezi and Manyawusa Sodidi

represents tradition, and the poet is dealing with the very stuff and image of tradition. In some regards, during the performance of a poem, the king is beside the point.

Tyabashe lamented the present of Diliz' Iintaba while extolling the greatness of past Mpondomise royalty: the royal cape that rested on Diliza's shoulders—tentatively, it turned out; he was to give up the kingship a few years later in favor of his brother—suited Tyabashe's themes. He praised the past, using it as a weapon with which to assail and reveal the weaknesses of the present. So critical did his images become that some members of the audience wondered that King Diliza endured them so stoically.

The poems are works of art that can be appreciated, understood, and analyzed only in the context of performance. The creation of the oral poem is a theatrical as well as social and political event. It is drama, ritual, that requires the presence of an audience in addition to the performer. At times, it includes other players—most frequently the subject of the poem's images. Members of the audience often take an active role, chanting perhaps to the measured organization of image clusters evoked by the poet, punctuating the images with, among the Zulu, for example, exuberant cries, "He has said it!" As event, oral poetry requires spontaneity. It loses its identity when it is frozen in memory or writing. Poetry, and this includes written as well as oral, has intricate interacting sounds, rhythms, and patterns. The spontaneous edge of oral poetry provides an added tension apparently vital to the drama of the event.

Tyabashe was the center of the poetic event, gathering into the rhythms of his rugged cadences large audiences at the royal residence of King Diliz' Iintaba Mditshwa. The king himself was present: "Otherwise," Tyabashe observed, "there will be no purpose for the poem." For Tyabashe, the poetry was not a reliquary preserved in the memory; it was an active art form, a vivid social force, performed always in the presence of the person being spoken of in the poem. The members of the audience, a living group of members of the poet's society, reinforce the images by reacting to them, applauding them; they are appalled by them, involved in them. If the observer is to fully comprehend such poetry, it is not enough merely to record the words of the poet. There is always the sense of the person to whom the work is directed: when that person is absent—if, for example, he is dead—the evocation of images relating to him or her requires a contemporary reason for performance. Tyabashe, therefore, refused to perform poems for the deceased Lutshoto as he had performed them in the past; they were not meant to be memorized. He could no longer perform poems about King Lutshoto, for Lutshoto was dead. He was able, however, to invoke the spirit of Lutshoto, and his poems functioned as a critical counterpoint or context to what he saw as the contemporary flaccidness and malaise of the Diliz' Iintaba period.

The audience must be there, too, and the audience, in the case of Tyabashe, must be Mpondomise. Without audience and without subject, the poetry, he argued, lost everything—immediacy, meaning, and purpose. Tyabashe was contemptuous of the thought of the poetry as an academic enterprise, repeated for an alien to be locked into the historical past in a book. Ashton Ngcama made similar demands. He required an audience, too, even though he insisted that he was oblivious to the members of that audience once the performance was underway. And he had to have the physical form of a subject; without that form, there was no reason for the poem—and no inspiration. When he created a poem in praise of King Jojo, long dead, he found it necessary to meticulously recreate the king, clothing a member of Jojo's lineage in fabricated Xhosa royal garb, and he thereupon addressed that surrogate figure. Ngcama would not—he asserted that he could not—praise the mountain, Nolangeni, without standing before it, facing it at dusk when it was at its most majestic. He could not address Xesibe greatness in poetic imagery without being in the presence of a symbol of the Xesibe past.

Such poetry, I have argued elsewhere, "cannot be produced artificially. It necessitates the intricate lacing of time and space; it requires event and spontaneity, and loses its identity when frozen in memory or writing. Performance reveals among the images links that are not always obvious beyond the poem's framework. Reaching outside the poem for guidance through its dense imagery and historical-cultural allusions can be enlightening, but it distorts the poem and its purpose if external devices interfere with its patterning and that critical network of relationships between poem, creator, and audience." The poet creates an artistic context for the experience of these images; that context must not be shattered in the interests of reclaiming a historical linearity. The poetry, as is clear, involves more than words. The sound of the poet's voice and the movement of his body are crucial to the success of the poetic event: the very person of the poet, posed in dramatic attitudes, his mien now fierce, now gentle, in a splendid broad space, facing the subject of the poem at a quite surprising distance. Is it the audience, the king, or both, who are the subjects? They are equidistant from the poet, all addressed equally by the poet, as he declaims his words vigorously and with resonance in bold rivulets of sound, image, and motion. The audience arcs around poet and subject, itself very much a part of the performance, the bodies of the members of the audience sometimes in dance motion, held and controlled by the calculated movements of the poet's body, the whole creatively enveloped in the rhythm of the images and the sound of the poet's voice, the sounds of the audience controlled and channeled by the rhythms established by the performer.

Tyabashe would not have performed outside the royal residence; he refused to do so. The king, perhaps aware of how he was being used as a mask, a token, was most often passive during the performance. He did not interfere, even when the poet was most scathing in his attacks. He allowed himself to be manipulated. The poet was the active force.

During the performance of a poem that has as its subject a reigning king, for example, the presence of both leader and a portion of the subject peoples constitutes an event ripe with aesthetic and social tension. It is a stirring event: the audience and the poem's subject become transported as they respond to the artistic devices wielded by the performer. It is a masque: with music and heightened language, with imagery of the past mingling with present actuality. The reality that is caught in the images of the poem is enveloped in uses of body and voice that are not realistic but are rhythmical reorderings of their routine images—the cadence of delivery, the sound of the voice—and are placed within patterns of imagery that have no relationship to reality except through metaphor. It is often a political statement expressed as an active *pièce de théâtre*.

The artist traps in his artificially induced and organized images both ruler (if the subject of the poem is a ruler) and ruled in a combination that links these entities to images of the past as well as to a matrix of images from the present culture. At that moment, the images of the past and those of the present enfold the living chief and his living subjects. Past cultural experiences, compressed and symbolized in artistic images, are blended in performance with more realistic images selected from the contemporary world. The relationship between the two is revealed by means of patterning. It is in the defining of this relationship between two polar worlds that meaning is experienced. The poet is doing more than providing the portrait of a king.

There are times when the poet looks to the past for the subject of the poem, and that subject may be long dead. In such cases, too, unless the poet is strictly an antiquarian, it is most frequently the present world that is the focus of the work rather than the venerable leader who is only the ostensible subject of the poem. The images of the past, no matter how urgent their presence in the performance may appear to be, are being used to bring the members of the audience into a unique, felt relationship with the images and experiences of the present. The poet most often stands in immediate proximity to the subject of his work.

Heroic poetry inevitably deals with the past, a golden dream time, a time of mythic feats and supernatural valor, of utopian communities and extravagantly triumphant armies. Historical personages and events are placed into this splendid antiquity, and are themselves mythologized. The poetry requires that past perfection as a measure for the present. It turns mortals into demigods and routine affairs into times of priceless moment. The heroic age is the age of myth and dream time for every culture, and is no less real, for all is fabrication. In Tyabashe, antiquity is equated with tradition, and heroes with the past. The "moderns" fight against growing old, they cling to the milk-skin: they refuse to embrace the past, that is to say, the wisdom of the past. Tyabashe's poetry really has little to do with the reigning king, Diliz' Iintaba Mditshwa, although it is to Diliz' Iintaba that the poet ostensibly directs his images. The very presence of the reigning monarch opens old wounds for the poet. When the bard sees Diliz' Iintaba, he remembers the past, and he seems also to be treating Diliz' Iintaba's break with that past. Tyabashe's poetry has to do with Diliza only in the sense that the poet is longing for the old times that Diliz' Iintaba now fails to represent adequately. But his office, the Mpondomise kingship, does represent it, and it is to the distinction between the office—its connections with the past, symbol of tradition, condensation of the greatness of the past—and the current officeholder that Tyabashe directs himself. The one is the measure of the other.

Such poets as Umhle Biyela and Nombhonjo Zungu deal with the heroes of the Zulu past, and so glory in tradition. It is when the heroes of the past are placed into a context of the present that conflicts and tensions are sparked between the two traditions, the two cultures, the two times, and a political statement is the result. And the poet generally comes out in favor of the past; he is, after all, the chronicler, the keeper, of the past, and has a vested interest in it—which will solve, he argues, the problems of the present. The past is mythologized, somewhat, as the poet moves from objective appraiser and historian to advocate, but always within the context of tradition, though the mythologizing of the past gives the poet enormous latitude for criticism: he is, after all, the mythmaker; the poet uses the tradition to condemn, criticize, and set standards for the present, and thus does not have to personally criticize the human leaders of the present. The poet speaks not for a king, for a person, but for tradition, and the king is praised or blamed to the extent that he represents that tradition, to the extent that the tradition is revealed through him and his actions and his office.

White-black relations thread through the oral poetry tradition. "I am the darkness of the Kwena," exults a Tswana poet, singing of Jacobina Nthile of the Mogopa or Kwena clan,

> . . . the shield of the family of Modiane of Tau
> [I am] the night such as causes people to curb their movements
> until daybreak when they can stretch their feet;
> Man of the family of the black crocodile of Modiane of Tau.[123]

Ernest Sedumeli Moloto provides "a stanza from the praise of Chief Mankuroane of the Batlhaping" of the Tswana:

> No-questions, son of Mmakeakgwile
> allows no questions and no jokes,
> not even a child is allowed a joke—
> no matter even if it be a lion on its haunches

its lips trembling with anger
its mouth cavity blood red
guns booming incessantly.

Moloto notes, "Quite clearly this had to do with a person in a big and powerful position: a lion on its haunches stands much higher than on all fours. It is in a temper, judging by its trembling lips. But this lion has guns . . . that boom continually." Yet, he adds, "In spite of all this, the outsize lion dare ask no questions." Mankuroane had overcome his white nemesis, "and his bard mocked at them. They must have made some stupid error if even their booming guns were of no effect."[124]

When poets in the oral tradition evoke images associated with their leaders, they do so as their artistic predecessors have done for generations, with a fine regard for the unencumbered image.[125] Mtshophane Mamba, a Swati oral poet, describes the unique might of Swaziland's King Sobhuza II:

You are a labyrinthine sea:
You confuse us,
You don't swim, you surge,
Leaving the crocodiles of the sea
Snapping at the water's foam.[126]

The Zulu poet, Nombhonjo Zungu, compares King Shaka favorably to a venomous snake:

Viper of Ndaba:
Erect, ready to strike,
It strikes the shields of men![127]

And the Xhosa bard, Mdukiswa Tyabashe, chants praises of Diliz' Iintaba (the name means Feller-of-mountains) Mditshwa, the Mpondomise king:

He is the grain of the people,
We are all given life's grain,
We are all given life's grain
He gives it to the favored ones!
It was given to Matiwane,
It was given to Bushula's people.[128]

Ashton Ngcama, a Xesibe poet, likens the power of the ancient Xesibe king Jojo to the bite of dogs:

> To the one who bites like a dog:
> The people of Nqabana's place remember him:
> He bit them,
> As he bit the Mpondo, then left them living,
> As he bit the Xesibe, then left them there,
> As he bit the Nguni, beating them back,
> As he bit the Thembu, then left them there.[129]

Images such as these are rhythmically linked, developed, and sustained by their arrangement and subsequent patterning, by the sounds of the poet's voice and the movements of his body. The effect is to harmonize all participating in the poetic event—poet, audience, and subject—into a community, and to merge past and present, history and the contemporary worlds.

E. W. Grant witnessed an old poet perform in kwaZulu. The poet wore a leopard skin, and, as he proceeded, "His voice became loud and strong, his face was uplifted. Shield and stick would be suddenly raised and shaken in the air. Gestures became more and more frequent and dramatic. The reciter would leap in the air, or crouch with glaring eyes, whilst the praises poured from his lips, until he stopped exhausted."[130] Brooks and Warren argue, "The relationship among the elements in a poem is what is all important; it is not a mechanical relationship but one which is far more intimate and fundamental," and "[A]ll poetry . . . involves a dramatic organization."[131]

The language of the poetry is elegant, "highly figurative," A. C. Jordan noted, and "abounding in epithets, very much like the Homeric ones."[132] It is composed, W. B. Rubusana contended, of "speech which concentrates all of the eloquence of the Xhosa language, comprising all the figurative aspects of Xhosa."[133] The heroic poem, Edison M. Bokako wrote, "is laudatory. The poet freely indulges in ornament, entertaining contrasts between major and minor personalities." He argued, "The might of heroes is exaggerated. This is because heroic poetry is not bare realism. For two reasons. Firstly, because the poet must secure that largeness of atmosphere which will produce the illusion of heroic ampleness. Secondly, because the 'grim resolution of heroic despair' does not allow him to use a less self-conscious style." He writes of "the spirit of poetry which in Matthew Arnold's words 'attaches its emotion to the idea.'"[134]

By locating his central figure in a historical and cultural framework, the poet assumes an intimate knowledge of history and culture on the part of his audience, and he freely selects details from that background necessary to the construction of his poetic imagery. If such references and details are frequently elliptical and often seem obscure, he is confident that the members of the audience will suffer no confusion. It is not simply that they will, as a matter of course, supply what is missing; the poet does not want or allow them to force the poetry into a linear mode, for historical narrative is not the key organizing device of the poem. Atomized history represents one segment of the raw material of which the poem is built. Those traces of historical narrative present in lyric oral poetry exist primarily as parts of a larger poetic scheme.[135]

In a conversation that I had with a Zulu poet, Umvuyana Nkwenyana, on September 13, 1972, in Yanguya, kwaZulu, a conversation that was continued on September 16 of that year, the discussion turned to the creation of oral poems. On September 16, we spoke after he had performed heroic poems for Dingane, Shaka, and Cetshwayo, Zulu kings. Then about eighty years old, he said that his performances were not what they once were, that he had mastered the poetic art by working with practiced poets from his teenage years. Mr. Nkwenyana insisted that the poems that he created were at once historical and commentaries, noting that images from nature and other sources are a part of the raw materials of the poet. He said that these repertories were widely shared, that what made a poem original was the uses to which the poet put these traditional materials. He also explained that materials from the contemporary world could effortlessly and seamlessly be introduced into events that had occurred scores of years ago, concluding, as so many poets and storytellers did, that it was the combination of all of these materials that revealed the world of today within the wholly necessary context of the world of yesterday. Our lives are never separated from tradition. Poetry is the means of connecting the two, the way we understand ourselves. We could never move forward without the past.

There is in the poem a grid that holds the emotions in form. It is feeling and the imaged containment and ordering of feeling that have primacy in oral poetry. The poem does not approximate history so much as reveal the graphic movement of the artist's private feeling, the progress of the poet's thought as it is made public in an artistic event through images of which narrative history is one contributory element. In the performance of the poem, the imbedded narrative is but suggested so that the movement of feeling is not hindered: feeling is the logical movement of the poem, not narrative. The poet is not being purposefully cryptic; his images seem inscrutable only when one looks to the lyric for narrative. The argument of the poem is an argument of feeling, the experience one of the movement of feeling. Images are aligned and juxtaposed in logical patterns. Complex associations are established between images as the poet brings past and present into sometimes uncomfortable union, generating novel emotional responses from the audience, the poet's feeling marshalling associated feelings of members of the audience into form. He depends upon his poetic tradition, the materials of his craft, and the historical and cultural experiences that he shares with the audience to summon feeling from its members.

By channeling these now externalized feelings by means of the new environments that he has created, the poet—as Ngcama and Tyabashe enthusiastically insisted—expresses his own feeling. He cannot make public his private feeling without the emotions of the members of the audience. History, with fantasy and myth, is reordered; images of history are worked into new, unwonted configurations by the rhythmical patterning of the images; new contexts are contrived that alter the images and their accustomed associations, giving them fresh, original meanings. The images are enlarged and reshaped by the poet's voice and body. The usual context of images has only vestigial echoes in the poem; the usual context becomes a part of the poem only through its fragmentation before its reshaping. The poet interferes with familiar environments in the interest of establishing new lyric tensions.

The poem exists to dismantle history and to make history lyrical. The disjunctive nature of the imagery allows for the unimpeded and unopposed flow of the poet's emotion, and tolerates a certain breadth of experience of the members of the audience in their identification with the images. The tolerance does not, however, extend to the overall gathering of images that establishes a unity of feeling within the poem—and without—moving the individual members of the audience to a common artistic experience. B. W. Vilakazi emphatically agrees that oral poetry can become emotional and therefore personal. Discussing the "Shaka" poem collected by James Stuart,[136] he notes that in certain imagery "is seen the height of lyric quality," and "reveals ecstasy of feeling of a perfect imagery." Such poetry, he concludes, "passes from being an objective presentation of great deeds, to become poetry of feeling and intuition."[137] The poet not only evokes and expresses feeling, he also comments on the feelings he has called forth. But when he does so, he does not step out of his role as artist, placing himself at a distance from his images by didactically examining them. He comments on feeling with the same materials used to summon feeling. He is able to do this because of the context of feeling that he has so painstakingly established within the poem—by means of his body and voice, the rhythmic patterns, the texture of image-arrangement. Feeling becomes progressively denser as more and more diverse emotions are tapped by the images. The poet organizes the dense feelings by means of the rhythmical patterning he is imposing on images that do the work of evoking audience emotions; he thereby traps within the images the emotions they are calling forth. A grid is established by the patterning, furnishing poet and audience with a regular and predictable emotional field. That grid is also charged with feeling, composed as it is of emotion-trapped images organized rhythmically. The poet plays his images off against the grid, the grid holding the remembered parts of the poem, holding audience memories and emotions, as he works them into a lively pattern. The poet works with other images, sometimes incorporating them into the grid and thereby changing the grid as well. All is emotion-trapped image; some of the images are worked into and held by the patterns, others flow across the grid.

The grid is early established; as the poet continues to evoke images and their corresponding emotions; these images first arouse tensions, and hence aesthetic energy, as they move across and are sometimes played against the grid. Then they themselves become a part of the grid, as new images are evoked. The grid is an active repository of emotion, the remembered parts of the poem; it holds audience emotions (and memories of emotions being tapped and nursed), and works them into a bristling pattern of feeling. The grid is alive, vibrating with feeling, feeling held in check and given form by the patterns; other feelings flow across the grid, later to be worked into the grid. The playing off of images against the grid creates a tension that is the combination of emotions of two or more images in conflict with each other, or an image in conflict with the pattern as poet and audience strive to work it into pattern.

There are two kinds of imagery in the poetry: one is the most visible, or audible, type. It is called into being by the poet, his voice, his body, a vocalizing of the cues that elicit the fully embodied images from the memories, experiences, and repertories of the members of the audience. These audible images, the most perceptible images, seemingly disparate and discontinuous, form the emotion-charged grid, and create another kind of imagery, depending as much on the patterning and arrangement given them by the poet as the poet's voice, as much on the imaginations of the members of the audience as that of the poet himself. This is the gradually evolving sum of the maze of images that comprises the poem.

Largely unspoken, it is nevertheless limned by the plethora of spoken images, moving slowly across the grid, not so much integrated into the grid (as the spoken images are) as accumulating, changing, and deepening it. A portrait is coming into being, with comments of the creator: hardly a photographic representation, it is more of a caricature, its lines and resemblance reflecting the views of the artist. The poet manipulates this evolving living portrait, composed as it is not of images, but of the feelings engendered by the images and patterned—given form—by the poet who is manipulating the grid. It is a new emotion-charged representation of the poem's subject—more than the sum of the images, partaking also of the very culture, tradition, and history of the people whose emotions being summoned emerge from those reservoirs in their experiences.

The poet comments on the images he is calling forth by creating a being composed of the emotions tapped by those images. By manipulating and controlling the emotions held in form by pattern, he comments on the subject. His commentary is, hence, also constructed of emotion, and is more than a didactic observation or homily. Feeling comments on feeling. It is the larger image against which the lesser images are aligned; this relationship is what gives those lesser images meaning. Comments, then, are largely unspoken. They are not the result of a single image; rather, they are generated from the crowded feelings organized by the grid, selecting and ordering the images as they move across it. And so a portrait emerges, the images contributing to it along with the audience's emotions engendered by those images. This, then, is how images from the past and present, the emotions of performer and audience, are woven into a texture that forms a portrait. By means of the grid, the poet influences the emerging portrait, controlling the developing experience of that portrait, commenting on it through the patterning of the images. The emerging portrait occurs within the sets of patterns established by the poet. These act as a narrow, binding control of an audience's perception and experience of the poem's subject. Another type of image is composed solely of emotions engendered within the poem. Unlike the more turbulent primary images that have much historical and contemporary experience adhering to them and must be forced into patterns, these images are less spirited, composed purely of the emotions generated by the activity of the grid. It is this sanguinary quality of the secondary images that harmonizes the members of the audience and their diverse experiences with the primary images and their historical, poetic, and cultural contexts, and for the period of the poem makes an aesthetic community of them and the poet.

A Page from a Journal

January 25, 1976

Images in oral narratives are experienced by members of an audience by means of a complex relationship between the body of the artist and the words she speaks. These have a network of threads reaching back in time to the ancient tradition, spreading throughout the contemporary culture and touching each person in the audience, the network weaving through the separate artistic and nonartistic experiences of those participating in the images evoked by the performer. It is not especially productive to consider body movement from the vantage of the spoken word, but we can begin that way. These movements seem both to complement and supplement the verbal elements of stories. Complementary actions include movements which reflect somewhat directly the verbally sketched images of a performance—body, face, and hands revealing more or less realistically the images summoned from past and present by words. The body and voice of the artist are vigorously unified in efforts to externalize narrative actions. Supplementary movements tend to occur apart from the verbally expressed images in any direct sense. Such movements provide, among other things, a rhythmic context for the development of the narrative; they shape the external form of the story performance, are most significant and functional aesthetically. A given performance is a mesh of these two broad categories of movement; it is not always easy to discern distinctions between them. The fact that many movements fit into both of the categories suggests a more than casual linkage between the two, and may finally make necessary a redefinition of such categories. The extremes are mime and shaping, rhythmic movements that have a relationship to the word in the harmony they establish with or reflect from the verbal images.

"Dinuzulu"

The Story and Its Poem

> If I describe my peach too perfectly, it's the poem which will make my mouth water . . . while the real peach spoils.
> —William H. Gass, *Fiction and the Figures of Life*

It is sometimes difficult for observers to appreciate heroic poetry, which because of the burden of historical and local allusions, seems hardly worth the effort—and certainly seems remote from aesthetic experience, the necessary research for comprehension diluting that experience considerably. This is because such frustrated observers do not know the story, and a familiarity with the story is crucial if one is to comprehend the poem at its center.

The poetry frequently seems beyond our grasp with its apparently interminable listing of names, battles, fortresses, places. There are too many footnotes for the outsider; too much historical and geographical research must be done. One cannot, more importantly, experience a cohesive argument when moving through such poems; they seem to consist of one detached image, even when somewhat developed, tied to another; the result is, at best, a mosaic that, albeit an interesting and perhaps useful portrait of the subject of the poem, is nevertheless not a very satisfying work. Or so it would appear. The logic of the poem escapes us, the inner laws seem distant and vague, and the movement of the imaged argument appears lost in the welter of disparate images and innumerable allusions. Of course, there is a logic, a cohesion, and the poems are without question often formidable works of art. The problem for the analyst of heroic poetry is not wholly unfamiliar to critics of literary works: readers in such societies who insist on reading poetry as a linear experience have the full force of the poem as fully denied to them as in an oral society. A quest for linear argument in poetry is futile. Oral poetry, no more than written, cannot be paraphrased into a philosophical statement or homily. Moreover, what the western observer considers distortion may result from an inability to comprehend the artistic system in which the images are lodged.

Dinuzulu

Even when the historical and local allusions are finally known, we remain confronted with the problem of unity in the poem. It is true that the subject of the poem is a unifying element, but it is also true that this is only a portion of the full argument in oral poetry. It does not account for the cultural and individual experience, deep and broad, that the images tap and bring into full and free flow in the poetic experience. The subject of the poem does unify the images and these released emotions in the sense that they all more or less cluster about that subject, but that is hardly adequate. The poems achieve their stature and resonance among the people because they touch deeper chords in the common and separate experiences. That is what the imaged argument is, and it is that argument that is most difficult for outsiders to manage, because the images simply do not have the same changed effects on them as they do on the members of the immediate audiences.

The Story

> I got the photograph signed by Dinuzulu yesterday, dear. I suppose you sent it. I like it greatly.
>
> —Olive Schreiner, in a December 1, 1908, letter to her brother, W. P. Schreiner, sent from De Aar in South Africa[138]

Dinuzulu (c. 1870–1913) was a Zulu king. He struggled with the British and Dutch settlers over the land of the Zulu. When Zululand was annexed to Natal in 1887, Dinuzulu resisted, and was tried for treason. He was arrested, found guilty, and in 1889 banished to St. Helena. In 1897, he was allowed to return to Zululand. During a later rebellion, he was found guilty once more, and again sentenced.

Senzangakhona (1760–c. 1810) ruled a small group known as the Zulu.[139] When he died, his son Shaka (c. 1788–1828) became the Zulu king. Shaka, a military genius, built the Zulu into a powerful nation.[140] In 1828, he was assassinated by his brother, Dingane, and others. Dingane (c. 1795–1840) then ruled for twelve years; when he was killed during a Swaziland military operation, his brother, Mpande (c. 1810–1872), who with the aid of the Afrikaners had been in rebellion against Dingane, took over. After a relatively peaceful reign, he died; and his son, Cetshwayo (c. 1826–1884) took over. The British, openly intervening now in Zulu affairs, removed Cetshwayo from power in 1879, restoring only a portion of his kingship to him in 1883. His successor was his son, Dinuzulu, who also came into conflict with the British, and was banished for ten years. He was finally allowed to return to his country, but the power of the Zulu was broken; and when his son, Solomon, succeeded him, it was with drastically curtailed powers.

When the youthful Dinuzulu assumed the kingship, the Zulu nation was torn and did not wholly support him. A cleavage had occurred during the reign of Cetshwayo between loyalists, called the uSuthu, and those who supported Zibhebhu, son of Shaka's cousin, Maphitha, and pretender to the throne. Open warfare between the two groups developed during Cetshwayo's reign. In 1883, Cetshwayo was forced to flee his royal residence at Ulundi when Zibhebhu attacked him. The quarrel, fed by the

Boers who wanted Zulu land for their farms, continued into Dinuzulu's time.

The British attempted to reduce Dinuzulu's power by giving land and power to such rival Zulu rulers as Somapunga, father of Mgojana. Dinuzulu fought not only the whites but such dissident Zulu as Sigwabugwabu, Mkashana, Dundu, Mgojana, Gidlana, and Mzamanantsuku. These and others are mentioned in the heroic poetry as having been defeated by Dinuzulu. The time of Dinuzulu was one of perpetual warfare, and much Zulu land and many kraals were reduced to rubble. The poet sings of the might of Dinuzulu, of his battles at various locations in South Africa—Zinyangweni, Banganomo, Nkandla, and others.

When the British imposed a settlement, Dinuzulu was exiled to St. Helena, and Zulu power was broken. Sir Arthur Havelock, governor of Natal had said, "Dinuzulu must know, and all Zulus must know that the rule of the House of Shaka is a thing of the past. It is like water spilt on the ground. The Queen now rules in Zululand and no one else."[141] When he returned, he became implicated in a rebellion; he was defended by W. P. Schreiner (Olive Schreiner's brother), but was found guilty, sentenced to four years imprisonment, and forced to give up his leadership of the uSuthu faction.[142]

Dinuzulu means "one who is a source of worry to the Zulus."[143]

The Poem

Meaning is of the intellect, poetry is not.
—A. E. Housman, *The Name and Nature of Poetry*[144]

IZIBONGO ZIKADINUZULU KACETSHWAYO

Udlothovu kabhekeki nangamehlo;
Ufana nemisebe yelanga;
Iso lakhe lifana nomnyazi wezulu,
Ingathi elengwe nengonyama.
Umavela-jahe, onjengeBhunu lakoPewula;
Ubhukuda ngomkhonto kwaDiki,
Usintshongo siyintuthu yamabhosho,
Edutyulwa ngoNongqayi,
Esikanisweni kwaNongoma,
Unxeba laphum' intuthu yesibhamu,
Uhlaba nangesikayise uMshweshwe,
Usilwane,
Unkunzumbili,
Enye eyakwaNgenetyeni,
Enye ingeyaseBanganomo.
Umagalelagase ngengengonyama;
Umashesha njengezulu,
Lapho eya kwaNdunu.
Umphangela-langa lingakaphumi,
KwaNongoma.
Lazithath' izihlangu zikaMandlakazi;
Usikhova kaMaphitha;
Ubusobengwe kaMaphitha;
Wamshaya phantsi uFata kaMaphitha;
Wamshaya phansi uMcasimbana kaMaphitha;
Wamshaya phansi Xhukwana kaMaphitha;
Wamshaya phansi uNdlovu kaMaphitha;
Wamshaya phansi uPoyiye kaMaphitha;
Wamshaya phansi uPhuzukumila kaMaphitha;

Wamshaya phansi uSewana kaMaphitha;
Wamshaya phansi uSikiza kaSomfula,
Wamshaya phansi akwabandaba zalutho.
Umagalelagase onjengenkosi yamanTshali.
Usinakanaka sezincwadi zabamhlophe,
Abelungu beziloba bezinakaza kakhulu,
Zilotywa ngamasosha namagumgedlela,
NabaNguni, namaSwazi,
NabeSuthu namaThonga,
NamaSulumani, namaZizimbane,
NamaPutukezi namaBhunu,
Umlomo owodwa usukuphendule,
Uyobona abamlomo ngamibili,
Bayavunana;
Kuvunana uZibhebhu noHamu,
Kuvunana uZiwedu benoMnyamana.
Usikhipha 'mbila ehlathini lakwaCeza:
Kuphelele yena.
Usiwolokohlo singamanzi oMkhuze,
Ugcwele izingazi zikaMashesha.
Isihlahla sombamba-mpala.
UMkhuze-vimbana
Bangakuphuzi abakwoNtini,
NabakwaDladla.
Uhlangabeza inyoni emhlophe,
Iza nomagagana.
UDinuzulu kabulali uyasizila.
Uqoth' imbokodwe nesisekelo.
Usikhuni simazinga.
Umpondo zamila enjeni,
Engabi enkomeni zesabani,
Lokhu sasiyokwenza amagudu okubhema.
Uthukuthela wawela Isikhwebezi,
Washona ngesikhala seQanda.
UNdaba, ulithiyathiya.
Unjengebutho likayise,
UNjininindi, ibutho lelo bekungelezintombi.
Umathanga adabula uMzinyathi,
Umfana kamSwazi khawula:
Ngoba uthi umakhakhamela.

Kawuboni yini ukuthi umakhakhamela
Ngowakithi eMkhontweni,
Ngoba wakhakhamela izinkomo zikaMashesha,
Okhethelwe ngamahashi,
Ngoba umuzi wakhe kuseMahashini.
Umfuyi wezinkomo ezifanayo
UNdaba.
Ulile ngomkhonto kwelakubo kwaZulu,
Ngoba udadewabo unguSililo.
Wagwaz' umuntu, wema,
Ngokuba udadewabo enguSimiso.
Wagwaz' umuntu, wameya,
Ngoba udadewabo enguMeyisile.
Wagwaz' umuntu, wabheda,
Ngoba udadewabo enguSabheda.
Wagwaz' umuntu onamandla,
Ngoba udadewabo enguNomandlambi.
Wagwaz' umuntu, wayeka,
Ngoba udadewabo enguSiyela.
Hamba sihambe wena waliwayo,
Siqonde kweleMbungumbu,
Kumbe kweloMgazi,
Lapho izwe lithe cebelele,
Yikhona sobona izintaba zaseSwazini,
Ngoba uyabizwa uNkunelana noMadevana.
Kuthiwa ubizwa oLakana,
Mbalake wathuba ufike oThaka,
Kwathi iBhunu, uPotolozi.
Wakuthwesa isigqoko,
Kwathi isigqoko sakufanela,
Nkonyane kaPhunga noMageba.
Izingqungqulu zibethene phezulu,
NgekaMaphitha enye,
NgekaNjinininindi enye.
Angiqedi nezobhabhalala,
Kwathi ekaMaphitha yabhabhalala.
Mamb' emnyama kaNjinininindi
Umdwengula dwishi alenz' iqhele
Alethwese amambuka.
Unkomo zawela zithwel' iningizimu ngezimpondo,

Zabuya sezithwele inyakatho.
Umathathel' ahlome njengezulu,
Inkunzi kaNdaba.
Umthente ohlabusamila kaDlungwana,
Umagwilika nango wakithi eMahashini.
Wakhethelwa ngemikhonto
Ngoba umuzi wakhe kuseMkhontweni.
Inkunzi edumela uMashesha.
Ubhensa bahlabe emuva nangaphambili,
Kabahlabi wena,
Bahlaba nantsi indlovu kaManqobizintaba.
Uphondo lwendlovu alungeni,
Lapha ezibayeni zamankengane.
Usifuba vungama inyakanyaka,
Umsishana ufinyelela kubafo.
Uzulu ladum' ekuseni kwaNongoma.
Useyidide wathiya izizwe zonke,
Ebezimhlaba zimhlanganyele.
Umakhangula-jozi elikoFalaza,
Ukuba kazi eleMbokodebomvu,
Uyakulikhangula nini!
Mhlahlela nhloko zabafo.
Inja kayisuke laph' emnyango,
Ngoba kukhona izikhulu,
Kukhona uZiwedu noMnyamana,
Kukhon' uTyanibezwe noMabhoko.[145]

THE PRAISES OF DINUZULU, SON OF CETSHWAYO[146]

Unshorn one who cannot be looked at;
You are like the rays of the sun;
Your eye is like a flash of lightning,
It appears to be that of a leopard and a lion.
He is the heedless one, like the Boer of Paul Kruger;[147]
He stabbed with the spear at Diki,
The wreath of smoke being the smoke of cartridges,
Fired off by the Nongqayi,[148]
At the fort at Nongoma.[149]
Whose wound emitted gun smoke,

Who stabs also with that of his father, Moshoeshoe,[150]
The terrible one,
He the overcomer of two bulls,
One being of the Ngenetyeni kraal,
The other being of the Banganomo kraal.[151]
He who strikes hard like a lion;
The swift one like lightning,
On the occasion he went to Ndunu.[152]
He who anticipated the sun before it rose
At Nongoma.
He took away the shields of Mandlakazi;[153]
Sikhova, the son of Maphitha;[154]
Busobengwe, the son of Maphitha;
He felled Fata, the son of Maphitha;
He felled Mcasimbana, the son of Maphitha;
He felled Xhukwana, the son of Maphitha;
He felled Ndlovu,[155] the son of Maphitha;
He felled Poyiye, the son of Maphitha;
He felled Phuzukumila, the son of Maphitha;
He felled Sewana, the son of Maphitha;
He felled Sikiza, the son of Somfula,[156]
He felled him in an overwhelming manner.
He strikes a lightning blow like the chief of the Tshali.
He is the butt of white people's writings,
The white people wrote them and adorned them extensively,
They were being written by soldiers and carabineers,
By the Nguni and Swati,
By the Sotho and the Thonga,
By the Arabs and Mozambiquans,
By the Portuguese and the Dutch,
One mouth chances to make a reply,
It goes to see those who have two mouths each,
They take one another's part;
Zibhebhu and Hamu[157] take one another's part,
Ziwethu and Mnyamana[158] take one another's part.
He is the expeller of the rock rabbit from Ceza:[159]
And he takes up the whole place.
He is the down-rush of the waters of the Mkhuze,[160]
Which are mixed with the blood of Mashesha.

He is the thicket of the impala-holder.[161]
The Mkhuze River withholds its waters
So that the Ntini[162] people may not drink of it,
Nor the Dladla people.
He is meeter of the Nyoni-mhlophe[163] regiment,
Which is coming with hungry beggars.[164]
Dinuzulu does not kill, he wipes out.
He destroys the grinding stone and the foundation stone.
He is the jagged firebrand.
He is the horns that grew on a dog,
I wonder why they were afraid of growing on a head of cattle,
Seeing that we would have turned them into smoking horns.
Enraged, he crossed the Sikhwebezi River,[165]
And went out of sight over the Qanda Neck.
Ndaba,[166] the stumbling block.
He is like his father's regiment,
Njininindi, that regiment consisting of girls.
He is the legs that crossed the Buffalo River,
The Swati boy, cease:
Because he is the one who goes at them furiously.
Don't you see that the furiously moving one
Is of our Mkhontweni kraal,
Because he rushed for the cattle of Mashesha,
Whose marriage ceremony was performed on horseback,
Because his kraal is at Mahashini?[167]
The keeper of cattle that are similar,
Ndaba,
He mourned by means of weapons in his country, Zululand
Because his sister is Sililo.
He stabbed a man, and he remained standing,
Because his sister is Simiso.
He stabbed a man, and scorned him,
Because his sister is Meyisile.
He stabbed a man, and he spoke nonsense,
Because his sister is Sabheda.
He stabbed a man who was strong,
Because his sister is Nomandlambi.

He stabbed a man, and let go,
Because his sister is Siyela.
Come, let us go, you who are in bad favor,
And let us make for the barren-soiled land,
Perhaps to the Mgazi District,
Where the land is level and open,
So that we may see the hills of Swaziland,
Because you are being called by Nkunelana and Madevana.
It is said you are being called by the hot-tempered ones;
As a matter of fact, when you arrived at the Ithaka,
It happened that a Boer, Potolozi,
Placed a hat on your head,
And it happened that the hat suited you,
You calf of Phunga and Mageba.[168]
The eagles fought high in the air,
One belonging to Maphitha,
The other belonging to Cetshwayo.[169]
I am uncertain which one will collapse,
It happened that Maphitha's collapsed.
Black mamba of Cetshwayo,
The tearer-out of a strip, which he turned into a fillet
And caused the traitors to emerge.
He is the cattle that crossed, bearing the south on their horns,
They returned carrying the north.
He is the speeder, the one who arms himself like lightning,
The bull of Ndaba.
The grass of Dlungwana[170] that pricks as it commences to grow,
There he is the seeder of our Mahashini kraal.
He was danced for with spears
Because his kraal is Mkhontweni.
The bull that rushes at Mashesha.
He who turns his back so that they may stab in front and behind,
He is not stabbing you,
They are stabbing this elephant of Manqobizintaba.
The horn of the elephant does not get in,
Here in the kraal of the destitute.

He is the chest seething with commotion,
He whose limbs reach right up to the foes.
He is the heaven that thundered at Nongoma in the early morn.
He has puzzled and barred all nationalities,
That stabbed him in unison.
He who initiated into use the stabbing spear that is with the Falaza regiment,
I wonder when he will initiate the use of the one
With the Mbokodwebomvu regiment!
He is the cleaver of the heads of the foes.
Let the dog move away from the door here,
Because nobles are present.
There is present Ziwethu and Mnyamana,
There is present Tyanibezwe and Mabhoko.

A Broken Linearity

The Move to the Poem

> Poetry is the spontaneous overflow of powerful feelings: it takes its origin from emotion recollected in tranquility.
> —William Wordsworth, preface to *Lyrical Ballads*

The poem was always there. In the historical events, looming behind the actual realistic events, in the poet's efforts to remember the historical event, the poem was always there. It is the poem that gives meaning to the event.

POETIC IMAGES

This Zulu heroic poem composed in Dinuzulu's honor is a network of names of people and names of places. These place the events into historical and geographical perspective and give the poem a sense of realism. At the same time that these realistic images are being recalled, the poet evokes images of fantasy, comparing Dinuzulu to "the heaven that thundered," to "the horns that grew on a dog," to a "wreath of smoke." It is by means of a combination of the realistic images from history and metaphorical or comparative images from nature, and the rhythmical grid that composes these disparate images and gives them their unity, that the poet moves the audience to meaning.

The poem is a mass of metaphors, a metaphorical labyrinth, each figure moving the audience closer and closer to the poem in the story: unshorn one, rays of the sun, a flash of lightning, heedless one, wound, overcomer, lion, thicket, jagged firebrand, horns, legs, calf, black mamba, tearer, speeder, bull, grass, seeder, bull, horn of the elephant, chest seething, limbs reaching, heaven thundering, cleaver of heads. The poem seems heavy with story. The story clings to the lines, to the images, so that a strong sense of place and event is assumed. The story holds hard to the sinews of the heroic poem: it is history within which a poem is struggling to emerge. The audience participates willingly in this struggle, which is at the heart of the experience of the poem, and the metaphors are the pathways to the poem's poetic center.

There are references to sun, lightning, and smoke that occur in the first nineteen lines of the poem, then again in line 33. At the end of the poem are references to lightning (line 110) and to "the heaven that thundered" (line 125). Occurring with greater frequency are the references to animals: in the opening sixteen lines, images of leopard, lion, bulls, and unshorn one; like the celestial images, they have the effect of organizing the historical materials. In the middle of the poem, between lines 46 and 75, are references to rock rabbit, impala, dog; and between lines 100 and 131, the final part of the poem, are references to calf, black mamba, cattle, bull, elephant, horn of the elephant. There are also human acts in the poem, from common (heedless one, meeter) to extravagant activities (jagged firebrand, legs that crossed the Buffalo River, keeper of cattle, tearer-out, speeder, seeder, chest seething, limbs reaching to the foes, cleaver of heads).

It is not that the images are ordered in a necessarily logical, chronological manner; it is the poetic accumulation and organization of images that slowly limns the image of Dinuzulu. A mosaic of images from the poetic tradition is interwoven with historical events, places, and people: Paul Kruger, Diki, the Nongqayi, Nongoma, Moshoeshoe, Ngenetyeni, Banganomo, Ndunu, remembering the struggles with Mcasimbana, Xhukwana, Ndlovu, Poyiye, Phuzukumila, the epic conflict with Zibhebhu and Hamu, the mountain fastness at Ceza, remembering such great ones of the past as Ndaba and Cetshwayo.

RHYTHMIC PATTERNS

The bard, manipulating the materials of his craft—the poetic images, the rhythmic patterns—poetically organizes and contains the released feelings of the audience, and so imbues the event with meaning. He strips it to its poetic essence and thereby makes it a part of the mythic experience of the people.

Of the one hundred and thirty-five lines in the poem, nine lines (in whole or in part) have to do with celestial images, mainly lightning; thirty-two lines (in whole or in part) have to do with images of nature, mainly animals; and the remainder focus on historical events. Of these remaining ninety-four lines, there are two refrains, each consisting of twelve lines.

The other seventy lines are historical, the story of Dinuzulu, fragmented, a broken linearity, with seemingly random references to Moshoeshoe and Cetshwayo, to Zibhebhu and Hamu, to Afrikaners Paul Kruger and Potolozi, to places like Ndunu and Nongoma, the Mkhuze River, Mkhontweni kraal. Some of these persons and places are worked into the refrains, others into the nature imagery, others remain apparently untouched by the poetic imagery. But all are worked into the rhythm of the poem, and so are already removed from reality. The rhythmic music of the performance has the effect of reordering the poem's imagery; historical images and the cadenced metaphorical references are transformed into celestial and natural phenomena.

The basic pattern is the "He who ______" pattern: this becomes the grid of the poem, the poetic tool used by the bard to organize the many diverse images. It is the pattern that runs through the work, becoming the identity of the poem, the means whereby other patterns are carefully woven together to form a seamless whole. So the texture of the poem is formed. All of the images organized by the poem's basic pulsating rhythmic pattern are images of violence, depicting Dinuzulu's relentless offensive and military prowess, the steady drumbeat of his conquests, his irresistible strength and his annihilation of war materiel and armies, and, in an image almost always associated with Dinuzulu, the destruction of peaceful images as well.

POETIC ORGANIZATION

This poet opens and closes the poem with a battery of metaphorical images, and between these provides two major litanies and a number of briefly sustained historical descriptions. We can watch the poet as he launches his efforts to convert history into poetry, as he actively seeks the poem in the story, and, through his images and their poetic organization, makes the audience a part of that quest.

These poetic images are themselves organized into patterns: "He is the ______," "He who ______." From early in the poem, beginning in line 5, the poet makes specific reference to people and events, and those references dominate the poem from lines 20 to 99 as he moves to almost wholly historical references. It is the rhythmical organization of these historical references that is significant here, because that organization links the several image categories, and unifies the natural elements, the animals, and the historical events and personages. As the poem advances, the extrahistorical references have their effect, becoming metaphorically joined to the historical references by the pulse of the poem.

After twenty lines of initial metaphorical imaging, the poet shifts to a clearly defined refrain of historical figures, all sons of Maphitha, who are vanquished by Dinuzulu, an impressive rout of an enemy that, in poetic terms, moves on for twelve lines to culminate with a return to metaphor: "He strikes a lightning blow." The poet inherits from the artistic tradition certain formulas, and here he brings one of the more preferred into play: "He felled ______, the son of ______." The other major formula used by the poet: "He stabbed a man and ______ / Because his sister is ______." The rhythm of the poem that in a shadowy way organizes the earlier part of the poem now becomes nakedly apparent and remains so for a sustained time, until that rhythm is again burdened with unlike images, again becomes metaphorical and the poet moves into a complex set of images, one dealing with the relations between Dinuzulu and Europeans, in the end working into the imagery the entirety of southern Africa. He moves to the major confrontation with Zibhebhu and Hamu, then, with the image, "the expeller of the rock rabbit from Ceza," he triumphantly moves the poem back to a series of metaphors, the essential organizing factor of this poem: "down-rush of the waters," "thicket of the impala-holder," "meeter of the Nyoni-mhlophe regiment," "the jagged firebrand," "the horns that grew on a dog." Some of these metaphorical images contain more historical commentary or description than others, the historical comments becoming fuller, the metaphors encumbered, seemingly less poetic, as the historical detail threatens to overwhelm the poetic imagery, but that is brief.

FEELING AND ITS CONTAINMENT

Dinuzulu's warlike prowess is absolute. It is a war of *imfecane,* total destruction. Everything is being pulverized: even the grinding stone, the foundation stone—images of home, of domestic life, not war—are destroyed utterly. Praise names used in the poem are Dinuzulu's praise names. The poet, by means of these images, slowly patterns a mosaic portrait of the subject of the poem. The poet's attitude towards the subject of the poem is expressed through these patterned images. But these are only the most obvious forms of image patterning. The next step in the developing complexity of the composition of heroic poetry is the creation of poetic texture of a richer variety.

All of the images organized by the poem's basic pattern are images of violence, depicting Dinuzulu's relentless offensive and military success, his irresistible strength and his annihilation of both peaceful objects and war materiel. The audience, through repetition and rhythm, soon becomes aware of the poet's purpose; the genealogical material, through its organization and patterning, becomes associated in this poem with destructiveness. This violent pattern dominates the poem and affects all other images and patterns. Around the basic pattern with its warlike theme, the poet develops associated patterns, some of them depicting the violence of lightning, which, through juxtaposition, is a reflection of Dinuzulu's strength.

The poet moves into a second litany, this one organized by the words, "He stabbed a man." and "Because his sister is ______." The historical elements are drained out of this twelve-line refrain, except for the names of the sisters. This is followed by a sustained historical description of Mgazi District, the hills of Swaziland, the Ithaba, the Boer Potolozi, and then the poet moves into a final fusillade of metaphorical images, quickly rendered, after indulging himself with the "calf of Phunga and Mageba": black mamba, tearer-out, cattle, speeder, bull, grass, seeder, bull, horn of the elephant, chest seething, limbs reaching, and heaven thundering. The poem ends with a historical reference to the use of the stabbing spear, tied to two metaphorical references—cleaver of heads, dog—and thence to the final references to historical figures.

This pattern of violence dominates the poem and affects all other images and patterns; the audience, through repetition and rhythm, soon becomes aware of the poet's purpose. But something else is happening here, something more subtle, a potent counterpoint paralleling the basic pattern and simultaneously subverting it: the poet adds brief passages that are not patterned. He is attempting to fathom the terrible fate of Dinuzulu, vital because Dinuzulu's fate is that of the Zulu people. So it is that the many conquests of the Zulu king, the dominant imagery in the poem, lose their balance at times, just as the rhythmical grid of the poem loses its balance with the unpatterned images: "He is the butt of white people's writings" (line 34) and "It happened that a Boer, Potolozi, / Placed a hat on your head" (lines 97–98), the historical reality that was undermining the Zulu nation. And so it is that the two dominant refrains of the poem, themselves major factors in the construction of the grid of the work, differ so dramatically. The first is a traditional rhythmical grid: "He felled Fata, the son of Maphitha; / He felled Mcasimbana, the son of Maphitha" (lines 24–25 and following). The second is also traditional, but there is a disturbing departure from the warlike confidence of the earlier grid, beginning with the disarming line, "He stabbed a man, and he remained standing" (line 79), which then moves into the pattern: "He stabbed a man, and scorned him, / Because his sister is Meyisile. / He stabbed a man, and he spoke nonsense, / Because his sister is Sabheda," (lines 81–84 and following). Underlying the poem, craftily worked into its rhythm, are the very images that will erode the power of the Zulu polity. The structure of the poem, then, is as much a part of the meaning of the work as the words themselves; the images are historical and natural. The poetic texture of a poem that ostensibly honors a king moves to much larger and calamitous issues. It is in this counterpoint that the most potent emotions are evoked.

THE MUSIC IN THE STORY

The mixing of patterns is evident. What this poet does is devise a series of separate patterns, each built around the two basic patterns. He then develops the poem by an artful arrangement and blending of the patterns, the basic ones forming the central characteristic of the poem's texture. Each pattern is usually fully repeated so that its character and emotional evocation can be divined. This becomes a part of the audience's experience through repetition. Later, the poet need only hint at that pattern, and the entirety of its emotional content is then blended with that of the new pattern. So it is that the various emotions evoked by the patterns are formed into the texture of the poem as well. They are trapped within the repeated patterns, then these patterns are richly plaited to provide a denser texture. The poet also provides brief, singular interludes that, counterpointed against the relentless litany of the vanquished, generate a potent sense of violence.

A part of the rhythmical experience of the story is the uneven relationship between historical images and the poem that is making sense of the historical images. The focus of this seemingly disparate assortment of images and commentaries is the historical character, Dinuzulu, but poetically, it is the organization of those images and commentaries, the rhythm of the poem, that establishes an illusion of unity when the materials seem anything but unified. The cataloguing of metaphors has the effect of building a tower of references to the subject of the poem, and to place him within a historical, geographical, and cultural context. But even as that happens, it is the poetic experience, the rhythmical experience, that attracts the audience and that will, in the end, be of much more significance than the listing of places and people and events. The poet is seductively moving us into the poem in that historical story. At times, the tempo becomes irresistible, as with the two refrains, and even when the poet moves on for two or three or five lines about a historical event, it is soundly a part of the rhythm of the poem, it cannot escape that rhythm. And so the poet takes the series of images, initiates the audience to the rhythmical embrace of these images, and then moves to the points where these rhythmically organized images move into full music: the two refrains at lines 21 to 32 and 78 to 88. When the poet moves to the final part of the poem, returning to the metaphorical cataloguing, all of history is enveloped by the poem in the story, it cannot escape that poem; it is inescapably and irrevocably a part of that poem in the story. It is then that the poet, depending on the audience's anticipation and its experience with these typical renderings of heroic poetry, becomes subversive.

There is a move to lyric here. History is forced, coaxed, edged into the familiar, eternal, mythic tones of tradition. Emphasis in all storytelling is on the familiar, which is to say, on the poem in the story. There is a stir to melic, a transit to the cantus of the people, of their history from ancient times, of society, of tradition: it is music that everyone knows, the music to which the audience responds.

I had a number of discussions about the performance of oral poetry with the Swati bard, Mtshophane Mamba, during the month of October in 1972. We spoke at the royal residence of King Sobhuza II. Mamba described his own feelings when he stood before the king. He said that he never prepared a performance in advance, but there was no question, he emphasized, that he depended heavily on two things: his memory, his repertory, of Swati images, historical and cultural as well as contemporary and poetic; and his craft, his ability to work these images into rhythmical patterns. At the same time, he asserted, the poetry always occurred within events that were of immediate moment to the members of the audience. As a poet, Mamba noted, his job was to work with all of these materials and, in a seemingly spontaneous way, to create music, to unite a king, an audience, and himself to history. It was that spontaneity within a tradition that seemed to fascinate and to challenge this poet above all else. He candidly added that his performances were not always towering successes. But with years of experience, he went on with some irony, he was able to work his way out of any poetic traps, to use his phrase, that his somewhat extemporaneous performances inevitably invited.

The song in the story, then, celebrates aspects of the warring Dinuzulu that are at odds with each other, and in the process, the poet comments about war and its devastating impact. Behind these traditional images lurks the force that will deal death to those images. The poet gives dimension to aspects of the story, selecting events and recombining them, so that the story is reshaped, its theme and central character given new definition. The historic images and the figurative details are the fragments that the poet works into unity by means of the rhythmical patterns that he employs. All is swept up in these patterns, and the way the interludes are integrated into the rhythm of the poem becomes itself a mirror of the way the poet works to move the disparate images of contemporary and historical life into the weaving spell of the poem within the story.

Another poem from the Zulu oral tradition reveals the essence of this heroic poem shorn of specific historical references, as if a poet were commenting on the musical purity of the poem:

Sikhulu les' isizwe, esithwal' imiqiqingo,
Sihamba nempahla, sitheng' izinkomo ngolembu.
Ngiya kuyiraya bo!
Iza kuliqed' izwe.
Iluzwambuzwambu,
Isuka phansi, yaqond' izulu.
Injengenyoka eyadl' isixabu sabamhlophe.
Bayicupha, yabanjwa.
Bayidons' amalang' amabili, 'mathathu;
Bayinquma ngomese.
Kwagqabuk' ilangab' esizibeni,
Labahangula.
Kwagqabuk' izintutu,
Zaqond' izwe lonke, lavutha!
NaseMbilane,
Lapha kade bethi iyaphuma,
Bethi igcwel' iziziba zonke, nya![171]

Great must be this people, who carry loads of goods around,
To barter salempore[172] for cattle here and there.
I shall sing a song about it.
It will overspread the entire land.
A long thin frame it has, bending to and fro.
Starting from the earth, it makes towards the sky,
Like that huge snake that ate the white men's sheep;
They set a trap for it and caught it,

Pulled at it two, and three, days long;
They cut it through with knives,
When a flame leapt out from its pool,
And scorched them.
Clouds of dust at once broke forth,
And streamed throughout the land, which was set ablaze!
And here at Mbilane, too,
From whence (as every pool, it was said, was full thereof)
They thought it must spring forth.

"I shall sing a song about it." It is the poem in the story of which the poet sings here, in the ambiguity of the work: That song "will overspread the entire land." It has "A long thin frame, bending to and fro," and "Starting from the earth, it makes towards the sky." The poet ties the song to the event: "Like that huge snake that ate the white men's sheep," and so the poet moves the song into the core of the historical event. Is the poet writing of an *impi* (army) here or he is referring to the poem?[173]

And so the poem is drawn to its essence:

Ubani oza kufel' esilungwini?
Mana, Nkosi!
Ungezwa bebubula,
Beyasola.

Who is going to die among the whites?
Stand firm, oh king!
Heed not their mutterings,
They are but finding fault.[174]

A Page from a Journal

A STORYTELLER

January 26, 1976

Nongenile Masithathu Zenani is a poet, and like all great poets her words spark and sparkle, and give new form to the way we think about and experience life. Her stories betray her love of life and her penetrating criticism of life's foibles. But it is her love of life that remains with you. What she did was take the ancient Xhosa storytelling tradition and reshape it for her contemporary world. And, like all great artists, she has a universal impact. She has the ability to capture the essence of an experience in penetrating ways and universal terms. An artist, she knows the members of her audience in some ways better than they know themselves, and she works their emotions and experiences into the fabric of her stories. Her stories rise out of the specific moment and locale, but in their artistry they transcend time and place: she is for all times and settings. In the alchemy of storytelling, when we hear her stories we are one with the Xhosa and their hopes and dreams. I meet her in the depths of apartheid, when the racist regime touches people in the remotest parts of the country; I am continually struck by the sense of humanity and the richness and universality of Xhosa tradition as communicated in the oral traditions. She knows the power of the word, its wonderful and terrible emotional force, and she uses that power to drive unerringly to the possibilities and the foibles in all members of her audience. Poor as she is materially, she lives the life of the mind, expressing in her stories and commentaries the life of the heart, and in the process enriches all members of her audiences.

—We had discussions long into the night about the art of the storyteller, and she always brought those discussions back to feeling. She was contemptuous of those who saw stories as purveyors of simple moralities, noting acerbically that this is what Christian missionaries did with the Xhosa stories, manipulating the stories and the tradition to suit Christian morality. Because the missionaries knew next to nothing about the Xhosa traditions, she said, they never understood what meaning actually is.

—Stories in the oral tradition are never meant to be memorized, she argues, nor are they meant to be frozen in time. The storyteller is constantly in the process of linking the present and the past: it is therefore crucial that the images be flexible, that their linkages be evanescent. Oral stories, these *iintsomi* in the Xhosa tradition, are composed of images, some of them ancient and often fantastic, others contemporary and realistic. A storyteller patterns images from these two repertories into a story, bonding reality and fantasy, uniting the present and the past, and providing an unbroken continuity between the generations so that the past, by means of its splendid images of fancy, imposes itself upon and shapes the modern world.

—Masithathu Zenani had recently taken me to a traditional Xhosa wedding, and she discussed this at length with me. She explained how the wedding ritual itself was a story, a theatricalization of real-life relationships. The bride, hidden in her mass of veils, was involved in a change, and the veils suggested this: the bride could not be seen, her identity therefore uncertain. The veils represented the period of transformation, as she made the transition from unmarried to married woman. The attendant events were all separate references to the bride's past and her future, symbols of her loss of her earlier state and her rebirth into a new and very different and challenging state. Simultaneously, there were symbolic suggestions that the bride, in her new role and environment, was not alone, that her past, tradition, family, society, remained a part of her human context. The ritual that we had observed was a living story, a testament, said Masithathu, to stories' power.

The Story

The tales of the people are a hidden lore.
—Henry Callaway, quoted in Marion S. Benham, *Henry Callaway*

January 26, 1969

It is a Zulu performance, and after the performance, I am expressing an opinion about the symbolism in one of the stories we heard. The Zulu performer stops me, and explains to me that the meaning of a story is the totality of performance, not a simple message. Performance is the thing. The Zulu performer explains to me, "If I am to tell you what this story means, I must tell it again."

The story is a construction. It contains the ingredients that immediately come to mind when one thinks of a story: characters, a plotting of events, perhaps some suspense as one moves from a conflict to a resolution, the clearly crafted prose of the teller. These are the obvious materials of the storyteller. But, as we have seen, they are not the essential materials. These include above all else the emotions of teller and audience, images that evoke those emotions, rhythmic patterns that hold and shape the emotions, and the poem at the heart of the story, which is essentially a metaphor composed of the emotions of the members of the audience. All elements in the story conspire to produce this essential internal metaphor that holds the story together in the sense that it becomes the vessel constructed of the feelings of the audience. The story is a construction.

A poetics of storytelling begins and ends with emotion. The question of the meaning of the story moves us into this complex webbing of emotions. Meaning is not the obvious surface morality or statement of the story, although that is what we sometimes discuss when stories are analyzed. Those surface meanings are simply one of the many ingredients, and hardly the most significant of those ingredients, that compose a story.

A Xhosa storyteller

It is music that provides essential insights into the inner workings of stories, because it is to the music of the story that the audience responds and to the music that it contributes. Music, which provides the sinews of the metaphorical core of the story, consists of the emotional responses of the audience, a combination of those responses and the rhythmical form given to those responses by the performer. Music may itself constitute the totality of this metaphorical center.

The full performance of the story is ritualistic in the sense that the audience has been there before, has had those adventures before, and regularly revisits the stories to recover those experiences. Storytelling always involves echoes, a shadowing of the past. Thus, stories are never wholly novel occurrences; they are always experiences of the known, of the past. Ritual partakes of the familiar,[175] a ritualized way of behavior, so that each time a member of an audience is a part of the performance of a story, that member weaves into that ritual a combination of old and new responses, and these responses are primarily emotional. When storytelling becomes ritual, each time a member of an audience experiences it there is a rich combination of that which is a part of his own emotional history and the new layers affected by recent experiences, as well as by that of this particular rendering of the story. The ritual experience in the story links an audience to its origins, so that there is a mythic stratum present as well. As with all such events, there are certain schema that must be followed; these guidelines are scrupulously adhered to by the storyteller and her audience. They know the rules, and within those rules they have all kinds of possibilities for originality and movement. They do not move beyond those rules, although there will be times when they stretch the boundaries.

The answer to the question, "What does the story mean?" often seems obvious and unambiguous. But even the story with the most obvious meaning is a complex mixture, a web of words, motifs, patterns, and emotions. The Zulu performer who insisted that the meaning of her story could only be apprehended if she told the story again knew with all effective storytellers that the apparent meaning was only the surface meaning. She knew that much more was transpiring between the storyteller and the audience. Emotions have always been evident when stories are told, but the thought that the emotions may be relevant to meaning has eluded many analysts and critics. Yet, emotions are at the heart of storytelling, emotions are the poem at the heart of stories. This is a study of that emotional core, the way storytellers manipulate images into patterns; then, from that rhythmic, metaphorical union of images, the way they work the emotions engendered by those images into beautiful forms that contain the meaning of the story.

The Riddle in the Story
A Propensity for Metaphor

"You got the words right, Livy, but you don't know the tune."
—Samuel Clemens, quoted in Albert Bigelow Paine, *Mark Twain, a Biography*[176]

In the oral tradition, artistic categories are interwoven; a common internal structure characterizes them, each with a rhythmical ordering of image and motif that controls the ties between the art tradition and the real world.[177] It is by means of this common structure, it is because of the metaphor or its potential (the organizing factor in each of the genres), that vital links are established with the visual arts, as well as with dance, mime, and music. Each of the forms in some way nourishes the other. The lyric poet partakes of the riddler's art, the tale operates according to the principles of the riddle and lyric and contains the germ of the epic. In all cases, the metaphorical core controls expansion and development into more complex forms. The oral tradition is never simply a spoken art; it is an enactment, an event, a ritual, a performance. Patterning of imagery is the most visible artistic activity, involving the blending of the contemporary world and the fanciful fabrication of the tradition. The combination of the images and their transformation into dramatic ritual is the result of metaphor. "The deliberate conjunction of disparate items which we call metaphor," writes the poet, James Dickey, "is not so much a way of understanding the world but a perpetually exciting way of recreating it from its own parts."[178] When the realms of art and reality are brought into contact, and that relationship is caused by metaphor, the audience is in the presence of myth. Metaphor takes an audience's routine experiences and, in a performance, links them to ancient, often fantastic, images from the art tradition. The combination renders contemporary experience comprehensible and roots the members of the audience in history. Metaphor implies transformation, from one set of images to another, but without giving up any of the original meanings or perceptions that an audience might have of them. This process becomes mythic because of the changes involved. Real world images may be cultural, historical, or personal. Their blending with fantasy, the movement from one state of being to another, is mythic and is coupled with a reenactment that is ritualistic. The drama of performance is an effort to capture both the ritual, the graphic images of transformation, and, more importantly, the fierce focusing of venerable emotions on contemporary change. Myth is not a tale; it is a process within a tale. It is related to stories of the gods because gods are creators and are thus involved in primal transitions. The shifts wrought by the gods have their parallels in those brought about by cultural heroes, epic heroes, even tricksters and tale characters. The audience may have moved from the place of the gods, but the tales and the shifting states stay stable. We remain in the presence of myth, which is always in transition. It is the dying and reborn god, the hero transforming his society; it is the tale character shifting identities through the dramatization of a cultural rite of passage. Myth is the engine of metaphor. Because of that, it is a narrative device, but it is more. Ancient motifs—condensed, symbolic, heavy with emotional potential—are embedded in the tradition; myth has the power to activate those motifs, to release and contain the intense feelings. Always in motion, myth is liberating, but its leap into the unknown is, in the oral tradition, seldom open-ended. It insists upon a return to origins, altered perhaps but ever cyclical. For that reason it obviates history while depending on history for its images.

The purpose of metaphor, at the core of the mythic process, is to harness the emotions of the members of the audience, trapped as they are in images of past and present, thereby divining paradoxes and resolving conflicts, and to move that audience into a new perception of reality. The riddle is a figurative form comparing "two otherwise unrelated things in a metaphorical manner."[179] In the comparison the problem is fathomed, but perhaps more important the attributes of each set are transferred to the other. When the Lingala riddler utters this poser, *"Mokonzi moko, akofandaka se o kati ya nzube"* ("A chief who only sits among thorns"), the answer, *"Lolemo"* ("The tongue"), reveals a description not only of the tongue but also of the chief.[180] Because the riddle involves paradox as well as imagery, it exercises both the intellect and the imagination of the audience. In its attempts to find the answer, it becomes a part of the metaphorical transformation. The delight in discovery characterizes the riddle, prepares members of an audience for the more complex coupling that occurs in the tale and epic, and reflects the relations among images in lyric poetry. The riddle operates in two modes, much as lyric and tale do: one is literal, the other figurative, with a tension and an interaction between them.[181] It is not that the literal mode acts as a block or misleading clue to the audience,[182] but that the literal level of interpretation interacts vigorously and creatively with the figurative; that is the full experience of the riddle. It is not simply a solution that is wanted, it is the prismatic experience of figurative imagery placed against the literal. The Zulu raconteur riddles, *"Ngendishi yami egubuzekile"* ("A dish of mine that is turned upside down"), and the answer participates in the metaphor of poetry as the solution is sought.[183] "A stupid little fellow who drags his intestines," riddles the Berber performer, and again, "My little meadow which is not mown," and again, "She gave four to the sky, she gave four to the earth, she gave four to her mistress":[184] the play is between fantasy and reality, between the figurative and the literal. In the riddle, the audience's imagination, made active during performance, is also made visible.

The riddle establishes a model for all oral art. The relationship between images has at least the potential for metaphor and complexity. In the African lyric, it is possible to see a set of riddles operating as the separate images in the poem relate to one another metaphorically[185]—and also, often, with paradox. Andrew Welsh notes, "The riddle is the root of the lyric element in the sense that both the riddle maker and the lyric poet developed their respective expressions through the same associations of picture and thought, the same process of seeing, knowing, naming."[186] The combination of figurative images creates the final experience of the lyric poem. It is often more complex than the riddle because it embraces a number of riddling connections, and a single riddle relationship may become more complex when it is introduced into the context of yet another, and so on as the riddling images of the poem interact. The poet supplies a series of images that repeat aspects of a basic theme or examine an emotion with intensity. Each metaphorical set, in itself a riddle, acts as a kind of clue, bringing the audience closer to an understanding of the poet's intent. *"Mon coeur est tout joyeux,"* in the Mbuti song that ends this book, establishes a theme.[187] It is repeated concretely and metaphorically, *"Mon coeur s'envole en chantant"*; then image follows image— *"Sous les arbres de la forêt / Forêt noire demeure et noire mère"*—as the poet contrasts herself with a bird, explaining the significance of the place. In that homely image and its suggestion of childbirth, the poet continues, *"Dans mon filet j'ai pris / Un petit, tout petit oiseau."* That is the significance of *"la forêt, / Forêt noire demeure et noire mère."* The poet repeats the image yet again, but with a thematic change: *"Mon coeur est pris dans le filet / Dans le filet avec l'oiseau,"* tying the separate image strands together. The lyric poet repeats the image, establishes the boundaries of the varieties of imagery that may be introduced into the poem, and creates the rhythm. These assure that the different sets of images will be experienced by the audience in a similar way. In the Mbuti song, the singer unites the images of ensnared heart and trapped bird. When we learn that the poem is performed by a woman while giving birth, the images of joy, forest, and snaring achieve a metaphorical union, and the lyrical riddling is at an end.

Myth is not a theology or body of dogma or a worldview; it is not so much a story as that which moves the story, and we find it in incipient form in the riddle, lyric, and proverb. In the latter, metaphor is achieved when a somewhat hackneyed expression is brought into contact with reality. *"Mlomo umoza upoke nyama ku nkaramo?"* ("Can one mouth take meat from a lion?")[188] asks the Tumbuka sage, and a contemporary instance of the uselessness of a minority opinion is linked to the tradition. *"Mahara mboya, ukwiza sima yamara"* ("Wisdom is like mushrooms that come in season when the porridge is finished"),[189] says the Tumbuka wise man, and a modern experience of the Monday morning quarterback touches the ancient lore of the culture. The proverb is a metaphorical relationship, tying an old saying to a situation with which it may or may not have a clearly perceived relationship, but with thought, it reveals a "valid cryptogram" for that real life experience. The proverb in this respect behaves similarly to the way image operates in lyric poetry, in which diverse images are brought into contact with one another. The audience knows what it must do, as it works toward an understanding of the relationship. The proverb form and the audience's experiences with it force a movement toward reason. Proverbs are tired clichés only when viewed in isolation; when they are placed into realistic contexts, they become vital, even dynamic. What gives them freshness is the experience to which they are giving form. In the lyric, linkages must be understood within the poem before they can be comprehended in the realistic context. In the proverb, the only way for the metaphor to be realized is by means of the instant connection between the art form and reality. The proverb is similar to the riddle in the sense that metaphor is intended, as the ancient truth of the culture touches contemporary experience. More perhaps than the riddle, the proverb establishes ties with the culture's sages. Ancient wisdom is carried by the proverbial expression that through constant use becomes easily remembered, and hackneyed until given new life. The proverb gives cultural and artistic form to present action. The riddle does much the same thing when problem and solution are harmonized. The Mende proverb, *"Manuma gbii na kambei hu"* ("There is no mercy in the tomb"),[190] possesses an ambiguity that gives it the potential for many uses; the equivocality is drastically narrowed and concentrated when creatively applied.

The storyteller

The three independent genres interact primarily by means of their identical metaphorical construction. As oral forms become longer and more complex, it is this same process that animates them, as if the riddle and lyric poem formed their core with the proverb adding a somewhat didactic bridge between the worlds of the real (that is, the present) and the fantastic (that is, the past).

The single most important characteristic of African oral performances is the patterning of images.[191] Children learn to organize like-images, establishing a model for the comprehension of more sophisticated forms in which unlike images are meant to be aligned. In the simple tale, patterns are built on the actions of a single character, as fantasy and reality are linked in a linear movement from conflict to resolution. At the same time, the metaphorical structure, not unlike that which governs the movement in lyric poetry, controls the patterning, and provides the possibilities for complexity, for meaning, and for the revelation of the mimetic relationship. That lyrical core assures that the potential for expansion and development are not lost. Out of a triangular relationship that includes a central character, a helper, and a villain, the basic movement is developed. The tale at this stage will not necessarily be metaphorical; it may simply bring like image sets into contact with one another for no purpose other than to move the tale effectively to its resolution. But the possibilities for metaphor are a part of the form because of the existence of mythic images and their patterning. The linkage between the real world and an illusory realm contains the possibilities for a metaphorical relationship, a set of worlds controlled and manipulated by the storyteller.

"Dulube"

A Story and Its Poem

> Music resembles poetry; in each
> Are nameless graces which no methods teach,
> And which a master-hand alone can reach.
> —Alexander Pope, "An Essay on Criticism"

In its simplest form, the story of Dubulihasa (or Dulube, or Tulube, or Ubongopa-kamagadlela) is literally a poem—the story is dominated by a song that provides the spine of the tale. Thieves attempt to steal an ox, but the ox refuses to move until the boy who herds it sings to it, telling it to move: "Dubulihasa! Dubulihasa! / You must go, Dubulihasa! / Because you can see / That I'll be killed, Dubulihasa!" The words of the song are altered slightly, revealing the movement of the story, as the ox and boy are taken far from their home and the ox is slaughtered and eaten: "You must cross [the river], . . . ," "You must enter [the yard], . . . ," "You must be snared, . . . ," "You must be killed, . . . ," "You must be roasted, . . ." But when the men go to a river to bathe, the boy sings his song to the carcass of the ox: "You must get up, . . . ," "You must leave, . . . ," "You must travel, . . ." And so it is that the boy's adventure away from home and back is constructed around the song.

How does the storyteller create metaphor in the poem? In stories dealing with transformation or rites of passage, secondary characters, sometimes fantasy in nature, become mirrors of, metaphors for, the central real-life character who is undergoing change of some kind. At the heart of the story is the poem—it may be an actual poem or a song, as in the various versions of this Xhosa and Zulu story from South Africa about an ox.

Four storytellers create their own versions of this story, developing its melodic line around that song: an ox is stolen, then slaughtered, and then brought back to life. The fate of the ox becomes interwoven with that of a boy by means of the song. The story parallels the boy and the ox: the ox responds to the commands of the boy expressed in the song.

DUBULIHASA, THE OX

Performed by a Hlubi Woman (Xhosa)

An *intsomi* goes like this—

There was a boy who herded cattle. He continued herding day after day, and then he would go home. Then he would return and herd the cattle, and again he would go home.

It happened one day that a man arrived and said to the boy, "Boy, I want you to come to my place!"

The child said, "I'm afraid!"

This man said then, "Now, I want you to bring these cattle and come to my place!"

The child fled.

The man returned three days later, and said, "There's no way out today! I'll beat you!"

The child said, "All right, then."

The man said, "Well, speak, boy, so that these cattle move!"

The child sang,

"Dubulihasa! Dubulihasa!
You must go, Dubulihasa!
Because you can see
That I'll be killed, Dubulihasa!"

The ox traveled on, it traveled and traveled, the ox traveled.
Again the man said, "Speak, boy, so that this ox travels!"
It stood there.
The child said,

"Dubulihasa! Dubulihasa!
You must go, Dubulihasa!
Because you can see
That I'll be killed, Dubulihasa!"

The ox bellowed, "Mpooooooo! Mpooooooo!"
The man said, "Speak, boy, so that this ox moves!"
The boy said,

"Dubulihasa! Dubulihasa!
You must cross, Dubulihasa!
Because you can see
That I'll be killed, Dubulihasa!"

At a river. The ox crossed over.
Again, the ox bellowed, "Mpoooooo!"
The man said, "Speak, boy, so that this ox moves!"
They were now fairly close to the home of this man.
Again, the boy said,

"Dubulihasa! Dubulihasa!
You must go, Dubulihasa!
Because you can see
That I'll be killed, Dubulihasa!"

The ox traveled, it traveled. Then, when it entered the yard above the cattle-kraal the ox stopped.

The man again said, "Speak, boy, so that the ox comes into the yard!"

The ox bellowed, "Mpoooooo! Mpooooo!"

Again, the boy said,

"Dubulihasa! Dubulihasa!
You must enter, Dubulihasa!
Because you can see
That I'll be killed, Dubulihasa!"

The ox entered the yard. It stopped and urinated.

The man said again, "Speak, so that the ox comes into the enclosure!"

The child spoke,

"Dubulihasa! Dubulihasa!
You must enter, Dubulihasa!
Because you can see
That I'll be killed, Dubulihasa!"

It entered the enclosure. The man took some ropes, and came with them.

He said, "Speak, boy, so that I can snare this ox and kill it!"
The child repeated,

"Dubulihasa! Dubulihasa!
You must be snared, Dubulihasa!
Because you can see
That I'll be killed, Dubulihasa!"

The ox was snared, and it bellowed now for the last time.
It said, "Mpoooooo! Mpooooooo!"
The man said, "Speak, boy, so that the ox may be pierced!"
The child said,

"Dubulihasa! Dubulihasa!
You must be killed, Dubulihasa!
Because you can see
That I'll be killed, Dubulihasa!"

He killed the ox then, and it was skinned, it was finished. Then it was necessary that it be roasted.

The man repeated, "Speak, boy, so that the ox may be roasted, so that we can eat!"

He said,

"Dubulihasa! Dubulihasa!
You must be roasted, Dubulihasa!
Because you can see
That I'll be killed, Dubulihasa!"

They roasted the ox, and it was eaten.

The man again said, "Speak, boy, so that we can bring the ox into the house!"

"Dubulihasa! Dubulihasa!
You must enter, Dubulihasa!
Because you can see
That I'll be killed, Dubulihasa!"

They took it and brought it into the house. When they got into the house, this woman could not eat it at all, this ox would choke her.

It appeared that the boy must speak again, and so he did:

"Dubulihasa! Dubulihasa!
The old woman should also eat this ox, Dubulihasa!
Because you can see
That I'll be killed, Dubulihasa!"

The old woman then ate the ox.

Time passed then, time passed, time passed, and then they got up. When they went to wash, the child remained behind with this old woman. When they had gone away and were on the other side of the homestead, when they had arrived at the river, they washed. The boy came back to the old woman and gave her some tobacco.

He said to the woman, "Smoke!"

The old woman smoked. When the old woman had finished smoking, the boy said,

"Dubulihasa! Dubulihasa!
You must get up, Dubulihasa!
Because you can see
That I'll be killed, Dubulihasa!"

The ox got up, it stood at once!

Again the child said, "Dubulihasa, I want you to go outside now, so that we can travel!" And again he said,

"Dubulihasa! Dubulihasa!
You must leave, Dubulihasa!
Because you can see
That I'll be killed, Dubulihasa!"

Dubulihasa went out. This child sat on the ox's horn, and he drove the other cattle.

Then the old woman said, "The cattle are gone, cowards! The cattle are gone, cowards!" Again the child said,

"Dubulihasa! Dubulihasa!
You must travel, Dubulihasa!
Because you can see
That I'll be killed, Dubulihasa!"

Dubulihasa traveled and went home. He got home then, and he was asked, "Where have you been?"

He said, "I was taken away!"

He told them everything that he had done, and there was happiness at home because he had returned.

The *intsomi* is ended, it is ended.[192]

In this version of "Dulube," the storyteller begins with a song that has the possibilities of slight alteration in the second line:

Dubulihasa! Dubulihasa!
You must ______, Dubulihasa!
Because you can see
That I'll be killed, Dubulihasa!

That song, placed at relevant junctures through a linear movement, creates a story. In a straightforward tale, the poem in the story is readily identifiable. The melodic line that is the linear movement is, in such a case, given richness but not complexity by the song. This combination of linear melodic movement and the regular pulsing of the song moves the story and the performance to their resolution. The song is clearly and carefully integrated into the linear movement by the modification in the second line.

There are various ways whereby the storyteller takes the central character and makes him more complex. One way is by adding further detail. In the hands of the gifted performer, Nongenile Masithathu Zenani,[193] further developments of that central Dulube song occur.[194] The song remains the pivotal organizing device in this rendering of the tale, but further detailing deepens the structure and melodic line. The skeletal song builds the spine of the story, holding it, giving it its incipient form. But a considerable amount of descriptive detail is developed by Zenani, providing greater motivation for the acts of the characters, linking the boy more clearly to the fantasy ogres (the villains are more realistic in the preceding story). As fantasy characters, they readily become a part of the boy as he moves through the transition in his life. The conflict between the boy and his father sets the frame for the contest that is to follow. The struggle between the boy and the ogres is more fully detailed, more graphically described. The storyteller links the ogres and the ox: "They tried to lasso the ox, but the rope snared one of the ogres instead." "Then they attempted to throw the ox to the ground. But when they tried to do this, one of the ogres fell to the ground instead of the ox." "But when they tried to stab the ox, one of them was stabbed himself."

A new pattern is developed that parallels the basic Dulube song. This subsidiary pattern has the effect of bringing the boy and the ogres into analogous relationship. A metaphor is developing, growing out of the simple song pattern. In the end, the return to the frame is complete when the boy and his father are reconciled: the boy and Dulube have returned, the villainous ogres left behind: "They knew that the ox that controlled their movements was gone." The ox and the boy are one: "The ox moved on then, the child riding on top of it." So it is that, in the language of storytelling, the ox and the ogres mirror the duality of the boy as he passes through a transformation, separated from his family as a boy, returning to them unified with the symbolism of the ox.

Another way to make the story more complex is by providing additional patterning around the poem at the heart of the tale. In a third Xhosa version of the story, "Tulube, the Ox,"[195] the same galvanizing song forms the center of the first section, with a development of that song to include a repeated refrain—"When they tried to ______ the ox, they ______themselves,"—building into the story the ineptness of the villains. With the final repetition of "Get up, Tulube," the song is interrupted and never allowed to fully develop. Instead, the storyteller weaves into that final rendering of the song a new pattern, the "Zemk' iinkomo" (The cattle are departing!) pattern familiar in chase sequences in a variety of southern African stories.[196] So it is that the boy-ox relationship is welded more closely to the acts of the villains. And so it is that the ox and the villains become a part of the boy's duality as he passes through a transformation. Fantasy, then, is not a necessary ingredient of subsidiary characters who are to be worked into metaphor: it is the organization of the images, the formal organization of the emotions engendered by the actions of the characters, that is responsible for the metaphorical relationship between the boy and the secondary characters. In this case, the negative meaning given to the villains is emphasized by the "Zemk' iinkomo" pattern, stressing also the movement of the boy away from what the villains represent and toward what the ox represents: "The cattle have gone off with the prisoner!"

In a Zulu version of the story, "Ubongopha kamagadlela," collected in 1868, performed by Umatshotsha umkaMafuta,[197] that same basic poem is present, developed and detailed somewhat, and now linked to other patterns. The simple pattern begins to take on other meanings. It remains obvious in this Zulu tale, stabilized at its center. Now the motif and the pattern take us into the psyche of the boy as he moves through a transformation in his life. But there are heroic possibilities here as well: there are mythic elements in his nature, and in the end he creates a new kingdom. The point here is that the formal structure of the story remains recognizably similar: What has happened to develop deeper meaning?

There is a brief introduction, necessarily establishing the pattern that will dominate the story. In this particular rendering of the song, an alteration occurs in the final two lines:

> Ubongopha-kamagadlela,
> Ubongopha-kamagadlela,
> ______, it is time to ______;
> ______, it is time to ______.

The variations:

> Awake now . . . ,
> Set out now . . . ,
> Return now . . . ,
> Enter the pen. . . .

Then there is the coming of the thieves, and the patterned song continues:

> Awake now . . . ,
> Go now . . . ,
> Go now . . . ,
> Stand still now . . . ,
> Go now . . . ,
> Go now . . . ,
> Go into the pen now . . . ,
> Let me get down. . . .

The pattern is interrupted by two other patterns, surely familiar to the Zulu audience, a lightning and a spitting pattern, along with an "I shall die if that ox dies" pattern.

The performer returns to the earlier and dominant pattern:

> Die now, it is time to die . . . ,
> Be skinned now, it is time to be skinned . . . ,
> Let your tail be cut off. . . .

This is followed by the resurrection of the ox and a return to the basic pattern:

> Arise now . . . ,
> Stand up now . . . ,
> Let me mount . . . ,
> Go now. . . .

Chase and destruction follow, with another repetition of the basic pattern:

> Stand still now . . . ,

and a destruction pattern: kill one and all die, and an inability to kill the youth, accompanied by the spittle pattern. The conclusion is next, and a final reprise of the pattern:

> Go in now. . . .

This story is a development of the Masithathu Zenani version, with the Ubongopha-kamagadlela song the primary organizational element that ultimately creates metaphor. The secondary patterns—the lightning and spitting patterns—augment and develop the dominant pattern. Identity is crucial to the story, as might be expected in a tale with a transformation at its core: "I do not get off, I do not walk on the ground, I remain on the ox. From the time of my birth I have never felt the ground." So it is that the storyteller weaves the ox into the boy. As the boy moves to manhood, the spittle pattern is interwoven with the main pattern, emphasizing the move to new identity: "King, child of the greatest, mysterious one who is as big as the mountains." And all of nature responses: "It thundered and rained exceedingly," and all houses leak except that of the boy, which strangely remains dry. The villains are not able to damage that essential boy-ox relationship, and when the ox is killed, a part of the youth dies. It is then that the ox can be brought back to life, appropriately by the boy: he is reborn, as the ox's rebirth shadows or mirrors that of the boy. Now the youth's manhood is tested, his new identity as a man is tried, with the pattern in which the villains attempt to kill the youth and they die instead. He returns to his home, and the relationship with the ox is again underscored: "I will live on the back of Ubongopha-kamagadlela till my death."

The poem within the story, which is evident in each of the four stories in this set, has to do with the relationship between the boy and the ox. The ox becomes the storytellers' way of revealing the changes that are occurring within a youth who is undergoing a dramatic transformation. In this final story, the performer broadens the metaphorical aspects of the ox to include nature itself—an element that has been present all along is now made clearer, and so the poem within the story is deepened.

As stories become more complex, the inner poetic-metaphorical activity will not be so obvious, but its function remains the same: to deepen the audience's experience of the central character and the realistic environment in which he struggles, to elicit emotions from the members of the audience by means of mythic imagery, and, through patterning, to make the audience a part of the story's song.

A Page from a Journal

June 13, 1975

The ancient and familiar diffuse feelings—fears, hopes, dreads, joy: these feelings are first evoked by the familiar narrative images (imaginative: everyone knows they are not to be accepted literally: they are not history, after all), then held there, trapped there. Then those feelings (no longer diffuse, caught now in familiar images which may already be molding the feelings if the images are fixed symbols) can be channeled, directed, molded, formed, given sense, particularity, given cultural and individual definition by the artist, brought into juxtaposition with yet other images holding (trapping) yet other feelings. Thus can feelings and images—the unique combination of these in art—lead to abstractions (they can be abstracted), symbols, to abstract thought: by a process of metaphor. This is the real significance of the several semiotic systems that comprise the oral narrative system. This is why the artistic experience is so significant: it deals with feelings, and through feelings the mind.

The move is from physical involvement of the members of the audience (feelings, body, gesture, images) to mental abstraction (juxtaposition of image, thought). And the significance of this for nonverbal aspects of performance?

Fantasy

The Storyteller's Palette

The absurd and fantastic reign supreme.
—G. Wilson Knight, *The Wheel of Fire*

MYTHIC IMAGERY

Fantasy is the combining of two worlds; one thought of as real, the other thought of as fictional. Metaphorical sparks fly when those two worlds come into contact. What we have to do then is understand the limits of the two worlds, how they intersect.

The critical function of the basic mythic image with which the storyteller begins is to rouse sensations from the members of the audience. In the storyteller's memory and imagination is a potent repertoire of mythic images. The important thing about storytelling is the way those images are remembered, elicited, and organized during a performance. What is a fantasy image and what is not? Certainly we can agree that there are images that tug at the edges of the real. Within the context of story, a variety of images can be found, running from the starkly realistic to the mysterious to the strange and otherworldly to the monstrous and violent. Some stories that seem to contain no such images are nevertheless placed into the category of fantasy tales. Fantasy is more complex than determining whether a given image is fantastic.

These are the tools: mythic images and contemporary images, patterns, and metaphor, the combining of which results in meaning. Two essential activities of the performer involve her choice of imagery and the form within which she envelopes those images. In the process of this organizing activity, the various images are perceived as one, and we move into the aura of metaphor. The fantasy images by themselves tell us little. It is the coupling of those images with others that creates meaning. By themselves, fantasy images are not the story. The story typically includes a real-life character who moves into mythic worlds. The story centers on this central character's rhythmical movement from one state to another, in various confrontations and contexts; it is a transition of identity for this person, with other events and patterns serving as commentary on his developing identity as a man. The important thing is this rhythmical activity, a blending of the real and the mythic, images that generate emotion.[198]

The mythic image contains an inner core that often has an aura of fantasy, the supernatural, beginnings. Fantasy may involve mythic archetypes of great antiquity and power[199]—enchanters, princesses, quests, looming towers, hidden cities, haunted forests, walled gardens—or myths not as ancient but no less potent, from ancient frontiers to a bomb that can destroy civilization. But the content of these symbols and images is not confined to fantasy, nor does it make a work a fantasy. Fantasy places the material in a fictional framework within which it is treated as empirical data, the common stuff of ordinary reality.

Fantasy contains history, fragmented history, reconstituted history, the marvelous, and myth. It is not an end, it is a means. It is not the image but the entire organizing apparatus that forms the fantasy world of storytelling. Images that we may characterize as fantasy, real-fantasy, marvelous, uncanny, or supernatural are joined in rich metaphorical linkages, so that the images blur and shimmer and blend. In the end, what is reality and what is fantasy? A study of fantasy is not a study of a flying carpet or twenty-league boots or whether Jonah was actually swallowed by the whale. Rather, a study of fantasy takes us to the very foundations of art because fantasy is, in the end, rhythm, the heartbeat of narrative production. When we move into the world of the storyteller, we are in the realm of fantasy, whether or not there is a talking crow, a rolling human head, a monstrous dragon.

A fantasy world seems different from the real world, but those who live in that world are familiar. Fantasy is constructed of mythic images, and each time such images are produced they are revivified. The fantasy world of the story becomes more than a mirror of the real world: when the audience moves into that constructed world of story, it has experiences that move it to a new truth.[200] It is not really a question of whether what happens in these fantasy worlds could or could not exist. Fantasy is ambiguity, a spectral presence, suspended between being and nothingness. It takes the real and breaks it. Fantasy recombines and inverts the real, but it does not escape it.

The crucial thing is that there are two realms, one that echoes in prismatic ways the other. In understanding the prism, we come to a deeper understanding of that world that is under investigation. The mythic world is the storyteller's tool whereby she analyzes the world that we inhabit.

Such investigation can take place in no other way. A congeries of characters may come to represent a single real-life character; a complexity of events may explain a single real-life event. But there is more to it than the two realms. The mythic world is not a contemporary world; it is ancient (or that is the belief), and it encapsulates images that are ancient and have the capacity to elicit strong emotional responses from members of audiences. It is the sense in storytelling that these ancient images contain the wisdom of the ages, that when they come into contact with the real, an audience's experience of the real world is given a new shape. Sometimes these ancient images are fantastic, but they do not have to be. It is their behavior that is the important thing.

The two worlds are not neatly separated: they fold into each other, so that the one seems at times an intrusion into the other. Fantasy is the joining of fiction and history.[201] It always occurs within the shadow of the real, but it frequently subverts the real and always provides the real with new dimensions and layers of experience and meaning. It is a world of rhythmical order, of connections and transformations, of metaphorical relationships often between the real and the marvelous. These relationships and other encoded materials are understood and experienced within the context of the mythic worlds. The basic tools of storytelling include these mythic and contemporary images, the rhythmical interweaving and patterning of these two categories of imagery, and the metaphorical relationships that result. Fantasy is the creation of mental universes with their own rules and laws. The raw material of stories is fantasy motifs and real-life images. The storyteller links these through patterning, bringing unlike images into relationship. Other images, image-sets, and minor patterns weave these larger patterns together. Without an understanding of these formal aspects of storytelling, there can be no appreciation of the poetry of fantasy.

What makes the story fantasy? Mythic images, for one thing, and narrative organization, for another. The fantasy images might be marvelous, they may be poetic or allegorical representations of the real, disguised versions of the real. But fantasy is also a part of the form of story: it is in fact the activator, the animator, of the images, moving them into metaphorical arrangements. Those metaphors may be primarily emotional. As the audience is moved closer to metaphor, fantasy slowly forms into poetic ordering. In the end, fantasy is no longer present: its residue remains, but it has been replaced by metaphor.

The movement of story is to metaphor. The material of metaphor is that with which we are familiar, and, more important, that with which we are unfamiliar. Fantasy, a poetic device that evokes emotion of one kind or other, takes us to the boundaries of our experience—out there, where all seems strange. Then fantasy moves us back to the familiar, but with a significant change: the world of the familiar can never be the same. It has been leavened, given new dimension by an experience in fantasy. In the end, fantasy becomes metaphor; that transformation is a part of the activity that we go through intellectually, imaginatively, and emotionally as we sort out items in the wondrous puzzle given to us by the storyteller. Fantasy, then, is always an active force. It is the engine of change, the activity in the betwixt and between area as the parts of the metaphor form themselves and slowly begin to coalesce. What begins as fantasy ends as an understanding, and fantasy, having done its work, fades, or, newly disguised, simply becomes a part of the completed poetic puzzle.

The engine that is fantasy includes the formal elements of the performance, the patterns or rhythm of story. The essence of metaphor is transformation, a move from one set of images to another, with threads of likeness connecting images that are unlike. Fantasy, then, is not just the furniture of the mythic world. It is the means of connecting the mythic and primary worlds. In other words, it is the stuff of metaphor. It is both a part of the image of metaphor, with contemporary real-life imagery, and, most importantly, the generator of metaphor, the union or the intersecting of the primary and mythic worlds, two worlds that are, in the language of storytelling, perceived as one.[202]

The melding of images into form involves rhythm and patterning, and results in metaphor. Rhythm, repetition, patterning—all of this is a form of structural fantasy. It includes the relationships between characters and events. This is the metaphorical part of the performance. All are encompassed in performance, in fantasy. Dance and music are engaged, orchestrating relations with the audience. So it is that we define fantasy as an image, an action, a pattern, and a relationship that occurs within a tightly manipulated and controlled narrative environment that partakes of the real world, but is itself a secondary world. That secondary world can only occur within the context and embrace of the real world. Thus, there is always an ironic encounter between them. But the relationship is only ironic; it is not a one-to-one relationship. The secondary fantasy world is fed by the real world. Indeed, everything in the secondary world can be seen to have its origins in the real world. But it is not the real world in its organization, in the relationship between images, and in

Mrs. Golomi Ntasambana

the images themselves when those images transcend in some way their real-life counterparts. This secondary world exists in its own right, with its own rules and laws. These rules and laws can be stated in broad terms, but they can only be worked out by an analysis of the individual narrative that exists within that secondary world.

A Page from a Journal

June 29, 1975

Gesture: Is there a hierarchy from the strictly complementary, mime, acting out of a character (by means of the performer's own body), to the ushering in and out of characters (now more removed from her own body; hence, gestures become more abstract, more supplementary?), to the rhetoric of storytelling (pure storytelling now, no character action, no ushering: purely abstract—and supplementary?)? This hierarchy is based on the artist's body and its relevance or proximity to what is going on in the narrative: the closer to her body (that is, the closer to mime, the closing of a perceived gap between verbal and nonverbal aspects of the narrative), the more complementary.

—Proximity of narrative action to the body of the artist determines the degree of abstraction of the nonverbal elements of a performance. The proximity of the body to the literal meaning of gesture and body movement. The movement away from the body is away from mime, complementary gesture, to symbolism, to abstracted gesture (to supplementary body movement and gesture?).

—Is there a move from the depictive to the discursive? Is it the same with ideophone? There is a move from ideophones as one moves from the depictive to the discursive. Does gesture thus follow the linguistic route?

—Hands and body for depicting character. Hands usher in and out, point, et cetera. Hands mainly for rhetoric. The body is rhetorical too, but very abstract.

—And the regular rhythm of the performance? Rhythm involves body movement and gesture—hands, feet, body, head, all. Is this regular rhythmic movement of the body and hands, abstract, symbolized (supplementary), a kind of grid or loom against which the more complementary gestures move and from which they originate? The individual complementary gesture thus grows out of the regular rhythmic body movement and language: the beat of the performance. This rhythmic patterned beat is the stuff of which complementary gestures are formed (or is the opposite true? or do they work both ways?).

—Is gesture an independent sign system? No, all elements are related, united, integrated. Nor are the verbal aspects of a performance a separate sign system.

—One must master a few structures (it is like learning a language), then hang images (words, phrases) on those generative structures. Structure is the thing: it makes sense of random images.

—Some gesture is strictly in tune or in harmony with the rhythm of content of the words: not at all complementary, not even apparently symbolic or rhetorical, or supplementary. Something else is operating here. Gesture and body movement just move along, in time with the music of the language and images, reflecting the rhythmic composition of the narrative performance. It echoes the rhythmic content of a tonal language in a work of art in which those tones, the inherent poetry of the language, are exploited, emphasized. The body and gestures move along with this, reflect, echo this.

Ritual

The Performance of the Story

> Above all else, poetry is a performance.
> —John Ciardi and Miller Williams, *How Does a Poem Mean?*

> But the genuine stories were never, at any time, written down. They were composed orally by the old people. And when we too asked how this tradition came into existence, we were told that it is a craft that had been practiced at the very beginning, in the old times. Such tales go back as far as ancestral time, to the age of the first people.
> —Nongenile Masithathu Zenani, *The World and the Word*

RITUAL, PERFORMANCE

Rituals have to do with change. They are the connections between the biological changes in our lives, on the one hand, and the needs of the societies in which we live, on the other. They take the momentous changes that occur during our lives and weave them into culture. Rituals are the means whereby we become acculturated, the means whereby we become functioning and productive parts of our societies. A major part of ritual is story, which provides both the context for these changes and the experience of change itself. Rituals include initiation ceremonies, marriage ceremonies, any and all of the formalized transformations that we experience as we move through life's trajectory. They provide us with our midlife corrections as we move through the adventures that comprise our lives. Rituals, then, are social, a means whereby we come into contact with the essence of our societies. They may be religious, mythic, a means whereby we come into contact with our gods. Without ritual, we are forever outside culture.

Ritual has to do with transition, very difficult periods in our lives. In his novel, *Smilla's Sense of Snow* (1992), Peter Høeg describes this transition: "People perish during transitional phases. In Scorebysund they would shoot each other in the head with shotguns when the winter started to kill off summer. It's not difficult to coast along when things are going well, when a balance has been established. What's difficult is the new. The new ice. The new light. The new feelings." He adds, "It's my only chance. It's everybody's only chance. To give yourself the necessary time to get acclimated."[203]

Arnold van Gennep writes, "An individual is placed in various sections of society, synchronically and in succession; in order to pass from one category to another and to join individuals in other sections, he must submit, from the day of his birth to that of his death, to ceremonies whose forms often vary but whose function is similar. . . . For groups, as well as for individuals, life itself means to separate and to be reunited, to change form and condition, to die and to be reborn. . . . And there are always new thresholds to cross: the thresholds of summer and winter, of a season or a year, or a month or a night; the thresholds of birth, adolescence, maturity, and old age; the threshold of death and that of the afterlife—for those who believe in it."[204] The rites of passage move one to a new birth. During the puberty ritual, the child dies and the adult begins life anew. As he passes through puberty, the young man becomes a fully qualified member of society. The initiation is a passage through death to a new life. During the marriage ritual, one moves from one state to another: one first becomes separated, moving to a liminal state. Then one goes through an ordeal and is thereby transformed. Finally, one returns, renewed, reborn. Myerhoff writes, "Rites of passage are often merged with messages and occasions that go beyond the change of status of an individual or age cohort. When the initiate is thought to embody messages about the cosmos, is considered a microcosm or miniature version of the largest concerns of the natural and the supernatural order, then what happens to the individual may transform the collectivity at the same time."[205] During the puberty rite of passage, a youth moves to adulthood, preparing to accept the rigors and responsibilities that such status entails. One of those responsibilities is actually another rite of passage—marriage, the movement of a person into a relationship with another human.

All rites of passage take a person or a community from one state to another, and in the process, change that person or community. In human societies, certain ceremonies and conventions are established to ritualize that transformation, the transition of a person. It is never easy, because we leave behind an accustomed identity and move into a new identity that is for the most part an unknown; it is never easy to leave the known for the unknown. But that is what the rite of passage is: a venture into a new identity, a new world of experience, it is a new adventure, a fresh journey that we thereby undertake, and some of us move into that adventure with excited anticipation, while others of us must be dragged into it with great reluctance.

But move into it we shall. These cultural rites of passage are essential parts of the human story, society's means of weaving humans into its fabric by creating a fiction with a deep cultural resonance, giving audiences the assurance that such changes are necessary facets of the human condition. William Frost observes that ritual "is presumed to be predictable, in outline if not in detail." He warns, "ritual also involves the danger of mechanizing action, of replacing possible real significance with an illusion of built-in significance."[206] When we move into these transformations, we are in a boundary state, a betwixt and between state that is neither one thing nor another, forsaking our former identity and moving into a new one—but for the moment of the transformation we have neither and yet possess both. It is a difficult and sometimes puzzling period, a time of ambiguity. For most of us, this move into uncharted territory is exhilarating. The ritual suggests the loss of identity, a confusion of identity, the ambiguity of one's character as one moves through these changes.

As van Gennep makes clear, the three stages of the rituals involve separation or isolation, ordeal or initiation, and return or reincorporation. Separation is the movement into adventure, the migration to the threshold. The ordeal dominates the pilgrimage, and involves tests and helpers and a singular struggle. This ordeal stage is the initiation into the new state of being; it is the betwixt and between area, the region of enormous energy that is initially undifferentiated. It is the area of the trickster that lurks within all humans,[207] and for the moment of change and transformation, the trickster is unleashed. The trickster is the force unbound when we move to the periphery. That force, however, is not outside us. It is the energy within us, forever masked (it is not a coincidence that the trickster is a master of the mask), ready to erupt whenever our guard is down. When we move into a new part of our lives, that force is released. Then we behave in extraordinary ways. This is the fantasy part of the tale, the part when the central character, having moved to the boundaries, is in a dangerous and unpredictable state. But he learns, and it is his wisdom that channels these forces and gives them the shape that will lead to the third stage of the ritual—the return, the movement back to the real world as a new being. Equilibrium has been attained, but the world is never the same.

The emphasis is on the second of the three stages, the ordeal or initiation stage, the betwixt and between stage. This is when we move away from our past and approach our new identities, and this is what the rituals and the stories focus on. The study of the oral tradition teaches us that our lives have a meaning that was laid down in the earliest of times. We progress in some respects, we change, we go through transitional periods that are, at times, frightening. These are the transformational rites of passage. Humans keep reliving those myths of creation through ritual; the myths are the prototypes of their own movement to fulfillment and maturity, of their own triumph over chaos as they move through the rites of passage and are reborn. The movement to the new identity is characterized by chaos and order, just as in myth, and, in the tales, the trickster is sometimes the embodiment of this chaos-order state. In the boundary state, humans are back to what they were in the ancient time, undifferentiated initially. A new time of creation is about to occur. The tale becomes mythic for the intervening period. As the world is in the process of re-creation in myth, so the individual is being recreated in the tale. The world is being reformed and redefined, and this is why myth is at the heart of all stories. This period of upheaval between two times of equilibrium is the key: it is the realm of the trickster. That intervening moment of change is theater, everlasting, the eternal moment. It is a season when everything is joined, everything is disjoined, when the world is formless yet harmonious, when all is movement: creation is occurring.

Performance of stories becomes ritualistic during the gathering of the emotions and images; transformation and life on the margins are at the heart of the story as metaphor becomes an experience, by its very definition, of change and transformation. The performer is the orchestrator, organizer, and shaper of audience's emotions into this metaphorical, ritualistic transformation. The role of the audience involves a willing participation resulting in an outpouring of emotions, as it moves to the periphery and into a state of limbo, into a frontier within the context of the story. Music, image, patterns move the audience into metaphor; through the evoked emotions the audience becomes a part of metaphor, a part of the story. In the end, it is a question of the audience as poem—the feelings or emotions of the members of the audience as the poetic heart of the story. The ritual that is performance moves the audience to the poem in the story.

"Sikhuluma"

A Story and Its Poem

Music oft hath such a charm
To make bad good, and good provoke to harm.
—William Shakespeare, *Measure for Measure*

Two brothers and their comrades are lured away from their home by splendid birds, and in the strange forest into which they move, as the brothers contend for hegemony, an unseen force destroys all of the boys except Sikhuluma, who is led back to his home by a dog. He goes in quest of a water monster, which he must first find and then entice to his homestead. There, the monster is killed, its skin fashioned into capes for Sikhuluma and his friends. They go to the far-off land of the villainous and supernatural Mangangedolo; Sikhuluma wishes to marry the villain's daughter, and is able to do so only after passing impossible tests set by Mangangedolo. It is with the assistance of a mouse that Sikhuluma succeeds. Even then, he is destroyed by Mangangedolo, only to be brought back to life by the daughter of Mangangedolo who becomes Sikhuluma's bride.

THE STORY OF SIKHULUME

By a Xhosa Storyteller

There was once in a certain village an old man who was very poor. He had no children, and only a few cattle. One day, when the sky was clear and the sun was bright, he sat down by the cattle-fold. While he was sitting there, he noticed some birds close by which were singing very joyfully. He listened for a while, and then he stood up to observe them better. They were very beautiful to look upon, and they sang differently from other birds. They had all long tails and topknots on their heads. Then the old man went to the chief and told him what he had seen.

The chief said, "How many were they?"

The old man replied, "There were seven."

The chief said, "You have acted wisely in coming to tell me; you shall have seven of the fattest of my cows. I have lost seven sons in battle, and these beautiful birds shall be in the place of my seven sons. You must not sleep tonight, you must watch them, and tomorrow I will choose seven boys to catch them. Do not let them out of your sight by any means."

In the morning the chief ordered all the boys of the village to be assembled at the cattle-fold, when he spoke to them of the birds. He said, "I will choose six of you, and set my son, who is dumb, over you, that will make seven in all. You must catch those birds. Wherever they go, you must follow, and you must not see my face again without them." He gave them weapons, and instructed them that if any one opposed them they were to fight till the last of them died.

The boys set off to follow those beautiful birds. They chased them for several days, till at last the birds were exhausted, when each of the boys caught one. At the place where they caught the birds they remained that night. On the morning of the next day they set out on their return home. That evening they came to a house in which they saw a fire burning, but no one was there. They went in, and lay down to sleep. In the middle of the night one of those boys was awake. He heard someone saying, "There is nice meat here. I will begin with this one, and take this one next, and that one after, and the one with small feet the last." The one with the small feet was the son of the chief. His name was Sikhulume, for he had never been able to speak till he caught the bird. Then he began to talk at once. After saying those words the voice was still. Then the boy awakened his companions, and told them what he had heard.

They said, "You have been dreaming; there is no one here. How can such a thing be?"

He replied, "I did not dream; I spoke the truth."

Then they made a plan that one should remain awake, and if anything happened, he should pinch the one next him, and that one should pinch the next, till all were awake. After a while the boy who was listening heard someone come in quietly. That was a cannibal. He said the same words again, and then went out for the purpose of calling his friends to come to the feast. The boy awakened his companions according to the plan agreed upon, so that they all heard what was said. Therefore, as soon as the cannibal went out, they arose and fled from that place. The cannibal came back with his friends, and when the others saw there was no one in the house, they killed and ate him. As they were going on, Sikhulume saw that he had left his bird behind. He stood, and said, "I must return for my bird, my beautiful bird with the long tail and topknot on its head. My father commanded that I must not see his face again unless I bring the bird."

The boys said, "Take one of ours. Why should you go where cannibals are?"

He replied, "I must have the one that is my own." He stuck his assagai in the ground, and told them to look at it. He said, "If it stands still, you will know I am safe; if it shakes, you will know I am running; if it falls down, you will know I am dead." Then he left them to return to the house of the cannibals.

On the way he saw an old woman sitting by a big stone. She said, "Where are you going to?" He told her he was going for his bird. The old woman gave him some fat, and said, "If the cannibals pursue you, put some of this on a stone."

He came to the house and got his bird. The cannibals were sitting outside, a little way back. They had just finished eating the owner of the house. When Sikhulume came out with his bird they saw him and ran after him. They were close to him, when he took some of the fat and threw it on a stone. The cannibals came to the stone, and began to fight with each other.

One said, "The stone is mine."

Another said, "It is mine."

One of them swallowed the stone. When the others saw that, they killed him and ate him. Then they pursued Sikhulume again. They came close to him again, when he threw the remainder of the fat on another stone. The cannibals fought for this also. One swallowed it, and was killed by the others.

They followed still, and Sikhulume was almost in their hands, when he threw off his mantle. The mantle commenced to run another way, and the cannibals ran after it. It was so long before they caught it that the young chief had time to reach his companions.

They all went on their way, but very soon they saw the cannibals coming after them. Then they observed a little man sitting by a big stone.

He said to them, "I can turn this stone into a house."

They replied, "Do so."

He turned the stone into a house, and they all went inside, the little man with them. They played the *icheya*[208] there. The cannibals came to the place and smelt. They thought the house was still a stone, for it looked like a stone to them. They began to bite it, and bit till all their teeth were broken, when they returned to their own village.

After this, the boys and the little man came out.

The boys went on. When they reached their own home they saw no people, till at length an old woman crept out of a heap of ashes. She was very much frightened, and said to them, "I thought there were no people left."

Sikhulume said, "Where is my father?"

She replied, "All the people have been swallowed by the *nabulele*."[209]

He said, "Where did it go to?"

The old woman replied, "It went to the river."

So those boys went to the river, and Sikhulume said to them, "I will go into the water, and take an assagai with me. If the water moves much, you will know I am in the stomach of the *nabulele;* if the water is red, you will know I have killed it." Then he threw himself into the water and went down.

The *nabulele* swallowed him without tearing him or hurting him. He saw his father and his mother and many people and cattle. Then he took his assagai and pierced the *nabulele* from inside. The water moved till the *nabulele* was dead, then it became red. When the young men saw that, they cut a big hole in the side of the *nabulele,* and all the people and the cattle were delivered.

One day, Sikhulume said to another boy, "I am going to the doctor's. Tell my sister to cook food for me, nice food that I may eat."

That was done.

He said to his sister, "Bring me of the skin of the *nabulele* which I killed, to make a mantle."

She called her companions, and they went to the side of the river. She sang this song:

> "Nabulele,
> Nabulele,
> I am sent for you
> By Sikhulume,
> Nabulele."

The body of the *nabulele* then came out. She cut two pieces of the skin for sandals, and a large piece to make a mantle for her brother.

When he was a young man, Sikhulume said to his friends, "I am going to marry the daughter of Mangangezulu."

They replied, "You must not go there, for at Mangangezulu's you will be killed."

He said, "I will go."

Then he called those young men who were his chosen friends to accompany him. On the way they came to a place where the grass was long. A mouse came out of the grass, and asked Sikhulume where he was going.

He replied, "I am going to the place of Mangangezulu."

The mouse sang this song:

"Turn back, turn back, Sikhulume.
No one ever leaves the place of Mangangezulu.
Turn back, turn back, O chief."

Sikhulume replied, "I shall not turn back."

The mouse then said, "As it is so, you must kill me and throw my skin up in the air."

He did so.

The skin said, "You must not enter by the front of the village, you must not eat off a new mat, you must not sleep in a house which has nothing in it."

They arrived at the village of Mangangezulu. They entered it from the wrong side, so that all the people said, "Why is this?"

They replied, "It is our custom."

Food was brought to them on a new mat, but they said, "It is our custom to eat off old mats only."

An empty house was given to them to sleep in, but they said, "It is our custom to sleep in a house that has things in it."

The next day the chief said to Sikhulume and his companions, "You must go and tend the cattle."

They left. A storm of rain fell. When Sikhulume spread out his mantle it became a house as hard as stone, into which they all went. In the evening they returned with the cattle. The daughter of Mangangezulu came to them. Her mother pressed her foot in the footprint of Sikhulume, and he became an eland. The girl loved the young chief very much. When she saw he was turned into an eland, she made a great fire and drove him into it. Then he was burned, and became a little coal. She took the coal out and put it in a pot of water, when it became a young man again.

Afterwards they left that place. The girl took with her an egg, a milk-sack, a pot, and a smooth stone. The father of the girl pursued them. The girl threw down the egg, and it became a mist. The father wandered about in the mist a long time, till at length it cleared away. Then he pursued again.

She threw down the milk-sack, and it became a sheet of water. Her father tried to get rid of the water by dipping it up with a calabash, but he could not succeed, so he was compelled to wait till it dried up. He followed still. The girl threw down the pot, and it became thick darkness. He waited a long time till light came again, when he followed them. He could travel very quickly. He came close to them, and then the girl threw down the smooth stone. It became a rock, a big rock with one side steep like a wall. He could not climb up that rock, and so he returned to his own village.

Then Sikhulume went home with his wife. He said to his people, "This is the daughter of Mangangezulu. You advised me not to go there, lest I should be killed. Here is my wife."

After that he became a great chief. All the people said, "There is no chief who can do such things as Sikhulume."[210]

In the "Sikhuluma" stories from the oral traditions of southern Africa, the complexity of poetry in storytelling becomes manifest. In the typical story of Sikhuluma, that having to do with his movement away from home as a child and his return as an adult, a dramatization of a boy's puberty rite of passage, a pattern reveals the outward movement to a far-off fantasy place. It is in that distant place that change occurs within the child, and that is where the storytellers locate their poem, in the metaphorical merging of fantasy imagery and realistic, within the metamorphosing character of Sikhuluma: the birds that he pursues, and the strange events that occur in the forest, including the deaths of his comrades even as he himself is reborn. The poem in the story is this gathering of images into a patterned vortex. In the second part of the story is another poem, one having to do with the water monster quested for by Sikhuluma or his surrogate, a poem consisting of a patterned quest and then a patterned chase. The third part of the tale is somewhat more complex, as a villainous and fantasy father and his beautiful daughter become woven into the character of the maturing Sikhuluma. The father comes to represent that which he is leaving behind, the daughter symbolizing his rebirth into a new identity. In the alchemy of storytelling and in the poem at the heart of the story, father and daughter become the contending sides of the real-life Sikhuluma. When all three of the Sikhuluma stories are merged, those poems become merged as well, creating a layered and dimensioned view of a transformation, a transition both occasioned and represented by the symphony of poems within the story.

Narratives that describe activities in the contemporary world frequently contain two themes: harmony between humans and nature, and rites of passage. Both emphasize the sustaining of unified societies. "Sikhuluma" is a tale that dramatizes the meanings of Sikhuluma's puberty and marriage rites of passage.

The name of the future king, Sikhuluma, means "eloquent speaker." This name is ironic, because he does not speak at all in the early part of the tale. But later, when he does speak, it is to save lives, befitting a future king and justifying the name, Sikhuluma. When he returns to his home after the first part of one version of the story, he speaks splendidly, this eloquence suggesting that Sikhuluma, born not speaking, has now come of age. The shift from no speech to eloquent speech signifies his movement from childhood to adulthood. The experience of the future king becomes a model for his subjects, as he moves himself and his society into a new dispensation: there are hints here of heroism.

Of the varied images in the story, perhaps the dominant one is an ancient image having to do with a quest that results in transformation. The patterning of that image dramatizes that movement of change. In each of the three segments that make up this pattern of mythic quest and transformation, the central character, Sikhuluma, is paired with a fantasy or mythic character—his threatening brother, a malevolent water monster, a fearful magician. Each of these characters has a balancing counterpart, and that counterpart has something significant to do with Sikhuluma: it may be the daughter of the magician, a sister, and it may be himself, his valor and plucky determination. Whichever the counterpart, the important character from the point of view of the poem in the story is that strange and threatening mythic character who contains within himself his opposite. Whether the story contains one, two, or three parts, there is a journey into a fantasyland, accompanied by a magical resuscitation. The pairing of characters, one of them mortal and the other ambiguous, becomes a poetic insight into what is transpiring within the real-life character as he experiences his transition. The relationship between the real-life character, Sikhuluma, and the fantasy characters is orchestrated by mythic image, patterning, and the ambiguity that in the end unites the characters.

Three separate stories frequently combine to form the "Sikhuluma" story. One of these has to do with the pursuit of birds. Sikhuluma and his youthful peers set out, moving to a fantasy land where the magical birds lead them. He is often set on this venture by a member of the old generation who urges the members of the young generation to follow the lead of the old. In that distant fantasy land, Sikhuluma and his comrades come into contact with villainous ogres who attempt to destroy them. In the end, it is Sikhuluma himself, isolated from or even isolated by his fellows, who must confront the ogres. Frequently his nemesis is his brother as well as the ogres. Sikhuluma triumphs and returns home to a warm welcome. There is a movement away from home, a transfiguring experience in an alien fantasy land, and a return to the home, transformed. At the heart of the melodic line is the poem, typically establishing a relationship fraught with emotions of danger, suspense, a movement into the unknown. Woven into that poem are two strands, usually: the fantasy dream-like ogres and the real-life hating brother. That rich emotional complex forms the center of the story, and is responsible for the metaphorical folding of the real-life Sikhuluma into the fantasy ogres and real-life rival-brother. In a Sotho version of this story, "Selomakupu,"[211] a straightforward and uncomplicated rendering of the tale, the crucial metaphorical relationship is that between the Sikhuluma character, here called Bulane, and the monster, Selomakupu. It is the life and death struggle between them that forms the essential rhythm, all other characters and such images as the return for a forgotten item and the falling spear are used by the storyteller to support and develop that essential pattern, the poem in the story, the relationship between a youth undergoing change and his other self.

A second story that comprises the "Sikhuluma" tale has to do with a swallowing monster. In this story, a youth, usually a boy, moves away from his home to a land of fantasy where he encounters, accidentally or by design, a swallowing monster, typically a water monster (examples are Sarah Dlamini's "A Boy Pursues a Water-monster" [Swati][212] and "The Nanabolele" [Sotho][213]). This is often a quest that the real-life youth himself initiates. At times, it is the sister of the central character who undertakes the journey, the sister being a brave counterpart of that real-life central character. The storyteller may use affiliated patterns—having to do with the magical birth of the central character from a calabash, for example—but the essential movement is to a far-off fantasyland where there is a quest. Sometimes it is to a variety of deep pools, and the initial quest is a vain one—seeking a fabulous river monster, seeking "a place where no frog cries." In the end, a water monster emerges. She is befriended sometimes, spirited away perhaps by friendly animals, and she returns home with the elixir—water, perhaps, from the place where no frog cries. Then she is sent on another fruitless mission, to get the liver of a fantasy creature, and again there is a patterned quest, and she escapes with the liver. Often, it is a dramatization of a male circumcision ritual, as a youth sets out to get a cape or a shield made of a water monster's skin. He may be assisted by a frog that shows him the way.

The nucleus of the story is the song revealing the nature of the quest. The youth has grueling and deadly experiences with the monster, and then there is chase. Sometimes, the monster is delayed by loaves of bread. There is a triumphant return home, and the cape or shield is fashioned from the skin of the destroyed monster. Or it is two brothers who refuse gifts associated with the emergence from the puberty ritual, demanding instead shields made of the skin of a water monster. Their sister sets out with a band of warriors, and they arrive in a country with vast pools. She sings a song at the edge of a pool, asking the creature to emerge. The pattern develops, with a frog emerging instead, and so the group moves deeper and deeper into the forbidden land. In the end, the water is agitated, and the sister and her group flee as the beasts give chase. The beasts give up, but not before the sister and her followers have killed two of them, making two shields of their skin. In the meantime, the brothers have killed a splendid bird and taken its plumes, and now a beast emerges from a pool determined to eat them. That is the pattern: the bird emerges, and the youths flee, but one of them leaves his plume behind. He returns to get it, and is chased by the birds, which finally give up and return to the pool. As the birds depart, the sister arrives with the shields.

Or a wife wants the liver of a river monster, and her husband sets out to get it. There is a quest, a flight, and the man slows the monsters down by throwing a stone that becomes a mountain. He gives the liver to his wife, and then she is thirsty. A pattern having to do with a quest for water follows, and she drinks copiously—from a pitcher, a calabash, a fountain, a brook, a river. And now the animals, having no water, find her with her enormous belly. Another pattern emerges: Which of the animals will pierce her? At last, the hare does it, and the pool and brooks and fountains are again flowing with water. The hare drinks in the pool, although the lion has decreed that no one should drink until the waters are clear again. The hare blames it on the rabbit, who is then beaten. When the hare boasts of what he has done, the other animals give chase, and the hare departs, together with the rabbit. The rabbit is destroyed by the trickery of the hare, as are other animals.

A girl seeks her beads in various pools. Finally, a pool informs her that it contains her beads, so she enters the water where she encounters an old woman who befriends her when a swallowing monster threatens her. In the end, the old woman transforms the girl, dressing her, telling her how to avoid the monster. She emerges from the pool, transformed. When her fellows try to do the same thing, they are not helpful to the old woman, and the monster devours them.

Humans are devoured by a creature; only one woman escapes. She gives birth to a son who has a necklace fashioned of charms. The child grows immediately, magically, into a man, and the woman explains that all humans have been devoured by the beast. He takes a knife, is swallowed by the beast, and cuts open the belly of the creature. But then those very humans he has saved conspire to destroy him, concluding that "He is a monster, not a man." He leaves, transforms himself into a stone, and is thrown to the other side where he escapes.

In "Manzabilayo,"[214] a Zulu version of this story, a young woman of another country marries a king, Manzabilayo, and bears three children. When the king's sheep eat plants at her home, the young woman abuses them. The sheep depart, and she goes after them, attempting to persuade them to return. But the sheep, insulted, vow never to return. A pattern ensues: the wife continues to follow the sheep, enjoining them to return, whereupon they refuse. When Manzabilayo asks about his sheep, his wife tells him that they were taken away by a cock. Manzabilayo sends his army after the cock. The army encounters a young man who shows where the sheep disappeared, then transforms himself into a young woman. When the army tells the king of this, the king commands that the young woman be brought before him. She says that she does not know what happened, and the king accuses her of lying. He sends the woman to marry in a certain village, a village that is filled with ravens. She meets a man who exclaims that he is happy to meet such a beautiful woman; he explains to her that his wives give birth to ravens. She remains there, but is unable to give birth. Then she is told to take a calabash and put it in a deserted place. In the meantime, she is excoriated by the ravens for being barren. In the calabash are children: they live in the wilderness, emerging to eat at the foot of a tree. As they grow up, they sing a song asking for their mother who had placed them at the foot of this tree. The mother hears the repeated song and she rejoices; when she reveals her children to her husband, he too rejoices. So the two children, a girl and a boy, grow up. They are children of fantasy. When the young man is older, he sets out on a quest to the land of Nqamundolo, a fabulous monster. He is carrying loaves of bread that have been baked for him. In the deep pool where Nqamundolo lives, there is commotion, and the monster appears. When it opens its mouth, the youth throws a loaf of bread into it, and this becomes a pattern: the young man delaying the beast by throwing it loaves. He lures the beast to his home, drawing it into the cattle kraal where his father stabs it. From within the beast comes much stock—cattle, goats, sheep.

There are many ways of telling the story, but central to each is the swallower who usually lives in a pool or a river. There is frequently a deliberate quest to find and conquer the monster. This expedition and struggle are metaphorical equivalents of the young person's quest for an adult identity. It is the patterns of quest and struggle that compose the poem in the story; it is into this poem made up of the mythic image of the dangerous yet seductive beast that the real life character and his quest and vision are worked and then tightly woven.

The third of the stories focuses on adventures in the realm of a villainous fantasy character whose daughter Sikhuluma wishes to marry. The mythic character in this story, variously called Mangangedolo, Mangangezulu, Dolosikuhlumba, often has magic stored in a huge knee. There is no returning from Mangangedolo's place. But it is to that forbidden place that the youth goes, seeking a wife. When he arrives there, he is given impossible tasks, and when he has satisfactorily completed these he is given a daughter of Mangangedolo in marriage. That is the essence of the Mangangedolo story: the youth moves into the forbidden place, he struggles with the monstrous figure of death, wresting from death life in the form of death's daughter.

In one version of the story, when he takes his wife home, she is not to work in the daytime.[215] She is forced to do so by her father-in-law after she has given birth. He insists that she go to the spring to get water for him, she is swallowed by the spring, and a pattern results: a girl brings the baby to the pool, sings a song, and the mother emerges from the pool singing of what happened to her. In the end, she is rescued by people of the community.

Dolosikuhlumba, his magic stocked in an enormous knee, has a beautiful daughter. Most young men are afraid to go to court her, but one young man does go. The father then sets what turns out to be an impossible task—herd his cattle. Dolosikuhlumba causes a huge storm to come up. A mouse assists Sikhuluma. The villain is impressed by the youth's wisdom. He gives him his daughter in marriage. But after a year, it is seen that the wife is barren. When she weeps because of this, doves assist her, making it possible for her to give birth by means of a calabash. Two children are in the calabash; later she puts them in a storehouse where she brings them milk. The husband is pleased. But after two years, she is again barren, and so he marries a raven who bears four ugly children. Now daughters of the barren wife and the raven wife are betrothed. During the marriage journey, the raven dies. The husband then kills his raven wife and remains with the other wife.

In another version of the story, a fantasy woman (she has one long toe) devours all men, not eating her daughters because their flesh is too bitter. A hunter comes upon the two daughters, loves them, and they love him. He is a king's son, and handsome. They hide him when their mother returns. One of them journeys with the hunter, but the fantasy woman gives chase, they climb into a tree, and the hunter's dogs tear her to pieces. He returns from the land of the dead with his wife.

The story is by now familiar: a real-life character encounters a mythic character usually by means of a consciously undertaken quest. The rhythm of the narrative locks these two disparate beings in a metaphorical yoke.

These three stories can be combined in various ways. The water monster story might be joined to that of the villainous Mangangedolo. The metaphorical dimensions of the story deepen as the storytellers bring two of the separate tales into a single story with an illusion of unity. It is in that illusion of unity that the metaphorical aspects of the story have their dynamic origins. In a Xhosa version by Nontsomi Langa, "A Boy Grows Up,"[216] the central character's time for circumcision has arrived, but he refuses to accede to this until a water monster is killed. All others fear to pursue the monster, but the youth will do it. He asks that loaves of bread be prepared and that the members of the community gather with their weapons; he will lure the monster to its death. At the center of the first part of the story is the song sung as the boy taunts the monster, telling it to come out of the pool and eat him. When the water monster appears, a second pattern, a chase pattern, is developed, combined with the throwing of the loaves. The pattern need not be developed at length: the audience knows it well. When he gets home, the members of the community kill the creature, and the earlier interrupted circumcision ceremony proceeds. But then the youth insists that he will marry "a daughter of Ngangazulu [as-great-as-the-sky]." But no one goes to that forbidden place, he is warned. On his way, two doves fly by and another pattern is established and evolved: nature giving advice to the youth as he and his comrades move into the alien place. When he arrives in that place, there is a song both associated with and sung by Ngangazulu, in which she wonders about these strange people. She tries to destroy them with her magic. In the end, the young man takes his wife and returns to his home. But the young wife cannot work in the daytime. The final pattern has to do with the forcing of the wife to work, the river devouring her, the rescue of the daughter by Ngangazulu, "And from that time on, she could work during the daytime."

In another version of "Sikhuluma,"[217] a child is born and hidden by his mother in a trough. When the father comes upon the child, he is delighted, calls him Sikhuluma, and declares that he will marry a daughter of Red Sun. The child grows and is never heard to speak. The counselors therefore decide to seek another chief. The youth says that his father insists that he wear a robe and shoes made of a water monster's skin, and carry a mat made of the same skin. His name is to be Sikhuluma, and he should marry the daughter of Red Sun. All are amazed at this child prodigy. Bread is then made, and Sikhuluma's aunt begins the pattern of the quest for the water monster. The familiar chase sequence follows. As she nears home, the aunt tells the people to heat an axe. The creature swallows the axe and dies. Then the storyteller moves into the second part of the story, the quest for the daughter of Red Sun. With the assistance of an old man and a wild rabbit, they move to the home of Red Sun, and a pattern of proper behavior is outlined by the skin of the rabbit.

As the storyteller unites two separate stories into a single narrative, the individual stories understandably become more involved, and the metaphorical nature of the central character and the mythic character is given another dimension. The fantasy struggle with the water monster is joined to that with Mangangedolo, and not only is there metaphorical union in the two stories, there is also metaphorical tension between the two stories and the two relationships. Because the same real-life characters are involved in each of the relationships, the audience more readily joins the two, and so a single musical relationship metamorphoses into a symphony.

Another way to combine the stories is to bring the pursuit of birds and the journey to Mangangedolo's place into union. In a Sotho version, "Sekholomi and Takalasi,"[218] Sekholomi sets out to marry Takalasi. A rat assists him, giving him a gall bladder that will provide him with instructions during his quest. The gall bladder warns him of an approaching lion, a developing pattern that results in the death of the lion. Then Sekholomi is prepared to go home with his wife. As they go home, they meet many birds, and Sekholomi and the young men pursue the birds and kill them. They come to a house, find no one there, and they remain in it. When the owner of the house returns, she prepares beer. Then she leaves. When they awaken, the young men drink the beer. But the gall bladder warns Sekholomi not to consume all the goods: leave some for the owner. They leave some of the bread, some of the birds. A pattern:

the owner returns, brews beer again, prepares bread. The owner and a friend go to the sleeping young men, and decide which they shall eat. They decide not to eat Sekholomi, as he is too thin. Now the gall bladder urges Sekholomi to depart. The young men leave, but Sekholomi remembers that he left his headdress behind. He plants his spear so that his fellows will know of his fate, and returns to the house. He finds cannibals at the house; they have come to eat the young men. He changes himself into a bee, gets his headdress, becomes a man again, and the cannibals pursue him. When they are near, he throws his knobkerrie behind him. It becomes a mountain and the creatures lose sight of him. Then he recovers his knobkerrie, thanks the rat, and returns home.

In a Ronga version,[219] the principal wife of Macinga is barren. She is ridiculed by the other women and mocked by her husband. She goes into the country and meets a dove, which tells her to return home; it gives her beans, maize, peas, and a packet of thorns. It tells her to bake the vegetables, pierce the grains of maize with a thorn, and then eat the grains one by one. The woman does this and becomes pregnant. The dove tells her she must instruct the child within her not to speak until the appropriate time. When the child is young, birds fly by, and Macinga challenges his son, telling him that when he was young he pursued such birds. Sikouloumé takes provisions and sets out with his brother, Mahoumana, and his servants, who are antagonistic to him. When Sikouloumé speaks, his servant is delighted, but Sikouloumé cautions him to say nothing. This becomes a pattern: the servant's joy, Sikouloumé's caution. When the birds are killed, the heavens respond with rain and thunder. Mahoumana's servants want to leave Mahoumana and join Sikouloumé, but Sikouloumé says that his one servant is enough. He magically builds a house (one reed becomes the fence, one strap becomes the roof, et cetera), and then he takes the heads of the slain birds and places them around the house. At night, the ogre comes, and he eats the heads of the birds, promising to return to eat Mahoumana and Sikouloumé, "killer of birds." Sikouloumé ties a string to the feet of the servants, and when the ogre returns, with the pattern revealing that he will eat Mahoumana and Sikouloumé and thereby grow fat, Sikouloumé pulls the string and they are afraid, wanting to go home. But the next day they return to the quest of getting the plumes of feathers from the birds. When they leave the house, Sikouloumé purposely leaves his feather plumes behind, and asks which of the servants will return with him to retrieve them. A pattern follows: the servants are afraid, refusing to return. Only Sikouloumé's faithful servant agrees to return with him. They find many ogres in the house, and there is a pattern: the ogres pass

Sikouloumé's plume one to the other, and in the end they give the plume to him. When an old ogress gives him the plume, the other ogres pursue him, and the song the pursuing ogres sing becomes a pattern. Sikouloumé and the others arrive at a large village. A dog lets them know what food can be eaten there. The people of that village kill their own daughter instead of Sikouloumé when Sikouloumé exchanges blankets with her, and Sikouloumé is able to kill the old woman who is a leader there. Then they take the people's cattle and depart with them. There is a pattern having to do with the dust raised by the cattle: the people of this village see them departing. They now pursue them. Sikouloumé and the others cross a river, and when their pursuers come to the other side of the river, Sikouloumé throws them a rope, and then lets go of it (a pattern) and the enemy is drowned. Then Sikouloumé transforms himself into a zebra and gallops away. His servant has his mother pour water on the zebra, and it transforms back into Sikouloumé. The brothers tell their father that it is Sikouloumé who saved them; they want to repay him, but Sikouloumé will take nothing. He is reconciled with his father, becomes the leader of the country, and his brothers go off to become leaders of smaller countries.

Once again, the fusion of two stories, each of which contains its own metaphorical relationship between mythic and realistic imagery, creates a more intensely poetic experience, as the members of the audience respond to two sets of relationships, each of which they know well. But now there is an additional emotion-eliciting experience as the two stories are unified and the separate poems in the two separate stories are blended, forming a richer, denser poem on a level at which the audience now has a much fuller role to play.

It is possible that all three of the stories—the pursuit of birds, the water monster, and Mangangedolo's place—might be joined. The story "Sikhuluma, the Boy Who Did Not Speak,"[220] by the Xhosa storyteller, Nongenile Masithathu Zenani, is in three parts, composed of the three separate stories already discussed: part one is the bird chase; part two, the quest for the water monster; and part three, the bride quest. These parts are worked into a unified whole: part one involves the bird quest, dramatizing Sikhuluma's puberty rite; part two has to do with the monster quest, dramatizing the end of puberty and preparation for marriage; and part three involves the bride quest, dramatizing Sikhuluma's marriage and his accession to the kingship. Each pattern in the story is built around a graphic mythic image. In part one, in Sikhuluma's puberty ritual, the mythic image is in the bird quest pattern: birds lure humans to their deaths. In the pattern built around Sikhuluma's speech and his warnings, the mythic image is the person hitherto mute who suddenly speaks: his speech is life giving. The third pattern is that of the serial deaths of the boys; the mythic image is the swallowing monster. Throughout the second and third patterns, there is another unifying pattern having to do with the rivalry between Sikhuluma and his brother, Sitshalotshalwana.

The second part of the story is a transition between the first and third parts. It is composed of two patterns: the monster quest and the chase, the mythic image being the swallowing monster in both patterns.

Part three deals with Sikhuluma's marriage ritual, and contains three patterns. The first pattern is built around the mouse's advice. The second has to do with the various murder attempts, and the third pattern details the slow death of Sikhuluma. The mythic images in the three patterns are, respectively, helpful animal, reluctant in-law, and dying and resurrected hero. Embedded within the second pattern, there is yet another pattern, this one having to do with the comments of Mangangedolo and his people: "This is a strange, a different groom's party."

The linkage, part two tying parts one and three together, consists of the symbolic significance of the monster's skin: it comes to symbolize Sikhuluma's satisfactory completion of the puberty ritual that will later protect him as be moves into the world of Mangangedolo.

The roles played by women become important. Sikhuluma's sister appears in part two; Sikhuluma's wife in part three. It is the sister who makes it possible for Sikhuluma to move finally into manhood. It is his wife who gives him rebirth.

Mangangedolo is a dualistic villain. His daughter, Sikhuluma's bride, is an extension of him. He is the death-dealing part, she the life-giving part. Together, they form a pair, and that dualistic, polar pair becomes the storyteller's comment on Sikhuluma's inner conflict as he moves through his marriage ritual.

Part one of the combined story is the initial sketching of the puberty rite of the boy, Sikhuluma. The final part can be seen as a further development of the puberty rite or of Sikhuluma's marriage rite, which is, in any case, the logical culmination of his puberty ritual. To deepen the poetry within the story, this final section is also the story of the bride of Sikhuluma, her transformation, her puberty rite, and her marriage rite. What binds Sikhuluma's puberty and marriage rituals is the activity of his sister in part two. She provides him with the monster's skin—the connective between his two rituals—and she makes plain that these rites are not simply the province of males. Her activities anticipate part three, when Sikhuluma shares the tale with his bride: the story of Sikhuluma's marriage ritual is equally the story of his bride's ritual. Her fantasy ritual functions as a shadow of Sikhuluma's real-life ritual.

Fantasy characters mirror Sikhuluma's transformation. In part one, in the forest, the land of fantasy, Sikhuluma's puberty rite occurs. The real-life character is Sikhuluma, and he struggles with his fantasy counterpart, his dueling brother, Sitshalotshalwana, the ugly part of him. The struggle with Sitshalotshalwana reveals Sikhuluma's readiness for manhood. Sikhuluma is the good side and Sitshalotshalwana, a fantasy character, mirrors his bad side. There is a pattern of struggle; others die as a result of this conflict, and the line of corpses represents Sikhuluma's break with the past. There are three important patterns in part one of this story: the bird quest, with the organizing mythic image of birds that strangely lure humans to their deaths; Sikhuluma's speech, a pattern containing the mythic image of a person hitherto mute who speaks, whose speech is moreover life-giving; and the deaths of the boys, presided over by a swallowing monster mythic image.

The movement to manhood consists of two stages, those stages indicated by a puberty rite and a marriage rite, with the second being the culminating test of adulthood. It is the combination of the two ritual movements that reveals the readiness of the main character for adulthood: Sikhuluma is born in a fantastic way, not speaking. He has an initial test, the beginning of the puberty ritual, involving at the nadir the struggle with his other side, represented by Sitshalotshalwana.

The second section is the pivotal part of the narrative. The cape made of the skin of the monster enables the puberty ritual to end—only then will Sikhuluma emerge from the circumcision lodge—and the marriage rite to begin. The two rituals overlap in part two. The water monster's skin becomes Sikhuluma's protection during his bride quest. The skin symbolizes the satisfactory completion of the puberty ritual and preserves the wearer in his mature life. What is being suggested here is that properly and successfully experiencing the puberty ritual sustains one as he moves into adulthood and its many dangers. In this second part of "Sikhuluma," there are two patterns, both having to do with the monster quest and both with swallowing monster mythic images at their organizing center: these are the "Come and eat me!" pattern and the chase pattern.

In part three, in the fantasy land of Mangangedolo, Sikhuluma's marriage ritual takes place. The real-life character is, again, Sikhuluma. The fantasy characters are Mangangedolo and his daughter; they come to represent the positive and negative sides of Sikhuluma as he contends within himself during this crucial period of change. They reveal Sikhuluma's transition from death to life, the culmination of his puberty rite: his marriage ritual. Mangangedolo's magic is dualistic; he is death, his daughter is life. In her fantasy struggle with her father, the daughter is mirroring what Sikhuluma is experiencing: it is in fantasy her marriage ritual, a reinforcement of Sikhuluma's ritual. She struggles with her father's magic, using it in a positive way: those negative and positive aspects of Mangangedolo's magic reflect the negative and positive aspects of Sikhuluma as he goes through a transformation. In the end, Sikhuluma dies, swallowed by an eland. The movement out of the eland's stomach, with the help of the bride, his better side, is the final symbol of his change, his resurrection to new life: he is reborn a man.

Storytellers tell the same story in diverse ways, so that there are complex interactions that deepen and comment upon aspects of the story under construction, interactions with other stories in the tradition and with fragments of other stories. In the three-part "Sikhuluma" by Masithathu Zenani, each of the parts can exist on its own, the paralleling of three stories within a single performance laying the foundation for metaphor. A single character threads through the three parts, acting as a connector. As this realistic figure moves into various fantasy lands—the strange forest, the distant realm of the water monsters, the fearsome world of Mangangedolo—mythic characters surround him, some attempting to destroy him, others nurturing and assisting him. The fantasy Sitshalotshalwana, swallowing monster, and Mangangedolo and daughter form the poetic center of the three parts; by weaving into the real-life Sikhuluma, they reveal his psyche, the change in identity that he is experiencing. These fantasy characters are linked with Sikhuluma by patterns that are constructed around mythic images; the swirling murmuring otherworldly beings envelop the real character, and when he emerges in the real world, those fantasy murmurs left behind him, he can never be the same. In the deep forest, he struggles with his alter ego, Sitshalotshalwana; the result is the deaths of their ten comrades and, as Sikhuluma shakes off his childhood past represented by those dead youths, the death of Sitshalotshalwana himself. Sikhuluma has rid himself of his past. Nature now assists him in his return to reality: the newly achieved harmony with culture has its counterpart in nature. In the alien place of swallowing monsters, Sikhuluma struggles with and overcomes one of them, and the cape fashioned of its skin becomes his means for a transition into the world of Mangangedolo. Sikhuluma moves into these realms as if into a vast chamber in which he will struggle with his demons, get them under control, and return an altered being. Magic symbolizes Sikhuluma's fate: Mangangedolo

A Xhosa storyteller

controls it, but so does his daughter. The struggle between father and daughter becomes emblematic of the transformation being experienced by Sikhuluma. In the language of storytelling, the mythic characters are a means of expression, a way of communicating ideas. Because these mythic characters are drawn in dramatic ways that have the effect of eliciting emotional responses, as the story's characters become a part of the transformation of the real-life character, the members of the audience through this emotional involvement are simultaneously worked into that transforming character, so that his transition becomes theirs.

Each of the three stories, as we have seen, possesses its own inner poem. But bringing the three stories together in concert means that the poetic, metaphorical center is going to be deepened. Nor is it simply Sitshalotshalwana, the water monster, and Mangangedolo that are consolidated. It is the figurative compact between Sikhuluma and Sitshalotshalwana in part one, between Sikhuluma and the water monster in part two, and between Mangangedolo (and his daughter) and Sikhuluma in part three that results in a much more labyrinthine emotional experience for the members of the audience: the poem at the center of the story has now become a synchrony.

The Metaphorical Leap

> The whole process is one of creativity: the big push, the metaphorical leap.
> —Leonard Bernstein, *The Unanswered Question*

The story is a self-contained artistic unit. It contains its own laws, its own reason for being. It does not necessarily obey the laws of the real world, but it utilizes the materials (the images, experiences, institutions) of the real world. It always does so on its own terms. We are therefore in danger of distortion if we seek to see a mirror reflection of the real world in these tales and poems. It is a reflection, but it is prismatic, seen through a glass darkly. Fantasy never wholly departs from the real world.[221] Such mythic images need not disturb our perception of the real. Fantasy is really meant to mirror that perception in its own way and to explore it. Indeed, in such exploration it sometimes subverts it. To deal with fantasy is not to suggest an experience that is somehow of lesser significance than a realistic experience. Fantasy is a material used by artists (with contexts that are also fantasy) to get at truth, not to tarnish or debase truth.

And if mythic imagery is fantasy in nature, so is the very structure of the story—fantastic, in the sense that its organization is artificial, its world walled, its materials necessary artistic elements with nothing that is extraneous. What renders the structure of the story fantasy is, then, not simply the images that make it up, but the melodic and rhythmic patterns that render it a performance rather than a mirror held up to nature.

It is, again, that poem within the story that makes it possible to approach the story as something more than a mere description of a conflict and a resolution. This is "the big push, the metaphorical leap."

THE POEM IN THE STORY
Myth, Music, Metaphor

> What we find beautiful in a work of art is not found beautiful by the eye, but by our imagination through the eye.
> —Gotthold Ephraim Lessing, *Laocoön; Nathan the Wise; Minna von Barnhelm*

Ambiguity, irony, metaphor: in the creation of a story, the performer selects images that seem unrelated, then establishes between them a bond that is initially ambiguous. When the audience begins to move along the path of images recalled by the storyteller, its members detect a union that was previously only dimly perceived if it was perceived at all; the images begin to form new configurations. It is this developing ironic journey to sameness, a blossoming sensation of recognition, that contributes to much of the energy and the excitement of the story. A musical form of masking occurs, as the storyteller, with body, voice, and resultant image, brings the images into harmonious linkage, a relationship achieved not with the didactic tools of preachers but with the mesmerizing murmurs of musicians. At this point, then, the storyteller having isolated and externalized the images, tied the emotions of the members of the audience to those images themselves and then to the images in tandem, that the possibilities for metaphor become manifest. Myth is in the images, music in the connections; the result is metaphor.

REBIRTH

The rites of passage move a person to a new birth. In the puberty ritual, the child dies and the adult begins life anew. As he passes through this stage of his life, the young man becomes a fully qualified member of society. He must learn which laws and rules are valid and, especially, how they are sanctioned. A central theme in a heroic life is redolent of both a god's first work of creation and its imitation in the initiation ritual. The initiation is a passage through death to a new life. But how is new life acquired? The basic model for this is found in the lives of the gods. A god become human moves to the earth and journeys through the primordial rite of passage before being wafted into the heavens or metamorphosed into the cosmological spheres. It is far from accidental that the heroic pattern also applies in many respects to the gods. The world is unrigged, and a new world grows from the shards.

Storytelling chronicles our great transformations, and helps us to undertake periodic transfigurations. The momentous rites of passage, birth, puberty, marriage, and death: as with all of life's crises, storytellers are there to provide imaged explanations, emotional cushioning. The stories become our means of making those corrections as we move through our life cycles. The earliest story that we know—the spare, splendid Gilgamesh epic of Babylon from 2000 B.C.—takes us even today into the anguished soul of a man confronting his mortality. Stories have to do with humans moving from one milestone in their lives to another. Storytellers dramatize the journeys through these great human crises.

They make space for us, enabling us to experience topics that are not normally discussed, taking us into the inner reaches of our souls, and, by means of luminous images, casting soul-shattering light into our deepest and most secret places. Storytellers are the mirrors of our nature, the guardians of our ideals, the means whereby we find our connections. They move us into new worlds, into realms blushed in cardinal colors, domains of fantasy in which we will be shorn of our identities and be recast, reborn, reemerging into our reality refurbished, rejuvenated, revitalized, and restored. They make possible the transformation of members of audiences into unique and rare entities with new and daunting responsibilities. Storytellers form our children, remind us of who we are.

Tradition keeps us stable, gives us the companionship and familiar wisdom of the past. It is a steadying influence: no matter how unsettling the experience of transition may be, no matter how confusing and disorienting the times, our lives are punctuated by these stories, these rituals, these recurring crises and accompanying crossings, which put down emotional channels to antiquity. We thereby become one with our ancestral past, and we are confident that, though we may be moving through turbulent times, the stabilizing authority of the past assures us, gives us meaning, keeps us balanced and secure. We are confident that life remains the same, no matter what the evanescent details.

The art of the storyteller involves an aesthetically crafted, artistically calculated movement of an audience into the heart of the story, the fusing emotional heart, that heart composed of the emotions of the members of the audience. It is the business of the storyteller to knit up those diverse emotions and work them into form, that form being the theme, message, meaning of the storytelling performance. In the linguistics that is storytelling, there is the arithmetic of the narrative surface, but there is also the geometry of the story's nucleus.

Whether the story emerges from the storyteller sitting before a hearth fire before an audience of listeners, a writer creating a story that will be read under a variety of conditions, a motion picture or television visual story that will be viewed in a darkened theater or a living room in a home, the essence of the story will remain very much the same. A journalist writing a story about an election in South America, about a fatal airplane crash in Asia, or a war in Europe; a historian creating the histories of Peru, of India, of Kosovo: both are storytellers and both utilize the essential materials of all storytellers.

Everything anticipates metaphor. That is the purpose of storytelling: to move to the heart of the varied images, to move to the poem in the center, to a poem that is at its core metaphor. The images catch an experience and reshape it; images that have the capacity to do this become easily recalled memories of experience.[222]

Myth is the core of the story, music is what links myth and other aspects of the story, and metaphor is the result of myth and music. It is performance that weaves the audience into the story, its memory of myth, its response to the rhythm, and so the members of the audience become a part of metaphor. They are not witnesses to the story, not listeners, not hearers, but participants in the story, a part of metaphor, their mythic memories rhythmically twined into the story. Story thereby becomes a rite of passage with the myth-bearing audience member the poem in the story. Myth is remembered, reborn, and becomes the heart of a metaphor that is composed of audience in the present with the storyteller as the alchemical orchestrator. The words of the storyteller become the notes that reveal the reality of the tune.

Story is always a rite of passage.

A Story from the Malagasy Oral Tradition

I describe things not because their muteness mocks our subjectivity but because they seem to be masks for God.
—John Updike, interviewed in *Writers at Work*

"RAMAITSOANALA"[223]

Once, Ravorombe, Big Bird, arose and built a house in the midst of the water. And when she had finished the house, she brought Iketaka to be housekeeper. And after Iketaka had remained there a long time, Ravorombe went away to seek prey, and, thus occupied, she swept up everything that she saw that belonged to men, and brought it to her dwelling.

After some time, she laid eggs and sat on them, and after she had sat some time the eggs were hatched, and the young birds went off to fly. But one egg alone remained unhatched, so she thought it addled, and removed it, placing it in the cover of a basket.

After Ravorombe had forgotten where it was, Iketaka said, "The addled egg is there in the basket, and we have forgotten to cook it."

Ravorombe replied, "Let it be until tomorrow, for the rice is all finished." So she stopped Iketaka.

On the next day, they forgot it again, and the same on the following day. And after a little time longer, Iketaka looked, and found that it was hatched, and had produced a human creature! She was astonished, and called to Ravorombe, "Come quickly! The egg is hatched, and has produced a human!"

She came and looked, and saw that it was really so. Then she said, "This is my offspring, her name shall be Ramaitsoanala, Green in the Forest. But there is no one to nurse it, so I'll go and steal a cow for milking, so that the child can feed on milk."

So Ravorombe went and swept off a cow in milk, and got it for her child's sustenance, for she, being a bird, had no breasts. Then she made a little box for the child and placed it there, telling Iketaka to mind it.

Then Ravorombe went away again seeking prey, and whenever she saw anything beautiful belonging to people she swept off with it and brought it to her child.

And when she came to her house, she cried out, "Ramaitsoanala there! Ramaitsoanala there! Why, say I, don't you peep out? Why don't you look about?"

But there was no answer, for the child was still an infant, and how could she speak and stand up?

So Ravorombe came in, and said again, "I smell humans! I smell humans!"

And Iketaka said, "Why do you say, 'I smell humans,' when we're the only ones here?"

The bird replied, "I thought that someone had come here and taken the two of you away!" Then she spoke again, "But have you given the child her milk?"

"Yes," replied Iketaka.

So Ravorombe stopped there for a time. But after a while, she went away again to seek prey, and again brought precious things belonging to people, and gave them to her child.

When she came home, she again called out, "Ramaitsoanala there! Ramaitsoanala there! Why, say I, don't you peep out, and why don't you look about?"

Again there was no reply, for the child was little, and how could she answer?

So the bird came in, and said, "I smell humans! I smell humans!"

Iketaka said, "Why do you say, 'I smell humans!' when we're the only ones here?"

The bird replied, "I thought that someone had come here and taken the two of you away!"

Then she stopped there, and said, "But how is my child? Is she getting big or not?"

Iketaka answered, "She's getting rather big now, and in a little time she'll be able to walk."

Then Ravorombe went off again, and the child began to learn how to walk.

Ravorombe returned, and called according to her custom, but no one answered for the child was still little.

After a time, Andriambahoaka came from the north, and he looked from the water's edge. He said, "Something very wonderful is over there on that island! Come, let's get a canoe and go there and see what it is." When he arrived there, he asked Iketaka, "Whose child is this? I want her for a wife!"

Iketaka replied, "This is Ravorombe's child—its mother is a bird, the child is still little. But please, sir, go away, for the day is windy and her mother will be here shortly. Please go away for a time, the mother will devour you all. Please go, and come again another time, for the child is still little."

So Andriambahoaka got up, and when he had gone only a little way, Ravorombe returned. She called the child as she usually did, but as there was no reply, she said, "I smell humans! I smell humans!"

And Iketaka, coming in, said, "What person can have been here? Every time you come in, you say that!"

Ravorombe replied, "I thought that someone had come here and taken the two of you away!" At the same time, she opened the box and looked at her child whom she saw to be getting big.

She said, "You remain here. I'm going to look for ornaments for Ramaitsoanala, she's growing up!"

So she went away.

In the meantime, Andriambahoaka spoke to his two wives and to his people: "There's a beautiful young woman, I'm going to take her for a wife because we've been most unfortunate in having no children. I'll be back after a fortnight. Tell the servants to fatten fowl and pound rice in abundance, for when I return I shall marry her. Make all preparations."

He set off, and, coming to the edge of the water, he sent for canoes, then crossed over. When he arrived there, he was welcomed by Iketaka, and he spoke to Ramaitsoanala: "What do you say, miss? If I take you for my wife, will you be willing?"

She replied, "Nonsense, sir, you can't manage me. So let it alone, sir."

He said, "Tell me why I could not manage you."

She replied, "This is why you could not: my mother is a bird!"

Andriambahoaka said, "If that is all, miss, I am equal to it. So come now, let us go."

Then Iketaka said, "But if you marry her, sir, will you not let her wait first for her mother?"

He said, "Let us go. When she comes, she can follow."

When the two could no longer resist him, Ramaitsoanala went away, and Iketaka was left to keep the house.

They took white rice and Indian corn and beans with them, in order to deceive the mother on the road until Andriambahoaka reached his home—in case the girl should be overtaken by her mother along the way and brought back.

After a while, back came the mother, and she called again as she was accustomed to.

Iketaka replied from the house, "Ramaitsoanala is not here, she's been taken away by someone."

"Who has taken her? Where has she gone?" asked Ravorombe.

"Andriambahoaka from the north has taken her, and northwards has she gone."

So Ravorombe went to the north. As she was getting near to them, the child Ramaitsoanala said, "Here comes my mother! That's why the day has become stormy. Just scatter some of the rice."

So they scattered it about, and went on their way.

When the mother came up, she said, "Here is rice that she has scattered, I'm forsaken by her!" So she sat down to gather the rice, then returned to take it back to the house.

After that, she went back to pursue her child.

But again, Ramaitsoanala knew by the wind that blew that her mother was following her, so the Indian corn was scattered on the road. The corn was also gathered up and taken back by Ravorombe, and so it happened with the beans.

By this time, her child was near Andriambahoaka's village. He sent people ahead, and said, "Tell the people to get ready, for Andriambahoaka is now just south of the village."

So the people made preparations, and the couple arrived. As the people sat there, Andriambahoaka's wives would not look into the house, saying, "How should a bird's offspring come in?"

As the couple was sitting comfortably there, up came the mother, and she said, "How is it, child, you have got a husband, and did not wait for me at all? did not even consult me?"

Her child did not answer.

Then Ravorombe arose, and took the child's eyes, she stripped off the child's skin, and she departed.

The child stood there stripped, and spoke to Andriambahoaka: "It's for this reason that I asked you if you could be bear with me, a person whose mother is a bird."

But Andriambahoaka replied, "I can still bear with you!"

When his wives heard that, they said, "Nonsense! What sort of wife is this, with nothing but bones and without eyes? We do not consent! Let the household property be divided!"

Then the wives brought Ramaitsoanala some *hisatra* (the strong tough peel of the papyrus) to make a mat.

So Ravorombe's child sat down.

Now when Ravorombe was going to cook rice, the eyes of her child dropped down tears from above the hearth—for it was there she had placed the eyeballs. And because of this, the mother could not by any means light the fire.

When she saw that, she said, "Come, let me go, for indeed grave trouble has befallen my child, because this falling down of her eyes is extraordinary!"

So she went off, and, coming in, she said, "What has happened to you, that I cannot light my fire?"

Her child answered, "Why, mother, the people are dividing the household goods, but I have no eyes, and that is why I am weeping."

So the mother said, "Where is it? I'll do it!"

Then Ravorombe plaited the mat quickly, and it was finished. Then she went away.

After that, Andriambahoaka's wives said, "Come, work away, and give her some silk" (for spinning or weaving).

And again, Ramaitsoanala wept, and her mother could not light the fire.

So she came again, and said, "What's the matter with you now, child, that I cannot light the fire?"

She answered, "Why, mother, they have brought me silk."

Then her mother finished the silk for her, and when it was finished she went off again to tend the fire on her hearth.

After a little while, Andriambahoaka's wives brought clothes and dresses for Ramaitsoanala to sew, and said, "Will she be able to finish these? And if we bring many other things, won't she run away?" But they were certain that she would not be able to finish them.

Then Ramaitsoanala wept again, and said, "This is too difficult!"

So her tears flowed again on the hearth, and again her mother arose, saying, "What can be happening to my child?" And away she went. She came to her daughter, and Ramaitsoanala showed her the clothes and dresses—which the mother finished, then went away as before.

After waiting a little, Andriambahoaka's wives said, "Now, let the three of us be compared, for we two are put to shame by this child of a bird! for people called her very beautiful, even though she had her eyes put out and has only bones!"

But Andriambahoaka said, "Enough of that, Ramatoa! What will you do, say I, to shame her? Enough of that!"

But she would not be quiet, she spoke all the more. As Andriambahoaka could not prevent the two women from speaking, he said, "When do you wish to be compared then?"

The two answered, "On Thursday."

He went to Ramaitsoanala and told her that she would be compared with the other two on Thursday.

Ramaitsoanala wept then, and again her mother was unable to light a fire. She rose up and came to her daughter. When she was told about it all, she said, "If that is all, don't be sorrowful. I'll go and bring ornaments for you, and then you'll be able to stand comparison with the others."

So Ravorombe went away, and brought her daughter's eyes and skin, and coral beads, and gold and silks, and all kinds of beautiful ornaments, and she also brought a golden chair for her to sit on.

When the appointed time came, Ravorombe adorned her daughter, restoring her eyes and replacing her skin, and she allowed no one to see her.

Then the three women were fetched to go in the open space to be compared, for the people were gathered together. The two wives did not adorn themselves at all: "This woman without eyes is coming, and what of her?" They got up and stood on the eastern side.

Then Ramaitsoanala came, and she went to the northern side. But as soon as she showed her face, the two other women fled. They ran off into the fosse in their shame and died there.

So Andriambahoaka took Ramaitsoanala home, and wedded her.

And she bore a child, she had a son whom they called Andriambahoaka, for he succeeded his father at his death. And the father rejoiced, for he had obtained what he had desired.

"And now for a story . . ."

Myth: The Raw Materials

Myth and Transformation

The myth-maker's mind is the prototype; and the mind of the poet . . . is still essentially mythopoeic.
—Frederick Clarke Prescott, *Poetry and Myth*

THE MYTH

In an East African myth, a human and a god become a mythic symbol of the nature of the universe.

❖

The Ganda people of Uganda and the Masai of Kenya have a myth about the marriage of a mortal, Kintu, to Nambi, the daughter of Gulu, king of heaven: human and god are joined as they move to earth to begin the new world. It is essentially a love story, of the attraction to Kintu by the heavenly Nambi, a relationship that is opposed by God until Kintu shows himself capable of satisfactorily completing the tasks set for him by his reluctant future father-in-law. The marriage complete, Kintu and Nambi move to the earth, and life will come into the world. They take with them domesticated animals. Gulu commands that they can never return to heaven. When they do so, having forgotten food for the chickens, God's son, Warumbe—Death—follows them to earth. Death now claims their children as his own, and Death has come into the world.[224] Nambi and Warumbe represent the duality of God, his life-giving and death sides, the two forces at large during the period of creation.

❖

Myth, the realm of the unknowable, becomes in the telling of the storyteller poetically linked to known human experience. The dynamism of story performance is the recognition of this connection, as the audience experiences a transmutation built on ambiguity and irony, involving a move from the realm of the enigmatic to metaphor—never crystal clear, always caught in the convex mirror of mythic mystery. The mythic image is masked by centuries of retelling, by shifts in the needs and visions of humans through time, combining each generation's historical and cultural experiences and perceptions, retaining its strength as long as successive societies discern within it a microcosm of their contemporaneity. The masks are never removed: the latest society continues, through its storytellers, the never-ending process of working its own hopes and fears, uncertainties and needs into the fabric of the myth; we see our world through a prism composed of composite worlds of our forebears, so that every story becomes a link to all time, a slight reordering of an unchangeable piece of human theatre. When we hear stories, there is a "willing suspension of disbelief" because we are embarking on an adventure of the soul that moves us, as it has our forebears, into a world at once familiar and unfamiliar, known and unknowable, the world of myth.[225]

The mythic image contains the essential energy of the story. The images are mythic because they reach back to primal times, to the times of the creator, of the earliest transformation when a new world came into being, when order converted chaos, when forces of creation and destruction struggled. That original mythic story is contained within the mythic image. Those remnants of that ancient time have a peculiar characteristic—they are deeply, primitively emotional, touching us in our deepest places. There are also images from the real world, the contemporary world, images both intimately and peripherally known by members of the audience. This is their world, their everyday world, a world with little that is rhythmic, that is framed. Open-ended, it is a fearful world. The ancient mythic images provide that frame, a sense of completeness and of belonging—an echo that resonates through the ages. The storyteller needs both of these images; these are the raw materials of story-making.

"Myth," wrote Mircea Eliade, "narrates a sacred history; it relates an event that took place in primordial time, the fabled time of the 'beginnings.' In other words, myth tells how, through the deeds of Supernatural Beings, a reality came into existence, be it the whole reality, the Cosmos, or only a fragment of reality—an island, a species of plant, a particular kind of human behavior, an institution. Myth, then, is always an account of a 'creation'; it relates how something was produced, began to *be*."[226] Myth is a story that has to do with first causes, origins, a story of cosmological transformation. Built on the storytelling images with emotional content, myths are recreated during performance. During such a performance of a myth—whether orally, in literature, in art, or in history—a contemporary audience becomes re-engaged with its past as the myth-maker reinvents that past, and, in so doing, reinvents those in the contemporary audience. It is at this juncture of ancient myth and contemporary reality that analysis takes place, focusing on the shaping relationship between the two. This involvement in the contemporary re-creation—or performance—of myth is ritual: it is the artistic, ritual re-enactment of an ancient story, frequently within a contemporary setting.

Myth depicts a struggle between antithetical forces, those of order and chaos. God, who is frequently composed of those dueling forces, struggles with chaos and order. Out of this primal strife emerges the world that we know, including humans, who, like god, are composed of the forces of order and chaos and, therefore, have the capacity for both. In a myth from the Dogon people of Burkina Faso and Mali,[227] the early story of the universe has to do with a struggle between Amma, the creator, and Ogo, one of her creations. Amma is alone and in the shape of a cosmic egg that contains the material and structure of the universe. The four collar bones fuse, dividing the egg into air, earth, fire, and water, establishing also the four cardinal directions. Amma plants a seed within herself, resulting in the shape of man. But there is a flaw within that creation, and the universe has within it the possibilities for incompleteness. The egg becomes two placentas, each containing a set of twins, male and female. After a time, one of the males, Ogo, breaks out of the placenta and attempts to create his own universe in opposition to that being created by Amma. Ogo is later transformed by Amma into Yuguru, the Pale Fox, who will always be alone, always be incomplete, eternally in revolt, ever wandering the earth seeking his female soul.

The ancient myth has to do with the supernatural, with god and with transcendental wisdom, with mystical behavior, and awesome activities. The gods are not wholly knowable, their activities not entirely explicable. There is an aura of mystery about the gods. We know them because they are so like us, yet we cannot know them, so remote are they in time, so magnificent their abilities, so mysterious their actions and motives. It is these gods—at once known and unknown, simultaneously recognizable and mysterious—who are at the center of the myths. These gods and their activities form the backdrop of contemporary belief. Regularly, ritualistically, through the theatrical re-enactment of the myths, we revisit the ancient times. We have to, for those times and those gods are our touchstones. They are the origins and the contexts for our lives. What we do occurs within the context of the ancient myths. Nothing is new; we only routinely re-enact the ancient myths, moving in the paths of our gods.

It is our artists who reclaim our gods for us. Through their art—poetry, story, painting, sculpture, dance, music—they recapture our past, our gods, our origins, our essence. They do this by revealing myth in contemporary life. The world of today is recreated within the context of the mythic past, and god and god's activities glimmer through contemporary man and woman and their activities. Our everyday lives are thereby given a sense of myth, of mystery, and our activities are imbued with a sanction, a sense of direction that they may not, in fact, have. Myth is the means whereby we measure ourselves, our world. More important, it is the means whereby we find our ways back to meaning. That meaning or essence is not wholly explicable, just as the gods and their activities remain not wholly knowable. But enough is known, enough is seen to assure us that the gods are our primordial kin: not just our origins, we are their earthly clones, possessed, as they were, of the forces of order and chaos. This is why the gods in myth are so intensely human. That is the "us" in "them." But if they are "us," they are also "them," meaning that they are something more than "us," and that is what gives them mystery, cosmological stature.

We do not allow ourselves to forget our gods. Storytellers bring the mythic and contemporary worlds into conjunction because of their memory of images and their sense of the necessity of linkage. So it is that when we read a poem, a story, a novel, or when we witness a dance, a theatrical performance, a symphony, the mystery of the gods glows in the interstices, and our lives thereby achieve a resonance that echoes back to a distant place, a former life. Always, we have the sense of having been there, a religious feeling of return to origins. Contemporary art is connective in that sense. The artist makes use of myth to give her work a resonance that it could not otherwise achieve. That resonance depends on the mythic motifs that we have inherited and that we deeply internalize at an early age, through our folklore, our religions, our cultural institutions. All is illusion; it is the storyteller's craft to evoke and sustain an illusory linkage during a performance.

What, then, is a definition of myth? Myth is an ancient story having to do with the gods who, struggling with the forces of chaos and order, are engaged in a cosmological transformation: the creation of humans and their world. Modern humans relive this through a ritual encounter. It is a lived metaphor, a tie between images of past and present, that constitutes the essence of the storyteller's craft. The restless and latent sensory life of the members of audiences contributes to the basic material of stories, the performer working the open-ended and seemingly meaningless routine of modern lives into the ancient stories that, through their strong emotional content, their clear meaning, and their tight narrative structure, give content, meaning, and structure to contemporary lives. Myth deals with dual forces, good and evil, energies of order and disorder, powers of destruction and creativity. These characterize the age of creation, a time when those forces were contending. Out of them grew the contemporary age. Most religious systems have myths about the origins, the creation, the coming into existence of death, and the struggle to maintain creative societies in the face of destructiveness. A creator god can also be a hostile, destructive god. Impulses of good and evil, order and disorder, destructiveness and creativeness: these characterize the Age of Creation. Often these forces are located in two separate characters. In the Egyptian tradition, they are Osiris and Set. But they are also often embodied in the same character, such as the dualistic Gulu, the dualistic Mantis, and the dualistic Winnebago god.[228] Most myth systems have stories about the creation, about the coming into existence of death, about the struggles to maintain creative societies in the face of destructiveness. And most myths deal with, if they do not answer, the problem of a god who is creative and benevolent, but who is also destructive and hostile. Myth-makers do not answer the problem, preferring to conclude that this is the human condition, it is in the nature of things. Thus, humans kill god's creation to survive, and in so doing upset the balance of nature, unleashing the vengeful forces of nature.

MYTHIC ALLUVIUM

Myth chronicles transformations, and this includes the rites of passage. The myth is "a large, controlling image that gives philosophical meaning to the facts of ordinary life,"[229] and thus orders our lives. It is "a sensible (sensuous, graphic), symbolic representation of an imagined situation or series of events."[230] It is ancient, and "always received from an already distant past."[231] Why is the creation so important to us? Why are the gods and their activities so significant to us? Why do we keep reliving the creation myths? Because these are the prototypes of our own movement to fulfillment and maturity, of our own triumph over chaos as we move through the rites of passage into adulthood. In the tale, Everyman or Everywoman possesses this duality, a mythic afterglow. That vast primal cosmological struggle is our struggle writ large. The dualistic god is Everyman and Everywoman, struggling with the two sides of their nature. The overcoming of chaos and the ordering of the world becomes our promise and our hope, but the divine trickster and the profane trickster, ever amoral and ever ready to obscure order with chaos, is a part of us as well. The myths are the tales on a cosmological scale, with gods taking the roles of humans. Wole Soyinka writes, "When gods die—that is, fall to pieces—the carver is summoned and a new god comes to life. The old is discarded, left to rot in the bush and be eaten by termites. The new is invested with the powers of the old and may acquire new powers. In literature the writer aids the process of desuetude by acting as the termite or by ignoring the old deity and creating new ones."[232]

Myth is the key here: the image that contains within itself the possibilities of creation, possibilities forever fraught with latent emotional residue. That is the poem in the story: the combination of mythic image, emotion, contemporary image, and the patterning that works these materials into metaphor. Story is built into the mythic process: "Any attempt . . . to explore the interactions of character and mythic beings or metamythic typologies inevitably involves us in the notion of narrative."[233] Myth, Frederick Clark Prescott argues, "is spontaneously created by the imagination, given belief, and told with no notion that it is anything but a story. . . . It is perhaps to us analyzable into story and thought; but the two are brought together, and are as inseparable as soul and body."[234] Myths are divine, supernatural, but "alongside the stream of religious imagination there runs a stream of purely narrative invention that can sometimes be identified with folktale but is really much broader."[235]

There is a unique mythic residue in certain storytelling images and motifs. They are archetypal, ancient, and retain the capacity to evoke emotions because of an echoing memory of those mythic images, because each contains a palimpset shade of a whole world or story, because in the mythic image the supernatural and the real come into momentary conjunction, because this is where God and man have their essential juncture. Myth, writes Santayana, "will translate into the language of a private passion the smiles and frowns which that passion meets with in the world." He notes, "Myth travels among the people, and in their hands its poetic factor tends to predominate."[236] The mythic nature of the image has to do with its power to evoke emotions, emotions having to do with memory, nostalgia, yearning. The mythic image, ancient and condensed, releases emotional energy, the center of the story. Two components of story, then, are the mythic image and the emotions the mythic image evokes. This mythic image links the contemporary audience to the past because of the presumed ancient nature of that image. The emotional energy is geared to transformation because of the composition of that mythic image. Deep in the mythic image is a story in microcosm, in bits and pieces, the fragmented story of a people, of origins. It is a kind of primal wall painting, remnants of a golden time, of an ancient struggle, still remembered but in pieces, patches of the past. It is our community memory, conjuring up a time of perfection, of union between God and man. It is also the memory of the shattering of that union, of the coming of death. Life and death, and all the associated parts of the emotional prism are there, but in their cardinal colors—the original myth broken into a thousand pieces, those pieces regularly put into new configurations with new images, contemporary images, by generations of storytellers. Each of these pieces summons an emotion, an emotion elicited by a recognition. A yearning is there, a sense of loss is there, and so is the promise of that primal time. This emotional vestige of our ancient past is the stuff of storytelling. John Updike wonders why "these people enjoy hearing them? Are they a kind of disguised history? Or, more likely I guess, are they ways of relieving anxiety, of transferring it outwards upon an invented tale and purging it through catharsis?"[237]

It is useful to watch storytellers as they create their works: they are sensitive to images that most effectively summon the feelings essential to the success of their performances.[238] Images that lack crucial vitality, or images that remain flat and hackeneyed and therefore without necessary evocative force, are discarded. That emotionally evocative image, or a clustering of such images, or a scattering of such images throughout the tale, assure a regular outpouring of a variety of usually cardinal emotions—of fear, joy, revulsion, attraction, and all of their variations. The storyteller is in trouble if she is not in the process of regularly eliciting such emotions. Sometimes she will pander to the audience, evoking images that she is assured will summon the needed emotional responses. Every storyteller learns quickly that without emotion there can be no story. Emotion is not just the essential building block of the story, it constitutes the vital meaning. Sometimes images of the real world are also emotionally evocative. Whatever the case, it is the chemistry between the fantasy and real world images that generates its own kind of emotion. The mixture of emotions is therefore complex and volatile, and without meaning until the storyteller rhythmically patterns them. It is then that the two kinds of imagery coalesce for the moment of performance, later to be returned to their separate categories. It is the mythic image, a part of the grand mythic epic, that the storyteller manipulates in a performance.

That image is the common denominator that links gods, heroes, and Everyman. It is the touchstone of the storytelling tradition, the means whereby members of audiences gain access to the deepest reaches of the story, to the poetic inner realm.

MYTH AND "RAMAITSOANALA"

Ravorombe, a cannibalistic bird, is the fantasy core of this narrative, the poem in the story. She gives birth to Ramaitsoanala, a human, who is therefore betwixt and between, both human and a bird. Ramaitsoanala moves from her home of birth to a liminal state, on the boundaries, to her home of marriage.

The relationship between the mythic Ravorombe and the real-life Ramaitsoanala is controlled by three significant patterns. The first pattern occurs during the activities that take place at the house of Ramaitsoanala's birth. This is the rhythm of this section: the mother brings the daughter items from her expeditions, objects that progressively transform the child into a human, moving her from her animal past (her mother is a bird, the child hatched from an egg) to full humanity, that is, from childhood to adulthood. The mythic image is the bird-mother, and the real-life child is at once worked into this mythic image by virtue of her relationship with Ravorombe.

So the storyteller introduces the fantasy bird mother and her real-life daughter, Ramaitsoanala. The child is in an ambiguous state, preparing to move from one state (her birdness) to another (her humanity), necessary to the establishment of metaphor. So the two types of imagery are now present, and the initiation of a transformation is introduced. The storyteller is establishing the materials necessary for metaphor.

THE MYTH IN THE STORY

A mortal is joined by two characters from the world of fantasy, a woman who becomes his wife, a jinni who becomes the realization of his dreams, and these two latter characters are the mythic aspects of the mortal man: they become the poem in the story.

❖

In an Egyptian story from *The Thousand and One Nights,*[239] Ma'aruf, a poor cobbler, has difficulties with his wife, Fatimah, who takes him to court a number of times charging him falsely of ill treatment. Finally, with the assistance of a jinni, he flies off to a far-off kingdom where he pretends to be a wealthy merchant waiting for his caravan to arrive. In the meantime, he borrows money from merchants of the kingdom and from the king's treasury, always promising that he will repay with dividends. He distributes all of this money to the poor. The king is captivated by his story and, thinking that Ma'aruf will make him rich, marries his daughter Dunya to him. But Ma'aruf's caravan does not arrive. Fearing that the king will kill him, Dunya sends him away. In a far-off place, he comes upon a jinni who controls large amounts of gems. The jinni, now under the control of Ma'aruf, has the great treasure loaded on camels and donkeys, and Ma'aruf moves back to the kingdom a very wealthy man. He is reunited with Dunya and, when the king dies, becomes the monarch. Fatimah, who has been seeking him, arrives, and she is killed by the son of Ma'aruf and Dunya.

A number of patterns organize the images in this lengthy tale. At the center of the story are patterns depicting the two sides of Ma'aruf, as a trickster who takes much money from merchants and from the royal treasury, and as a patron of the poor. He creates an image of himself that he later moves in to. Other patterns comment on Ma'aruf's activities, including patterns having to do with Fatimah's perfidy, with the deepening suspicions of the king and the merchants, and with control of the ring that in turn controls the jinni and his largesse. The metaphorical heart of the story is the triad of Ma'aruf and the two women, Fatimah a mirror of his ugly side, Dunya of his positive side. This set of relationships is held in place by the rhythmical patterning of the story. From that set of relationships grows the tale's meaning.

Kintu and the combination of Nambi and Warumbe, Ma'aruf and the combination of Dunya and Fatimah–myth and tale are identical in the sense that each contains the mythic germ that animates and gives dimension to the real-life characters.

Notes on Performance

Children's tales now; but not the invention of a child's intellect.
—Henry Callaway, *Nursery Tales, Traditions, and Histories of the Zulus*

NOKAVALA NTSHEBE

June 8, 1975

She is very demonstrative; she uses many ideophones and complementary gestures. Are supplementary gestures so conscious? Her narratives are basically all action, all physical movement. They therefore build on ideophone and gesture (and body movement). This is understandable. Therefore, considering gesture from the complementary vantage *only* for a moment, a single narrative should be *all* gesture. It is not. Why not? Which narrative actions enlist and invite gesture, which do not?

Consider first the body itself and its possibilities for movement, for dance—and so consider the possibilities of the voice, too. What is the relationship between body and voice? Do they exist separately? Or are they utterly reliant one on the other? Does the body express itself as the voice does? With a like vocabulary and syntax? Does it communicate experience or even information as the voice does? How do body (and gesture) and voice interrelate? This includes facial expressions, which seem more intimately connected to the word than gestures. Is this so? Why?

Gestures that move with word sounds and word rhythms and verbal patterns: do gestures follow patterns of their own? Gestures, body movement that occur in concert with verbal noise: not complementary. The end of a statement may be explosive, and the body reflects the explosion. This explosiveness may become rhythmical, a pattern—that is, a number of statements working to the same volume climax, with identical gestures and body movements each time. No apparent *meaning* in the gesturing, just a reflection of verbal volume. To what extent are narrative and artistic gestures images of feeling? How do the verbal aspects of a performance control or limit gesture?

June 9, 1975

Some questions: How do these images trap, hold, lock significant cultural experiences, artists' (society's) feelings regarding these experiences? Gestures—Are they physical only? Or do they move beyond representation to thought and abstraction and symbol? The narrative images, repeated often and apparently very old: Why are they remembered? What do they really mean for the culture? Does that meaning alter through the generations? How? Does alteration of meaning require alteration of image? Or does the ancient image continue to trap and to hold similar human feelings, yet adapt them to current contemporary realities? And, therefore, the old question about the relationship between the mythic image and reality. How are the gestures related to the verbal aspects of performance? Even those that are purely complementary? And how do abstract gestures differ from representational gestures in their relationship to the word? Why do these images continue to stir audiences? Why are they so universally remembered over long periods of time, pretty much intact? What human feelings do they express? Reflect? Hold? Sound, structure, image, statement. Sensuous beauty—the body, its normal movement versus its movement in the story: how do they differ? One is functional, the other virtual reality? An abstraction?

Functional movement now consciously altered by an artist, the superfluous omitted, the symbolic included. Now a closed world, whereas functional movement occurs in an open world.

Gesture now harnessed to a thought, not to a physical deed. Gesture now harnessed to an imaginary story, not to the bewildering chaos and open-endedness and uncertainty of real life.

The narrative images are very familiar—securely familiar—touchstones—artistic touchstones offering security, familiarity, the warmth of the familiar. Life in the world of the story flows evenly and predictably along ancient cultural lines and molds. The narrative images capture and hold human feeling in these lines and molds, thus providing security and order to an insecure and potentially disordered existence. The narratives accomplish this, but they also transmit data. They are not only a secure and well-lighted place; they also communicate information. They mold our feelings in our youth, they nourish those feelings as we move beyond youth. The narratives trap feeling and give it meaning in our youth; they trap feeling and affirm that meaning as we grow beyond youth. The narratives deal with diffuse human feelings, uncertainties, fears, joys, hopes, dreads; they trap and hold these feelings in images. When this has been done, it becomes possible to manipulate these feelings and give them meaning, to manipulate them

A Xhosa musician

by bringing them into relationship with yet other feeling-locked images, and in that juxtaposition imbue them with meaning.

The familiar narrative images thus first indoctrinate, in the sense of acquainting the members of the audience with the rhythmic nature of the story, then affirm that sense of acquaintance, giving meaning and shape to diffuse experience by shaping feelings, thereby giving them meaning. The images are the repositories of feeling. They call up feelings, purposely dealing with feelings of, for example, fear and dread, trapping those feelings, immersing us in images thereby, and then juxtaposing those feeling-packed images with yet other feeling-packed images. Meaning is the result. It is meaning achieved through images that mold our feelings. Often nameless fears find form in the villainous *zim* or roguish *imbulu.*[240] These become understandable, controllable in a cultural sense, in a performance.

Feelings—particularly concerning the great rites of passage—are provided with cultural identity, meaning. The artist calls up images, through her own feelings, and traps the feelings of the members of the audience in those feelings. The movement is from diffuse and nameless feeling to thought, idea, cultural ideal. The process is made possible by the image.

The move is to the abstract, to the symbolic, from the representational image to nonrepresentational thought. The material acted upon is the feelings of the members of the audience. The molding tool is the image. The concrete image takes the diffuse feelings, the many different feeling experiences of the members of the audience, gives them form, and thereby insures a common experience.

The *zim* holds a certain feeling, evokes a certain feeling, for the Xhosa audience, as do, for example, a hapless girl, an *imbulu,* an ox. Bring a hapless girl image (evoking and trapping a certain feeling) together with a *zim* image (evoking and trapping a certain feeling), and you begin to channel feeling, to give feeling particularity, form.

October 24, 1975

Narrative technique: a series of layered image sets: with transformations (paralleling sets of imagery). Everything is the expansible image, with transformations: it is an art work because each seemingly diverse image set is actually identical in structure. The act of identifying, of experiencing that identical nature of diverse image sets is both the artistic and the experiential message. Is this not also the nature of the short story, poetry, novel?

The separate work of art is drawn from a larger community of images. Does the separate work of art also organize the larger repertory?

Nokavala Ntshebe

The allied details cluster about the lexically identical core. The repetition of the expansible image: as often as necessary. That is, until sufficient new data has been supplied for adequate static-proof communication of message.

The performer has one kind of experience during a performance, and the audience has another, an apparently quite different experience from that of the performer. The intervening transformation of the art experience of the performer to that of the audience is an essential area of aesthetic inquiry.

October 25, 1975

Stories held together by a stitching process, through repetition. Oral narrative tradition is a communication system, requiring an aesthetic experience for the satisfactory control of the message and its movement from a performer to members of an audience. Communication of a message is achieved by means of complex systems of signs which interrelate within the performance, a closed system that has relationships with other closed systems in a society which itself is a closed system. But the performance contains within itself all elements necessary for the efficient and successful transformation of a message. Verbal and nonverbal sign systems operate in oral narrative tradition. These sign systems are not a part of the inherited plotting of the story; they become functional only in performance.

October 26 and 27, 1975

Another kind of gesture: "in this place," "in this part of the body," demonstrates this, or points it out.

The temporal tense *(bathi bakugqiba ukuhamba . . .)* a part of a lexical stitching process in narrative structure. *bahlala,* a transitional and less complex stitching.

The performer: her consciousness of the/her body as a *social* entity and her consciousness of it as an *artistic* entity.

The human body in the narrative (no arms, money for beard, etc.) vs. the human body that is a part of the performance (gesture, dance, etc.) vs. the human body as a social entity, vs. the human body as a physiological entity.

Another gesture: hand keeps time to the rhythm of the performance at the same time as it emphasizes. Keeping time and emphasis.

Music: Ordering the Raw Materials

The Creation of Metaphor

> Music is feeling, then, not sound.
> —Wallace Stevens, "Peter Quince at the Clavier"

Hear the chorus of poets in the oral tradition discussing their art:

> It's a feeling! It's a feeling! . . . I feel it, I feel it.
> —Ashton Ngcama

> The way a poem is expressed depends on the poet himself. Some people are slow and gentle, others are more forceful. That's because their spirits push them. . . . If my feelings are indifferent to what's going on, then my poem will reflect this. The poetry must come spontaneously.
> —Mdukiswa Tyabashe

> It is a stirring up of emotions.
> —S. K. Lekgothoane, "Praises of Animals in Northern Sotho"

> The bard . . . is a loving critic.
> —Ernest Sedumeli Moloto, "The Growth and Tendencies of Tswana Poetry"

Gabriel García Márquez wrote, "Ultimately, literature is nothing but carpentry." He explained, "Both are very hard work. Writing sometimes is almost as hard as making a table. With both you are working with reality, a material just as hard as wood. Both are full of tricks and techniques. Basically very little magic and a lot of hard work are involved."[241]

The work involves organizing the emotions evoked by mythic images; this is the rhythm of the story. The organization of any story entails a combining and ordering of the primary emotions evoked by the mythic images, the rhythmic movement being a secondary emotion, the patterns whereby the images, mythic and real-life, are worked into form. The "magic" of the story has its origins in the "hard work" of rhythmical organization. This form is the ultimate meaning of the story, leading as it does to metaphor.

The story becomes performance when the audience experiences the narrative surface of the tale subverted by another organizing device, a more powerful one. This is the rhythm of the story, the patterning that breaks up the narrative flow, even as that narrative flow continues unimpeded to the denouement. This relationship between the rhythm of the story and the narrative flow is the crucial artistic one, the relationship that makes possible an internal linkage between the sets of imagery in the story—the imagery of the real and of the mythic. There are two kinds of music in storytelling: the melodic line of narrative and the rhythmic music of metaphor, that is, the rhythmic music that produces metaphor—that *is* metaphor.

So it is that music is the essence of metaphor. "Music," said Leonard Bernstein, "is supposed to be a metaphorical phenomenon, some kind of mysterious symbolization of our innermost affective existence."[242]

But the essence of music is feeling and not sound. So the emotionally evocative images are the place to begin. The storyteller relies heavily on the separate histories of the members of her audiences and upon the individual experiences that they have had with the familiar images of the story that she recreates; she has many such diverse feelings as her raw material. When she organizes these feelings into patterns, the music of the story is the result, and it is the essential experience and meaning of the story.

"Music," wrote Aaron Copland, "has four essential elements: rhythm, melody, harmony, and tone color. These four ingredients are the composer's materials. He works with them in the same way that any artisan works with his materials."[243] These ingredients, and most particularly rhythm and melody, are a part of the materials of the artisan who creates stories. Music "is an arrangement of time. It is a series of patterns scrawled in the air, constantly shifting, changing, and disappearing as rapidly as they come," writes James Lincoln Collier. He adds, "These patterns in the air, however, are not random." When he argues that "music is an organization of sound," noting that "the mind automatically begins searching for patterns, for organizations," he is also speaking of the creator of stories, who devises patterns as well, organizing the imagery even as the linear movement of the story continues.[244] The story's patterns also shift, change, and disappear as rapidly as they come.

The words of the story and the music of the story: do we react in different ways? Is the reaction to the music "a sheer sensory factor in experience" quite apart from the reaction to the words of the story?[245] Do these complement one another, the one touching our intellect, the other our imagination? So that while the story is being told, our emotions, evoked by the images in the story, are given form by the music generated and controlled by other aspects of the performance: the body of the performer, itself composed of both the purity of music and the specificity of the mimed use of it; the music of the words, tonal, poetically expressed; patterning; the tightly and intensely emotional relationship with the audience; and the memory of stories and music. It is this music that governs the development, force, and, in the end, the meaning of the metaphors created within the story. These metaphors are the result of an interaction between the images in the story, but they are also metaphors constructed of the story's pure sounds—gesture, music, et cetera, taking the raw materials and working these into patterns.

THE MELODIC LINE

The melodic line of the story involves a cause and effect movement and the consequent ordering of the emotions. Story, as García Márquez notes, is construction. There are two categories of construction in a story: the organizing of the mythic images and the emotions evoked by those images. These are the melodic line and the rhythm that subverts that line. The mythic images are worked into a cause and effect narrative line, a melodic line carefully developed by a storyteller who works the mythic images into a relationship with contemporary real-life images, into a line that tells a story. This is the obvious construction element of the story; in the end, it is a mask, it is the face of storytelling, but by itself it is not the essence of storytelling. Still, there can be no story without this obvious surface, the organization of images into an attractive movement from conflict to resolution. This is what we think of when we think of story, but to analyze only this surface part of the storytelling performance is to miss just about everything that is most combustible, most memorable about the story. Narrative organization of images, then, is crucial to storytelling, but it is not the only form of organization. This is the form of story that most observers and analysts treat: this is the Proppian dimension,[246] the obvious moral surface of the story. It is crucial, but one cannot stop there.

"Melody is where music begins."[247] As with music, so also with story. "Melody is that inscrutable, magical element of music that captures the imagination and lingers in the memory to be recalled, hummed, and whistled long after words and accompaniments have been forgotten." The linear movement of narrative is the melodic line in stories. "A melody is a succession of musical notes conveying an impression of continuity—a series of pitches arranged in a logical sequence."[248] Copland argues, "A beautiful melody, like a piece of music in its entirety, should be of satisfying proportions. It must give us a sense of completion and of inevitability."[249] Of the two kinds of music in storytelling, the narrative music—the melodic line—is most accessible. But it is not the music that evokes and holds emotions, except in a somewhat superficial way.

Narrative has its own ability to rouse emotions: suspense, anticipation, puzzlement, the response to character and action. This is the immediate and essential arresting aspect of story. Without it, there is no story. It is clearly an organizing device. The linear movement from conflict to resolution, with perhaps a myriad of conflicts and resolutions along the way, is a crucial ordering instrument. The thirty-one functions outlined by Vladimir Propp essentially involve the narrative surface: the hero leaves home because of a quest or a lack or a violation of an interdiction. He encounters villainy, he is tested, gets a magical helper or agent, struggles with the villain as he continues his quest. The villain is defeated or the lack is liquidated, and the hero returns, is recognized, and ascends the throne.[250] The familiarity of the ancient images involved in such movements also provides an emotional aura to the story.

The linear movement is composed of the two kinds of imagery, the real-life and the mythic images. As the storyteller moves the story from conflict to resolution, emotions other than those of suspense, anticipation, familiarity, et cetera, are being evoked: these are emotions associated with the familiarity of the contemporary images and the prism of feelings tied to those, and—most significantly, because these are the most potent emotion-generating aspects of the story—the emotions associated with the mythic images.

These, then, constitute the emotional stew on the surface of the story: feelings associated with and roused by the two kinds of imagery and by the linear movement (and all affiliated elements) itself. By itself, the linear movement provides a certain amount of ordering of those emotions; the movement itself is both emotionally evocative and an organizer of those emotions. That surface activity in itself is an aesthetically attractive part of the story. If one remains on this surface then one will typically link these organized emotions with an obvious moral or message.

The linear movement of the story, the advance to resolution, is its melodic line, and the rhythmic grid, the harmonic aspects of the story, the tone colors provide the story its depth of feeling. These musical aspects of the poem are based upon, feed upon, the emotions generated by the motifs and associated images. But the rhythmic organization of the images provides its own emotional character, and it is the rich combination and interaction of the two varieties of organized emotion that generate meaning in the story.

RHYTHM, PATTERN, REPETITION—THE LURE OF THE FAMILIAR, THE SHOCK OF THE NOVEL

"Music," wrote Susanne K. Langer, "is a tonal analogue of emotive life."[251] Stories, like music, consist of melody and rhythm, the essence of poetry. If melody is not the ultimate experience of the story, it provides the line, the contour, that provides balance and organization. "A graceful melodic contour can strike as pleasing a balance as a line in a Picasso drawing."[252] It is also true that "melodies do not exist in a vacuum; . . . they are heard as part of a total musical work."[253] In a story, the melody is the story line, the narrative movement. This melody is on the surface of the work and involves the maneuverings of the characters. Worked into the melodic design of the story, among the many images that constitute that design, are potent mythic images. These are critical elements of the story, because it is these images that elicit emotional responses from members of audiences. We have seen that the melodic line provides some organization of these emotional responses, but it is not the key organizational factor. That factor is the rhythmic character of the story. The combination of melody and rhythm forms the core of the story, the poetic heart of the story. The melody of the story is the organization of images "one after another in a logical, meaningful series."[254] This melody is not the essence of storytelling; rather, it becomes "the springboard for a long work of music."[255] Copland notes, "As far as mere construction goes, every good melody will be found to possess a skeletal frame which can be deduced from essential points in the melodic line after 'unessential' notes have been pared away."[256] When two lines are developed simultaneously, we are in the presence of counterpoint: story is as contrapuntal as music.

As "melody is only second of importance to rhythm in the musical firmament,"[257] so the melodic line in story, the linear narrative organization of images, is second of importance to rhythmic organization of images. The two modes of organization are linked: "A sensitivity to rhythmic flow is also important in melodic construction."[258] This narrative thread is crucial to the success of the work: "Whatever the quality of the melodic line considered alone, the listener must never lose sight of its function in a composition. It should be followed like a continuous thread which leads the listener through a piece from the very beginning to the very end."[259] The plotting of images may become more dense; there may be more than a single narrative thread in a story. So also in music, where one might find "two melodic lines simultaneously. This method is called *counterpoint.*"[260]

As the melody develops, it is accompanied by rhythm. "Melody is made of rhythm too."[261] Charles R. Hoffer writes that "probably the most fundamental component of rhythm is the *beat,* the recurrent pulse found in most music." But "the beat and rhythm are not one and the same. . . . The beat is the simple pulse. . . . Rhythm is a larger concept, including the beat and everything that happens to sounds in relation to time."[262] The beat, the meter, "gives order to time. It organizes small groups of notes, and sometimes larger ones, and thereby provides a grid upon which music is drawn."[263] Hoffer observes, "The beats occur evenly in each case, but now they exhibit a pattern, and this pattern is called *meter.*"[264] Jourdain writes of the long sonic units provided by music: "A brain requires some way of breaking these objects into pieces so that it can analyze them piecemeal. It can't wait until the end of a ten-minute composition to figure out what happened. And so a brain is always on the lookout for clues about where musical objects begin and end." He explains, "What we call 'rhythm' exists in music to help the brain in this task. Rhythm draws lines around musical figures."[265] Plato wrote, "rhythm and harmony enter most profoundly into the soul and take the strongest hold upon it, bringing grace with them."[266]

Counterpointing of narrative lines begins the merging of the layers of the story. "Counterpoint reflects a linear, horizontal view of music. *Harmony,* on the other hand, stresses the vertical aspect, the effect of sounds heard simultaneously."[267] But "music . . . confirms what is already present in society and culture, and it adds nothing new except patterns of sound."[268] The linear motion of the story is subverted, then, when the images, with the mythic images at their core, begin to be repeated, patterned by the storyteller. This patterning is the essential quality—children master it even before they move to the linear organization of the images. The images are patterned, and these patterns become the essential rhythm of the story. The images are emotionally evocative; they also take the emotions and give them form. This is the patterning effect of the rhythmic grid. Emotions are at the core, perhaps in song, certainly in repetition. It is the rhythm, the patterning, that takes emotional outpourings and works them into form, so that the emotional responses of a given member of the audience are joined to those of other members, and the combination worked into a community of form.

Each repetition results in a new experience for the members of the audience; even if the repeated material is lexically identical, it can never be emotionally, experientially identical. The repetition by itself provides a new experience, each repetition deepening the artistic experience, exploring it. Each new set of details or images, no matter if identical to those that have come before, is experienced in a new context, and it is the context that defines the message. The storyteller starts with the core mythic image and allied details. She will then repeat the core mythic image and allied details, with new information provided with each new layered repetition. The patterning continues until all necessary new information has been communicated. Sometimes there is much repetition, sometimes not so much, depending on the designs of the artist. Repetition acts as a divider and provides layering, resulting in the decoding of the message.[269]

The incompleteness of form, the evolving transformation, means that the audience remains uncertain about the ending, about the future steps: the form remains incomplete until the end of story. The audience will have ideas of where the story is to go, and its predilections and sense of this will be altered, fulfilled, or wholly crushed by where the storyteller moves the story. This contributes to form, tension, suspense, and provides its own form of emotional response. The certainty and uncertainty, anticipation and frustrated anticipation evoke a complex array of emotions. The storyteller begins, then, with images, gatherings of images organized in linear form, but with the kernel of subversion built in. Moving beyond the story's surface without disturbing that surface is the raconteur's sleight of hand. The chemistry between the fantasy and real-world images generates its own kind of emotion. The mixture of emotions is therefore complex, volatile, and without meaning until the storyteller rhythmically patterns them. It is then that the two kinds of imagery coalesce for the moment of performance, later to be placed in their separate categories.

But story goes much deeper than this, and the message of the performance is considerably more complex. The music of the story, the rhythmic patterning of the story, subverts the linear narrative. In musical terms, the melodic line is manipulated, developed, textured by a patterning that seems to undermine that linear activity, at the same time that it develops a harmonious relationship with it. All of this has the effect of ordering complex emotions: those emotions educed by the linear narrative—including suspense, familiarity, the forward push of the cause and effect movement of the narrative, and those evoked by the mythic images, the latter very strong and tending to dominate, even to interfere with, the narrative linear movement. There are also the separate autobiographical and historical emotions having to do with individual members of the audience, their interrelationships, their societies, their beliefs. It is then left to the rhythm of the story, the patterning, to organize these various emotional responses into form, to harmonize them.

The harmonic aspects of the story, the tone colors, provide the story with its depth of feeling, that is, with its meaning. Not only words are involved; the body of the storyteller, the voice, the rhythm of the language—dance and music—are fully engaged. The body of the storyteller is itself an emotionally charged grid. The rhythm of the language, whether oral or literary, is purposefully enhanced and artificially emphasized by the performer. When a language is expressed orally, its rhythmical properties are manipulated in obvious ways—vocally and physically. The writer heightens the poetic qualities of the written language, employing more strictly literary devices. Both oral and literary poets deal with sound, and each strives to shape an audience's emotional and intellectual responses to images and the organization of images. Sounds and the rhythmical ordering of sounds are the primary focus of both oral and literary poetry.

The rhythmic ordering of the emotional experience of story, then, is an essential aspect of storytelling performance. In this sense, it is dance: "Like other cultural codes and patterned interactions, dance is a way of ordering and categorizing experience."[270] It is that combination of narrative movement, the melodic line, and rhythmic organization that is crucial to storytelling, as it is to dance: "Rhythm refers to patterned, temporally unfolding phenomena," writes Judith Lynne Hanna. She argues that "dance must involve more than just rhythmical movement, the pulsing flow of energy in time and space."[271] Olive Schreiner, the South African writer, said, "Perhaps there isn't any music on earth like what I picture to myself."[272]

MUSIC AND "RAMAITSOANALA"

The storyteller fine-tunes this relationship between fantasy and reality, emphasizing Ramaitsoanala's medial state: Ravorombe complains that she smells humans in her home. She thereby reveals her daughter's intermediate state of being, and Ramaitsoanala's developing separation from the mother. A human is indeed in her home: it is her daughter. This fact, along with the mother's fear that a suitor may come and take her daughter away, gives these suspicions a sharper edge. But something more important is happening: the two characters are actually a single being, the one a mirror of the other, the fantasy bird the symbol of the transformation of the real-life girl. The mother's birdness represents the childhood of Ramaitsoanala, which she must give up to move into adulthood. At the same time, clear contradictions in the mother suggest both this boundary state and the mother's inner turmoil as she resists giving up her daughter to adulthood and simultaneously prepares her for this state. The first pattern simultaneously shows the mother preparing her daughter for womanhood, yet resisting and wishing to keep it from happening.

The second pattern involves the flight of the bride, Ramaitsoanala, and her groom, Andriambahoaka. It takes place on the prairie, the land between the two houses—a liminal setting. As the prince spirits Ramaitsoanala away, the mother's furious pursuit is delayed when rice and then corn are thrown to the ground. This pattern reveals the mother's anger, her determination to keep her daughter to herself, and it also moves her child into the isolation stage of her puberty ritual. As with the first pattern, this one simultaneously shows a part of the puberty initiation and the mother's determination to block its progress. This pattern has at its poetic center mythic images having to do with flight, a bride quest, and a reluctant in-law.

The third pattern reveals the ordeal or initiation stage of Ramaitsoanala's puberty ritual, consisting of mythic imagery, a series of impossible tasks imposed by jealous co-wives and the continued reluctance of Ravorombe to allow her daughter to leave home. The mother's contradictions again reveal Ramaitsoanala's uncertainties as she moves from one state to another, as she quests for her new identity.

Notes on Performance

NONGENILE MASITHATHU ZENANI

June 19, 1975

Performance of three rites of passage. Another gesture: The artist talks directly to the members of the audience, or picks out a single member, with associated rhetorical gestures, eye contact, et cetera—points to him, uses him as an object for illustration, et cetera. Gestures: hands and arms gracefully moving, hands clapping, carrying on in an abstract way the last (most recent) complementary gesture. Gestures punctuating, complementing the rhythm of the narrative's verbal elements, the natural rhythm of the language, the poetic uses to which the performer puts that natural rhythm. Gesture and dance, vocal drama and song: how these blend in a performance. The complementary gesture is explicitly created, then it becomes abstracted and it continues now as an abstract (seemingly supplementary, but actually developed from a complementary) gesture; then it may go back to the complementary and then yet again be abstracted. Some gestures, then, are abstracted complementary gestures.

Gesture: from complementary to supplementary; the abstracted gesture: it carries on the complementary; it is rhetorical; it is formal; it shapes the narrative. Hands: one hand doing one thing, the other doing another; the two hands doing the same thing; one hand is busy, the other at rest; both hands are at rest. Hands: one hand demonstrates on the other—not as hand, but the hand is a substitute for what she is actually speaking of. Gesture: hand in the air, forefinger up, the hand shaking. Gesture: open hand, palm claps the other hand which is formed as a hole. And silences?

Plot, oral plot: simultaneous plus serial development. Picaresque vs. complex.

The full body: its nonverbal use in performance.

June 15, 1975

Hands forming a strictly complementary gesture may become purely supplementary, diffuse, and then again return to complementary gesturing. Masithathu Zenani does this frequently. Her hands, for example, forming a miming gesture, midway: hands still miming, the miming stops but the hands remain in the gesturing position, and continue to gesticulate. But now they are

Nongenile Masithathu Zenani

no longer mime, are no longer complementary. Now they are moving about not as miming gestures, but as supplementary gestures, with no mimed content. This may continue for a time, then the hands, still moving as a supplementary set of gestures, revert to the complementary, to the miming that originated this complex set of gestures. The miming may have lost its verbal associates for a time, and the supplementary gestures take over during the nonverbal activities: but not complementing this new verbal material, remaining instead a vestige of the earlier complementary gesturing, now supplementary, attractive, balletic, graceful. Then the verbal elements of the narrative recall the earlier mimed material, and the supplementary gestures (still an abstracted form of the earlier complementary gestures) return to the earlier gesturing, again complementing the verbal elements of the narrative. Here, then, is a series of uninterrupted gestures, moving from the complementary to the supplementary to the complementary, with opening and closing gestures identical, and the supplementary having its origins and destiny in the opening complementary gesture.

What if the narrative itself is the *form,* but not the *content?* The form reveals the idea, the feelings that the narrative's images hold.

Narrative tradition is a mass art form, insuring that whoever performs the images, whenever they are performed, the feelings of the members of the audience are evoked, made the same, captured, held, juxtaposed, given cultural definition, directed, ultimately reduced in intensity . . . catharsis.

July 3, 1975

Are gestures essential to the performance? Masithathu has periods of great calm as far as gesture and body movement are concerned, then periods of sustained animation (as today, the first half of the day was relatively calm, the second half very dramatic with gesture and body movement). Much traveling linking the various parts of her fine narrative.

The hands (for both Masithathu Zenani and Nohatyula Miyeki) leave the body during the ushering-out movements. The performer may develop a series of identically repeated gestures which have a life for one part of one performance only (or for one performance only), as with Masithathu Zenani. These gestures may grow out of or otherwise be related to surrounding gestures and body movements, or they may be wholly isolated as far as such influence is concerned.

July 14, 1975

The use of gesture, body movement, and other nonverbal aspects of performance continue, of course, to be significant in this sprawling performance, now almost seventy hours long. There is much incipient ballet in the movements that requires further exploration. The graceful wave of the back of the hand when indicating a distant occurrence, this wave taking on urgency or anger if the context demands them. Or a vague wave of the hand, again indicating something physically removed from the performer's body. Or a point may be made with the hands that seems to lack complementary significance. But in these apparently noncomplementary, ballet-like, dance-like (dance-like because abstracted, and hands used in ordinary conversation are more often more tied to the distinct work at hand) gestures, movements of the body, there is a certain stylization, abstraction, which really is quite complementary—or would be, if we were able to trace its history, perhaps. Is all gesture complementary, with gradations of abstraction from the distinctly mimed gesture to the seemingly "purely" abstract or noncomplementary movement?

Random notes from July 20, 1975, to October 15, 1975

For Masithathu Zenani, it is often a mixture of traditional story, Xhosa custom, and autobiography.

The language is a matter of rhythm. Thus, *uya kukhwela* may become *uyokukhwela* which may sound *uyokhwela,* but which may have an unspoken beat—a silence, a rhythmic silence, harmonious with sound—instead of *-ku-* = *uyo'khwela.*

The storage capabilities and functions of gestures.

Repetition as the divider and the layer, the message and the decoder: all.

The images: catch an experience in the "cage of form"[273]—becomes an easily recalled memory of an experience.

In repetition, patterning, expansible image: what new information is communicated with each repetition? Some new details (lexically different from those that have come before), but mainly a new experience (emotional, deepening the artistic experience; exploring) of the core with each generally precise repetition—so that even if the repeated material is lexically identical, it can never be emotionally, experientially identical. Thus, each new set of details or images, no matter how identical to those that have come before, is experience in a new context, and it is that context that defines "message."

Mythic image plus allied details: repetition. Mythic image plus allied details: new information with each new layer. Repeated until all necessary new information has been communicated. Sometimes there is much repetition, sometimes not so much, depending on the thematic designs of the artist.

June 29, 1975

Masithathu Zenani's histories and biographical narratives move toward the discursive, so there is frequently not a lot of gesture and body movement. True? But there is frequently much gesture and body movement in the histories and biographies: still oral tradition. And, after all, the images of fictional stories do constitute discursive reasoning.

The move from the house of birth to the house of marriage: always away from something. The hierarchy of gesture: away from the body, complementary. The hierarchy of words: away from mime, ideophone. Is the short-lived rhetorical gesture in a biographical or historical narrative, for instance, left over from depictive-then-symbolic complementary gestures?

June 30, 1975

"Feeling embodied in 'form.'"[274] But the form is so communal, so utterly determined by the art tradition . . . the words composing the verbal configuration of the narrative, the gestures and body movement building its nonverbal component. The artist has a lot of latitude here, but essentially the narrative images remain quite constant. There is no doubt but that the feeling of the artist is involved in the evocation of these images, and she quite obviously seeks to involve and trap the feelings of the members of the audience in these narrative images. . . . But is she—are her images—is her performance reaching for more? Is she reaching beyond her feelings and those of her audience, for a feeling or set of feelings that is purer, more basic, mythical, at the foundation of the culture? Is her feeling then but a part of a performance which seeks more than the mere unique expression of the particular feelings of one artist? One must not confuse the feelings—her feelings are a part of the performance, along with gestures, et cetera. And she enlists the feelings of the members of the audience because that must occur if they are to experience the "larger feeling," the cultural feeling, the mythical, folkloristic feeling, the pulse of the entire tradition. The "feeling embodied in the object,"[275] then, is not the idiosyncratic feeling of the artist. She uses the elements of the tradition that are available to everyone, then, with her own imagination (feeling) and genius, transmutes them, reaches that deeper cultural, mythical core. But even the most mediocre performer reaches that core, it would seem.

The "aesthetic object"—the narrative performance—is composed of images "abstracted from physical nature and manipulated to serve the artist's purpose."[276]

As with gesture, we move away from something, and as we move away, things are apt to become abstracted, symbolized, removed in appearance from the original appearance in physical nature. In stories, the *amazim* and *imbulu,* magical creatures involved in fantasy occurrences: the move is always away from something, away from the house of birth, away from reality, away from the body (reality) of the performer, and always to something unreal, abstracted, symbolized. For the audience, too, the move is away from their own physical reality to the reality—that is, the symbolized physical reality—of the narrative performance.

Why is this? Why the abstractions? Are these necessary to the objectification of feeling? Apparently. We take our actual experience and transform it. For we are not really interested, an audience is not really interested, in the experience of an individual audience, but rather in the new and more culturally universal phenomenon that the artist's experiences, mingled with those of the members of the audience, leads to.

The materials we work with, however, are the experiences of the artist, those of the members of the audience, and hence with the objects of physical reality. In performance, these become transformed, transmuted, into something else. They owe their origin to the objects of physical reality and the experience (and feeling) of the artist, and they use these materials to go beyond physical reality and the experience (and feeling) of the artist.

November 26, 1975

The body as the measure of all things, especially in a story. The storyteller, constantly using the body as a reference point, constantly referring to it. Measurement, distance, et cetera. Everything is measured, et cetera, in terms of the body. The body expresses the full world of the story.

November 27, 1975

The body and time. Narrative, the body as history (it lives and dies), and time. The body has an existence in physical time, is therefore itself a narrative: it has a beginning and an end. As such, it and the narrative are analogous. Significance of this? Is the body therefore a metaphor of the narrative? Then, by extension, of the society? The body, the narrative, society: their relationship. The body of the artist: How does it complicate, enrich, make cogent this relationship? Is this the crucial aesthetic relationship of the performance? And how does space enter this mix?

February 6, 1976

Characters not wishing to be circumcised, *intonjane*-ed, or married at the appropriate time: compare physical defects of characters, deformities, inability to speak or to speak properly, et cetera.

The story builds on feeling. Basic human feelings are channeled and given meaning; better, they become vehicles for meaning, but meaning is nothing other than contemporary feeling given ancient form. Contemporary fears, hopes, et cetera, are brought into contact with cultural (ancient) fears and hopes (more than this?) through the ancient images that contain those feelings. Thus, a fundamental difference between contemporary and ancient feeling: the contemporary feelings that are given cultural form in the ancient. One should distinguish clearly between contemporary and ancient images.

Metaphor: Preparation for Performance

Myth, Metaphor, Meaning

> "Pray for us. And pray for us. And pray for us. Good idea the repetition."
> —Leopold Bloom in James Joyce's *Ulysses*

Hear the chorus of scholars, a catalogue of comments about metaphor:

> It is metaphor above all that gives perspicuity, pleasure, and a foreign air, and it cannot be learnt from anyone else; but we must make use of metaphors and epithets that are appropriate. This will be secured by observing due proportion; it is when placed in juxtaposition that contraries are most evident. . . . Metaphors . . . should be derived from what is beautiful either in sound, or in signification, or to sight, or to some other sense.
> —Aristotle, *The "Art" of Rhetoric*

> When metaphor is used well, the vehicle is seldom flat or single-valued; the images belonging to it have physical qualities that suggest a tenor of feeling or idea with more than one component. In fact, the vehicle of a good metaphor spins long webs of association in which complex ideas are caught.
> —Mary Kinzie, *A Poet's Guide to Poetry*[277]

> Metaphor creates a new reality from which the original appears to be unreal.
> —Wallace Stevens, *Collected Poetry and Prose*

> Metaphor is a device for seeing something in terms of something else.
> —Kenneth Burke, *A Grammar of Motives*[278]

In general, when we speak of a relatively simple metaphor, we are referring to a sentence or another expression in which *some* words are used metaphorically while the remainder are used nonmetaphorically.
—Max Black, *Models and Metaphors: Studies in Language and Philosophy*[279]

What really matters in a metaphor is the psychic depth at which the things of the world, whether actual or fancied, are transmuted by the cool heat of the imagination.
—Philip Wheelwright, *Metaphor and Reality*[280]

Each word contains a certain plurality of virtual meanings; the moment a word is associated with others to constitute a sentence, one of these meanings becomes actualized and predominates.
—Octavio Paz, "Literature and Literalness"[281]

[Metaphor] provides us with a way of learning something new about the world. . . . In metaphor one expression supports two contents: one is a content the expression supports literally, the other is a content the expression supports only in the given metaphor.
—Eva Feder Kittay, *Metaphor*[282]

A work of art is like a metaphor, to be understood without translation or comparison of ideas; it exhibits its form, and the import is immediately perceived in it.
—Susanne K. Langer, *Mind*

To appreciate fictions is, to some extent, also to fictionalize ourselves, so that we may involve ourselves in a kind of metaphoric participation with fictional characters in some fictional world. Fiction then becomes a metaphor for life and our life is transfigured into the character in whose life we participate.
—Bijoy H. Boruah, *Fiction and Emotion*[283]

Art, if a metaphor at times on life, entails that the not unfamiliar experience of being taken out of oneself by art—the familiar artistic illusion—is virtually the enactment of a metaphoric transformation with oneself as subject: you are what the work ultimately is about, a commonplace person transfigured into an amazing woman.
—Arthur Danto, *The Transfiguration of the Commonplace*

> The aesthetic satisfaction derived from metaphor, imagery, and related techniques . . . depends on the *emotive potential* of the matrices which enter into the game. By emotive potential I mean the capacity of a matrix to generate and satisfy participatory emotions.
> —Arthur Koestler, *The Act of Creation*

MIRRORS

Metaphors have to do with transitions, transformations, the movement from one state to another.[284] That movement is the engine of storytelling, revealing a prismatic view of nature. Michael J. Arlen remembers a dream of his father and him driving through France. His father goes to get on an airplane, motioning to the boy to follow. When the boy looks inside the plane, "There all is darkness. *Black.* I have never seen such empty darkness as in that dream airplane I peer into, and then, somehow, I am standing on the grass again, the wind is blowing, and the blue plane is gone." Now in present time, he and his wife are on a plane: "Half asleep, I looked out into the night and saw my father's face looking in, squinting, trying to see something. I sat up. But, of course, it was my own face, my reflection in the glass, squinting, trying to see something, looking out."[285] James W. Fernandez thinks of this event as he writes of the Fang initiate who is going through his puberty rite of passage: "Often the initiate is aided by placing a mirror on the ground some six to eight feet directly before the initiate, who is also sitting spread-legged upon the ground," and a "significant moment in initiation comes" when he "recognizes his or her ancestor or troubling spirit in the virtual image of the mirror."[286] R. E. Dennett wrote in 1906 of the Vili diviner who held a mirror. Only this diviner was "allowed to look into it, to discover the successor of the defunct Maluango, made, as they say in the image of God. This mirror-gazing is called Ku Sala Fumu."[287]

The poem in the story acts as a mirror in a similar way. We all engage in "mirror-gazing" when we participate in storytelling. The mirror is the poem in the story. "What the poem is," writes the poet and critic, John Ciardi, "is inseparable from its own performance of itself. The dance is in the dancer and the dancer is in the dance." He insists, "Above all else, poetry is a performance."[288] Ciardi considers metaphor, image, and thought: "'Man,' said the critic Kenneth Burke, 'is the symbol using animal.' He might as well have said 'Man is the metaphorical animal,' for symbolism is simply a special case of metaphor. Carried a step further, the statement might have been, 'Thoughts are made of pictures.'"[289]

METAPHOR

Talking about metaphor in a lecture at the Library of Congress in 1967, James Dickey spoke of "the most miraculous thing in the whole of existence . . . those pictures of the world inside one's head; pictures made of the real world, but pictures that one *owns,* that one infuses with one's own personality. They are fragments of the world that live, not with the world's life, but with ours."[290]

Those "fragments of the world" are at the core of the story's engine, having the power to manipulate members of the audience into the developing metaphor that will in the end dominate all, at once telling a story and constructing the interpretative materials that will give the story its meaning. From that animated interior, the metaphor and its properties eddy until everything becomes a part of the inspirited parallel, from ancient imagery to audience to real world. This audience becomes one with the past, and that unity envelops the surrounding world. It is the storyteller who, with her memory, her imagination, her body, and her voice, controls these elements and the glimmering, fragile metaphor that will glow for the moment of performance, then dissipate.

Transformations are at the heart of the poem in the story; they are organizers of emotions, rhythm, and patterns. Metaphor is reached by means of the narrative, the melodic line, and the patterns, rhythm. It cannot be achieved in any other way. It is the vessel of the story, the form, containing within itself and thereby organizing and giving body to the various elements of the story—and especially to the emotions engendered by the narrative and rhythmic flows of the story. The two different sides of the metaphor are the real-life and the mythic sides. The storyteller's business is to bring them into a parallel relationship. Everything in the story moves to this parallel; an emotional intensity is achieved as the two unlike sets of imagery come into union.[291]

Fantasy or mythic images are "fragments of the world" that summon singular responses. These images are resonant: they are the carriers of tradition. When transported into the story, contemporary images achieve their own fantasy dimension once they are introduced into the secondary world of story. That is, they retain their real-world significance, but take on the coloration of those fantasy images because of the imposition of the parallel relationship.

Metaphor is the result of a combination of emotions and music. Emotions evoked by the images and the musical evocation of those images are given form by the rhythmical patterning imposed on the images and their musical accompaniment. Music is also basic to the patterning activity.

Within this musical context, the diverse images are brought into geared relationship: within the musical context, that is to say, metaphor is born. Because the images and the music evoke emotions from the members of the audience, the members of the audience are woven into the metaphor, are an integral part of the metaphorical process.

Metaphor deals with the unlocking of mystery, the unknown.[292] It must be "fresh and carefully devised," and it expresses reality.[293] Metaphor speaks about one thing in terms that suggest another,[294] involving the presentation of the facts of one category in the idioms appropriate to another,[295] two things active together interacting and in the interaction producing meaning—tenor and vehicle.[296]

RHYTHM AND METAPHOR

Earlier, Freud was quoted regarding his notion that experiencing something identical is pleasurable.[297] Repetition is, said John Hollander, "a powerful and diversified element of formal structures."[298] But, as Freud made clear, repetition for its own sake is not effective: "Novelty is always the condition of enjoyment."[299] And Arthur Koestler concurs, "When rhythm assumes a rigidly repetitive form, it no longer recalls the pulsation of life, but the motions of an automaton; its superimposition on human behavior is degrading."[300] Something more than pure repetition should be aimed at, said Paul Klee, "the way" of the creative process "should not tire us. It must rise higher, branch out excitingly, rise, fall, digress; it must become by turns more or less distinct, broader or narrower, easier or harder." He writes of how "the work becomes structured 'along the way'; the first even rhythm develops into several rhythms. The different segments of the way join into an articulated whole."[301]

Rhythm, writes Seymour Chatman, "is a phenomenon of time: it consists of events which recur with sufficient regularity within a certain time span to allow us to *feel* (technically, *perceive*) that regularity, and hence to imitate it or to predict future recurrences with demonstrable accuracy."[302] It has to do with tension, argues Alfred Corn: "For an artist, rhythm arises from the tension between regularity and irregularity, monotony and variety. . . . The play of regular against irregular rhythm is one of the most important expressive resources available to a poet."[303]

Rhythm is the visible form of the story as the mythic and contemporary images are worked into a poetic relationship. Metaphor is a process, a move to awareness—psychological, emotional awareness. Storytelling involves the combination of mythic and contemporary imagery, emotion, and the patterning that works these materials into metaphor, into the poem in the story.

Fantasy is crucial to this relationship, the fantasy mythic images perhaps more than other images eliciting emotional responses, and the fantasy images are then locked with realistic images. To make metaphor work, the mythic image must be worked into the equation. The reality that the audience discerns within the fantasy images has its own metaphorical effect, an understanding that the fantasy elements are not so distant, not so fantastic after all. We recall the images separately. The image is thus made discontinuous, shorn of its accustomed contexts and relationships. This is crucial for metaphor to occur. Images are then placed into new contexts. The mythic image contains within itself the possibilities of creation, possibilities forever fraught with latent emotion-tapping potential.

Mircea Eliade suggests that "the *actualization* of a symbol is not automatic; it occurs in relation to the tensions and vicissitudes of the social life, and, finally, with the cosmic rhythms."[304] It is a dance-like rhythm that moves the audience to the metaphorical center, a rhythm that is itself the essence of that center. Rhythmical patterning reorders the images, bringing them into unwonted linkages—metaphorical ties—with other images. Patterning reshapes the images, removes them from their normal contexts into an interaction that produces the metaphor. I. A. Richards has argued that the effect of the rhythm of a poem "is not due to our perceiving pattern in something outside us, but to our becoming patterned ourselves."[305]

Two lines move to metaphor, the narrative line and the poetic rhythmic line. It is the combination of these that results in metaphor: the poetic line in the story organizes narrative linearity. The metaphorical center of the story is dependent on the melodic line, the narrative line, at the same time that it is in the process of subverting that line. That combination of melodic or narrative line and poetic rhythmical line is the crucial story-making operation, its mechanism. The driving force of narrative, the melodic line, is also the driving force of story performance. Interfere with the narrative, and the performance comes to a confusing end. Two things are critical: the narrative or melodic line and the mythic rhythmical core. One without the other is only a story's shadow.

Transformations that occur on the surface of the story are woven into that metaphorical nucleus, themselves a part of and evocator of that nucleus. The storyteller unleashes considerable poetic force here: the music of the images themselves, the rhythmical binding of those images through patterning, and the new rhythms that are both producers and product of metaphor. This drive to metaphor occurs within the context of frames that provide artistic boundaries.

EMOTIONS AND METAPHOR—A SUMMARY

Performance involves the gathering of the emotions and images into a performance; there is a transformation of imagery, a move to the liminal, a mythic center. Liminality, transformation, change are the materials of metaphor. The audience is itself on the periphery, in a state of limbo, in a liminal position, and the audience becomes the poem in the story, its feelings the poetic heart of the story.

Metaphor is made possible through emotion,[306] which necessarily weaves the members of the audience into the metaphorical process, unifying the mythic and the contemporary images, even as it is elicited by such imagery. This is the crucial movement of the story: patterns gather up this welter of emotions. The images, patterned, are worked into the metaphorical heart of the stories where meaning resides.

This is the music of the storytelling process. Metaphor, constructed of the two kinds of imagery, becomes suffused with emotion, as the emotions of individual members of the audience become worked into the form of the story. The members of the audience are a part of the story's texture which is constructed of their own emotions as evoked by the story's images and also by the memories that they have of other renderings of the images and by the biographical-cultural-historical experiences that are conjured by the images.

The storyteller awakens dormant or moody emotions, feeling-inclinations, and brings them into openly felt and expressed feelings. The storyteller works "'inclinations' (or 'motives'), 'moods,' 'agitations' (or 'commotions')" into feelings, which are distinguished from inclinations, moods, and agitations as "occurrences." These feelings are "thrills, twinges, pangs, throbs, wrenches, itches, prickings, chills, glows, loads, qualms, hankerings, curdlings, sinkings, tensions, gnawings and shocks."[307] This diversity of emotions from the diverse members of the audience is mixed into the story, deepening and enriching its form.

At the same time that this mixing of emotion-charged images is occurring, other emotional activities are taking place. The rhythmical patterning generates its own brand of emotional release, that provided by regularity. The storyteller manipulates this regularity, injecting dissonant images that break the routine of the pattern. And there are images that are not emotion-charged, images that alter or interfere with the regularity.

Taken together, mythic and real-life imagery, narrative (or the melodic line) and rhythmic organization, and emotions generated and controlled by these, result in the performance, during which all aspects of the story are blended into a seemingly indissoluble whole. That is the illusion of storytelling—and we allow the storyteller almost complete access to our emotions. It gives form to audiences' lives for the moments of performance, and they keep returning to story because they routinely thirst for that order . . . and they routinely lose it, only to return again and again to the storytelling font, to sources, origins. Storytelling performance is a process that takes an audience deeper into itself, into the well-springs of its cultural roots. It is a mythic experience, bringing those roots into sharp conjunction with present-day experiences, giving those present-day experiences a form and a meaning that they do not in themselves have, making the ultimate poetic argument, that members of the audience are nothing until they blend their past and their present. Stories are composed of the scraps and parings of human lives, lived lives and dreamed lives, each shard a latent likeness of the larger mythic reality that forms the backdrop, the meaning ultimately, to daily existence—virtual images that are reconstructed within the members of the audience by a combination of memory, participation, and the artistry of the performer. That is the ritual nature of the story, a mythic retelling using the images of the present that have no meaning without the emotion-evocative images of the past. Emotion is at once the path to the past and the glue that fuses past and present in meaningful union.

Finally, there is the move to ritual, the full performance—performer and audience, the past artistic, cultural, personal, and historical experiences of performer, of audience, the prism of emotions engendered by these experiences, then worked into form by the metaphorical movement of the performance, the storyteller controlling the flow of those emotions and the working of those emotions into form.

Performance allows two essential movements to transpire, that between narrative flow and rhythmic patterning, and, within the story, that between real-life images and mythic images. The first movement (narrative flow and rhythmic patterning) is the external face of the story; the second movement (real-life and mythic images brought into union) is its internal workings. The internal movement, composed of the emotions of the audience evoked by the mythic imagery, occurs within the frame of narrative and rhythm: the combination of these is story, and the combination assures the evoking of emotions of the audience and the working of these into form.

It is the music of performance that makes it possible for the mythic images to mirror our lives, to create metaphors of our feelings, to make members of audiences more than an audience, to make them a part of the performance itself.

METAPHOR: MIRRORING IN "RAMAITSOANALA"

At her home of marriage, Ramaitsoanala is reborn. The mother has robbed her daughter of her identity, yet she regularly returns to assist her when the girl's removed eyes shed tears, which means, in the language of storytelling, that she is teaching her daughter to be a worthy woman. She teaches her by doing her tasks, making mats and weaving silk, sewing clothes, and finally restoring her daughter's beauty, a mark that the child has an identity, that she has become a full woman, that she can now take her proper place in her home of marriage as a complete woman and a knowledgeable wife. This is the reincorporation stage of her puberty ritual. The tasks pattern continues to link Ramaitsoanala and Ravorombe as a single entity, the fantasy character poetically revealing the psychological indecision being experienced by the youth who is undergoing a transformation.

Ramaitsoanala's liminal state is her incomplete state. The ordeal is the move from incompleteness to completeness, with the ambiguous attitudes of the mother—now hindering, now assisting the transition—revealing the ambiguity of the real-life character. She is leaving her birdness behind, as she emerges into full womanhood.

If this is the story of Ramaitsoanala's puberty rite of passage, it is also the story of her mother's contradictory feelings as she prepares her daughter for adulthood. Those mother's feelings are mirrors of the internal struggle of Ramaitsoanala. The fantasy mother, and the patterns that swirl around her, become the poem in this story, a poem fashioned of metaphor, the essence of poetry and therefore of storytelling.

Notes on Performance

NOHATYULA MIYEKI

June 28, 1975

She directs the rhythmic movements of the narrative with her hands, forefinger often outstretched, a supplementary movement when complementary gestures are not being used. An abstract movement, frequently growing out of very particular complementary gestures. Her hands also act as "stage directions." There are a lot of directions in her performances, as she moves things about on the stage—that is, the space that she carves out for the verbal and, mainly, nonverbal elements of the performance, moving characters on, moving them off, calling them on, pushing them off. Her hands also provide time-passage movement, usually an abstract motion. Complementary gestures become more important as she herself takes the roles of characters, and acts, mimes. She points to various characters, directions, things that are "off stage." She shows dimensions of things, people. But when the attention is on a character, she becomes that character, gestures it, mimes it. When she is out of the role of a character, then she assumes the role of storyteller, and as such she moves things and characters around her "stage." Note then that she has two important roles to play: as a storyteller and as the characters in the story. These two roles define her functions in her performances, and may have much to do with her gestures and body movement. When she is in the role of a character, her gestures are more complementary. When she is telling the story, she is more apt to be supplementary . . . though not always—there are complementary gestures in her role as storyteller, too. There is the rhetoric of the storyteller, mainly figuring in her role as storyteller, not as character. As storyteller, there is a full range of supplementary (sometimes quasi-complementary) gestures: gestures of emphasis, punctuation gestures showing ends and beginnings of sequences, for example. These seem very important.

We can now isolate complementary and supplementary gestures, functions of the performer as character and storyteller, storytelling having its own special range of gestures, for example, punctuation, emphasis, other gestures that are rhetorical. Then she is Nohatyula Miyeki, storyteller. But she can suddenly submerge herself in her character, and she is no longer Nohatyula Miyeki.

Nohatyula Miyeki

The performer does everything a character does. When she goes beyond character, she reverts to her role as storyteller, and gestures are apt to become more abstract. Note, of course, that she is always in her role as storyteller. When she creates characters, she is still in her role as storyteller. Thus: Nohatyula Miyeki as person; Nohatyula Miyeki as person, as storyteller; Nohatyula Miyeki as person, as storyteller, as character in the story.

There is bound to be a certain amount of abstraction in any case, because actions like eating are mimed. Gestures become more abstracted with walking actions, because the actual walking motions are tightened, telescoped, symbolized. For passage of time, very abstract; usually gestures and body movement are involved.

A Gcaleka woman's use of *heyi!* to mark divisions of her narrative. Bonisile's *ngoku ke,* Mhlangabezi's *hayi ke,* Mjithane's gesture-device.[308] How do these dividing elements in a narrative work? What are the divisions? Are these significant? Similar in structure and image? Compare other narratives by children. Compare these divisions with songs: Do songs perform the same function?

June 20, 1975

Gesture helps to make the form, the inner form, of the narrative performance perceptible and comprehensible. At the same time, of course, it is integral to the external form of the work. External form: The spoken words, the silences, gestures, body movements, facial drama, the audience, the place of performance. Internal form: The feelings trapped in the materials of the external form. The internal forms are expressed by and in the external forms. The feelings that compose the internal forms are made perceptible and comprehensible by the external forms. But we are not dealing with form as opposed to content here: these are one and the same thing. For oral narrative performance, the external forms are obvious. But what are the internal forms, and how are they manifested in the external forms? How are they revealed? released?

June 22, 1975

The reasoning process takes place against a regular background characterized by repetition, a grid. But why repetition? How do the images work with repetition? How do the images work generally?

The image and narrative. Discursive reasoning: How does it work? Why the image? The image and feeling: the image evokes and holds feeling, but it is not feeling itself; it is not composed of feeling. Is it held together by feeling? or is its function limited to evoking feeling? Yet it evokes feeling. Is its evocative function more important than its narrative role?

What precisely is the image? How is it constructed? And of what? How is it retained in the tradition over the years? How does it change over time? How does it hold feeling? Is the holding of feeling within an image the purpose of repetition of image? Once trapped in the image, feeling is kept there through repetition of the image. Is this so? And what then does repetition do to the feeling trapped in the image? Heighten it? Dissipate, dilute it? Repetition of the feeling-trapped-in-the-image: this image is then blended with yet other images which evoke and hold yet other (related?) feelings.

November 6, 1975

Gestures: Do they become more pronounced during verbal repetition? Implications of this.

November 10, 1975

Presence of the body of the performer: real body, artistic body, and social body, with the artistic body mediating between the physical and social bodies. The artistic body indoctrinates the physical body, makes it the social body. The body of the performer is the center of the performance; all flows from it. The hands help, the body movements condition all aspects of the performance.

November 25, 1975

Expansible images and patterned sets have obvious layering characteristics: certain images are precisely repeated—not necessarily a lexical precision but an image precision, with new data being provided and processed with each repetition, whether that new data are verbally new or experientially new, achieved simply through the layering process and not by means of new words. This process is carried to a new level with parallel image sets, in which there are no longer identical images or an obvious verbal representation. But the process remains the same. The layering process is retained, but now it is a structural layering, bringing diverse image sets into relationship, and making possible much more complex message-communication. Disguise as a plot factor. Illusion. Mediate between conflicting categories. Categories may be very different, of different weights. Resolve problems and opposites.

A Storyteller Guards the Poem in Her Story

The new metaphor is a miracle, like the creation of life.
—Donald Hall, *The Pleasures of Poetry*

Stories are constructed improvisationally within a traditional frame that provides a loom that challenges a storyteller's freedom. The melody that is the narrative thread evokes strong emotions which are softened, leavened, balanced by rhythmic patterns imposed on the narrative by the performer. Themes flow from this musical relationship. Melody, rhythms, and themes grow out of the organization of words and silences. Meaning is this complex nexus of word and sound, feeling, silence. Narrative time, fragmented, is reshaped into precisely defined melodies, which are worked rhythmically into metaphor. That metaphor, at once familiar and arcane, approachable and mysterious, is the center of the storyteller's activity. The storyteller's words are liberated when they are moved into a metaphorical connection; the emotions engendered by those words are knotted into new shapes, with a shimmeringly familiar aura about them, but normal human endeavor takes on new dimensions, and, when these inner images are mythic, is given an ancient resonance. The storyteller has this in her imagination as she tells her story. A story may be more complex than its surface may suggest, so that when it is worked within another art form, like film, distortions may result if care is not taken that the integrity of this inner poem is preserved. This is what concerned Olive Schreiner, the South African writer, when her novel, *The Story of an African Farm,* was being considered as the subject for a motion picture film. She created a set of characters who are mythic in the sense that they are caricatures, farcical renderings a clear distance from reality. Within the context of those mythic characters are sets of real-life characters, and the storyteller, in revealing their stories, links them to these fantasy characters. When the realistically drawn characters are linked to the mythic characters, metaphor is created, and the combination of characters and their trance-like interactions become the poem in the story.

A Poem in a Story

The story takes place on a farm in the Karoo Desert in South Africa. The farm is owned by a middle-aged woman, Tant' Sannie. Her stepdaughter is Em, a gentle and innocent girl. Em's cousin, an orphan, and the central character of the story, is Lyndall, who is ambitious and independent. On the farm are an old German overseer, Otto, and his sensitive, dreamy son, Waldo. The Karoo, drought-stricken, hot, is the backdrop for the unfolding of their stories. Lyndall constantly strives against Tant' Sannie, and she and Waldo have a close relationship. A trickster rogue called Bonaparte Blenkins comes to the farm, woos and wins Tant' Sannie, and when she responds favorably to him, he moves to take total control of the farm: he fires old Otto, who dies the same night. Then, having turned Tant' Sannie against Waldo, he ties him to a pole and beats him. But when Tant' Sannie's young and wealthy niece, Trana, comes for a visit, Blenkins courts her. But Tant' Sannie overhears his expressions of love, and throws him out. It is Waldo who gives him food and money, before Blenkins disappears. Tant' Sannie has leased half of her farm to Gregory Rose, who proposes to Em, then falls in love with Lyndall. Both Lyndall and Waldo venture forth. Waldo goes off to seek his fortune and wisdom. He never meshes reality and dream. Lyndall cannot accept Waldo, although he seems prepared in the end to accept her. She is his guide and measure, as she pushes forth to expand women's boundaries, and seems to fail. Lyndall departs with an old lover, and Gregory Rose seeks her. He finds her as she lies dying after childbirth, and he looks after her. Then, Gregory Rose, because Lyndall so desired, marries Em, and Waldo, lonely and sad, returns to the farm.

In her preface to *The Story of an African Farm,* Olive Schreiner writes, "Here nothing can be prophesied," referring to the setting, the Karoo. This is the story of children, two of whom die young. Em will continue to live, but much altered. Marriage to Gregory Rose cannot be what it might have been before he met and loved Lyndall. Em and Gregory Rose change. They will not evolve into Tant' Sannie and Bonaparte Blenkins, though there were earlier indications that they might. But Waldo and Lyndall change things. They are dreamers, not sufficiently realistic; they can only die. Em is a survivor, as are Sannie and Blenkins. Sannie is a caricature of the married woman, going through men because that is the way it was meant to be. Blenkins is also a parody, the exploiter of women. And that is the way Gregory Rose starts out. In fact, Em begins modeled on her mother, and Gregory Rose begins patterned on Bonaparte Blenkins. This is the story's basic parallel. But Em and Gregory Rose come into contact with Waldo and Lyndall who do not fit into these marriage stereotypes at all. The humorous first part of the novel is crucial to the development of the second part. The Blenkins-Sannie/Gregory-Em set is opposed to the Waldo-Lyndall set. The "youth & genius & beauty" of Lyndall and Waldo are "counter-poised," to use Schreiner's words, against the temporal realities of the world of Sannie, Blenkins, Em, and Gregory Rose. Waldo and Old Otto are paralleled: Lyndall loves them both. Old Otto will be destroyed by Blenkins and Sannie. Waldo will not remain with Gregory Rose and Em. Does he see them going the way of Blenkins and Sannie?

It is a story that is at once realistic and mythic. The basic pattern consists of the two pairs, Bonaparte Blenkins and Tant' Sannie, and Gregory Rose and Em. Blenkins and Sannie are exaggerated and unreal; Sannie is a machine, and Blenkins is so cynical as to be devoid of feeling. Gregory Rose and Em are patterned on them. But they are sympathetically drawn characters. Slowly, the storyteller brings the two realistic characters into metaphorical embrace with the two mythic characters, and the poem in the story is formed. But that inner space in the story is made complex by Lyndall, Waldo, and Old Otto, who go against the basic pattern. It is the pairing of the two dreamers, Waldo and Em, that deepens the metaphorical relationship between the other two pairs of characters, and so renders the poem in the story dense and rich.

Later, when the story was to be made into a motion picture, Schreiner would struggle against any interference with that poetic interior.

The poem in the story is the quest for the unity of reality and dream, yet the impossibility of the attainment of that unity. In a letter Schreiner wrote to the Rev. J. T. Lloyd, a clergyman whom she met in 1892 after he gave a lecture at the Kimberley exhibition on "Literary Life in South Africa," she observed, "I have never been able to conceive of God, & man & the material Universe as distinct from one another. The laws of my mind do not allow of it. When I was a little child of five & sat alone among the tall weeds at the back of our house, this perception of the unity of all things, & that they were alive, & that I was part of them, was as clear & overpowering to me as it is today. It is the one thing I am never able to doubt.

"The agony of my childhood especially from the time I was 9 till I was fourteen, was the impossibility of reconciling this direct *perception*."[309]

A Page from a Letter

OLIVE SCHREINER

I don't quite know what answer to give as to the proposal about the S. A. F. Long ago Wilson Barrett (a celebrated actor & theatre owner in the old days who was a friend of mine wanted to dramatise *[The Story of an African Farm]*, & told me I should make money from it) but I scornfully refused. I should of course rather *not* have anything of mine on a stage or bioscope: but if there was any chance of my making any money by it, I must consider it. I don't know in such a case whether one would be paid anything! I need never read what was said about it, & need never go to see it!

I don't quite see either what there is to put on a bioscope. The commonplace parts, by being shamefully exaggerated i.e. the parts about Bonaparte and Tant' Sannie could be made humorously perhaps—but of course they were just put in to counter-poise the tragedy & sorrows of Lyndall & Waldo—& that tragedy cannot be put into a picture because it is purely intellectual & spiritual. The tragedy was not at all vulgar tragedy that Lyndall had a baby got a disease & died, or that Waldo died suddenly. That is a common vulgar tragedy enough. The tragedy of whole book the eternal tragedy of youth & genius & beauty struggling against the adverse *material* conditions of life & being beaten by them. It is a cry out against *"fate."* How any of this could get into a picture I don't see. It must be absolutely vulgarised. I hardly see how without altering it, it could be made dramatic to the eye. For instance Waldo when he hears of Lyndall's death would be simply a young man howling, & the last scene where he sits in the sun & the chickens sit on him *might* seem simply comic. Still if there were a chance of my earning anything by it I should perhaps. If I could have a talk with the actress. I have seen only two things that were so well done as to be "artistic" in a bioscope, "Les Miserable" by Victor Hugo, a little Russian thing that moved me to tears, taken from some Russian. It was so *splendidly* acted, that you read the whole *character* of the people, all they were suffering & thinking simply in their faces.

Of course the whole point of An African Farm turns on Lyndall being a child of seventeen when she dies, with a tiny body with dark brown hair & large intellectual brown eyes. If she had been a full grown woman of twenty or twenty two the book couldn't have been written. Because Lyndall at 20 would have been much too *wise* to act as she did, & a fair haired blue eyed Lyndall would have been impossible, because then her character would have been different! If I were in London I should like to see the lady & have a talk with her: but I doubt whether without altering the story they could make it telling.[310]

A Page from a Journal

July 20, 1975

Rites of passage orchestrate one's movement through life; such ritualistic movements are often the focus of stories, as stories themselves become ritualistic experiences. Image sequences in stories sometimes parallel cultural rites of passage without actually directly reflecting such rites. They may be a continuous undercurrent, tacitly connecting the linear images to this universal pulse. The movement of characters in the story parallels similar movements in real life but in abstracted or symbolic fashion.

—The narrative usually concentrates on a single rite, but in longer stories, the rites may be repeated and themselves become images capable of being worked into patterns.

—Movement in a performance is never precisely that of reality. The performer may mime walking, for example, but this miming is not a precise reproduction of life: the movement is already abstracted to a degree.

—Some storytellers use SILENCES as in music—beats and rhythmic patterns, harmonizing (tonally and rhythmically) with the verbal elements.

—The *songs* in stories—the music as well as the words have a unique aesthetic relationship to the prose elements and the images of the narrative (in the same way that gestures and body movement do), but the prose elements are never wholly prosaic: there is a wave-like rhythmical movement linking them to the songs, as they eddy out from the songs. Nor need stories have actual songs in them to be musical.

Postlude

> Accordingly, he did not know whether her case was to be put down as good or bad.
> —Ryunosuke Akutagawa, "Rashomon"

We are a symphony. The storyteller plays us like a finely tuned instrument. The mythic images call forth cardinal emotions of love, fear, joy, hate, and we provide the emotional nuances from our own storytelling and biographical experiences. It is all music, the music of human feeling. Fernando Pessoa wrote, "My soul is a hidden orchestra; I do not know what instruments—strings and harps, drums and tambours—I pluck and thrum within me. I only hear the symphony."[311]

Are stories true? Our responses are truth, and the story thereby becomes, if not truth itself, an avenue to truth, a form, a vessel shaping our emotional responses. This is truth.

We all have our stories. The storyteller weaves our stories into her universal story, and so we become a part of the music of all time, our experiences resonating through the past, assuring us that we have value, that we are not alone, giving our uniqueness an aura of the universal, a pervasive context and meaning.

We all have our stories, or story-fragments. The storyteller gives these wholeness and community, so that my song is joined to your song, and a symphony is born. Here is the essence of metaphor. It is evanescent, but for a moment the music of story weaves into the linear movement of our lives, imposing its rhythm on that linear motion and recombining it into a grand myth, a universal story. There may be more than one poem at the heart of the story.

Long ago, the Mpondomise lived on the Hlangeni near the Dedesi where the Mzimvubu River comes from, and in spreading they came as far as Umthatha. They began with Phahlo, to be circumcised by putting up a

woman—Mamani by name, born of the wife of the Great House of Phahlo—to become an heiress on the death of the said chief. This did not satisfy the other house and there began to be the Right Hand side.
Phahlo begot Hlontso the heir, and Mgabisa on the Right.
Hlontso begot Mgcambe; and he begot Myeki; and he begot Matiwane; and he begot Mhlontlo. . . .[312]

THE STORY

The End of Mahlangeni

Then, a chief of Matatiele, Magwayi, refused to pay his taxes, the tax that the Mpondomise were supposed to pay. The magistrate of Qumbu District his excellency, Hamilton Hope, said, "Mhlontlo, there is a subject of yours who refuses to pay his taxes. He has been warned. Now a force must be sent out."[313]

Mhlontlo said, "That won't do! I cannot send out a force. My wife, a daughter of Sarhili, has just died. According to Mpondomise custom, I cannot even begin to talk about an armed force. I must remain silent, and not speak about such things as armed forces."

His excellency, Hamilton Hope, then said, "You're a liar! You're a liar! You said that you would obey the government. And now, you're not being obedient to the government! You're a liar!"

Mhlontlo calmly departed, and when he got home a Mpondomise meeting was called. All arrived. He slaughtered a bull, and the meat was eaten. When the eating was at an end, he said, "Mpondomise, I have called you together because I have been insulted by the magistrate. Did you hear?"

They said, "We heard!"

He said, "What do you say?"

Gxumisa said, "That magistrate should be expelled for what he has done! The government must be told that the magistrate must go. You, a king, should never be insulted! The magistrate must be driven out!"

He said, "What do you say, Mpondomise? Considering that I have been so insulted?"

The Mpondomise said, "We all agree!"

"We say the magistrate should be expelled!"

When that had been concluded, a colorful citizen of Mpondomiseland, Mahlangeni, a great provocateur of Mpondomiseland, very great, got up. If he happened to come to any homestead in which a creature was being slaughtered, meat with the name gebhe was cut and placed before him while he was eating—some meat from the chest of the slaughtered animal was cut and placed before him, this most prominent firebrand, who surpassed all others living among the Mpondomise.

Mahlangeni, this agitator who rivaled all the fomenters of those days, said, "What is this you're saying? What cowardice are you speaking? Just name me!"

It was said, "*Ntsuke-ntsuke*!"

And he said, "Please name me!"

It was said, "*Ntsuke-ntsuke*!" and he took his gelding and drove it through the kraal fence, then fell over with it inside the kraal. He swung it back, and drove it so that it came to fall on the outside of the kraal.

He said, "Mpondomise, who is this who's insulted? The king of the Mpondomise! Insulted!"

The Mpondomise said, "This magistrate must be expelled!"

"It's not the government that insulted the king! It is this person!"

"He must be expelled!"

And the meeting came to an end.

When the meeting had ended, his excellency, Joseph [Hamilton Hope], called a meeting, and it was held out on the veld. When everyone arrived there on the open veld, he said, "I still insist that you go to Magwayi! He refuses to pay taxes!"

Mhlontlo then said, "Well, I have heard what you have to say. But I shall not be able to go. Gxumisa will take my place. He shall listen to all the directives that you make. Here, then, are your Mpondomise. You shall speak to them. Come here, Sunduza!"

Sunduza was the son of the missionary; they went off.

Then his excellency, Hope, got up and said, "Mpondomise, I have called you to insist that you go to Magwayi in force, because he's been disobedient! I've talked with him a long time, Mpondomise!"

As the magistrate spoke, Mahlangeni said, "Please say '*Ntsuke-ntsuke*!'"—that flamboyant incendiary over there at the royal residence.

It was said, "*Ntsuke-ntsuke*!"

He said, "I say, 'Please say, "*Ntsuke-ntsuke*!"'"

It was said, "*Ntsuke-ntsu*—"

Oh! He leapt up and fell on the magistrate with a spear. He stabbed him. And he stabbed another person, and another—for there were three white men there, and he stabbed all three of these white men. As he was stabbing the third one, Thethani, a policeman who was nearby, shot at

Mahlangeni, but he missed. When the shot missed, Mahlangeni jumped on the policeman, then he ran into the tent.

As Mahlangeni was entering the tent, Mhlontlo arrived. "What is going on?" And he restrained Mahlangeni.

But all three of the white men had died.

Mhlontlo restrained him. "No!"

"These policemen?"

"No!"

Then there was a pause. They were wondering what to do. They did not know what to do, what would happen now.

Mhlontlo said, "Let all the white people come here."

It was necessary that the white people go to the mission station at Shawbury, for otherwise they would be hurt by the Mpondomise. There was confusion now, and some people broke into shops and looted them.

When the shops had been looted—in Tsolo here, there was a magistrate, [Alexander R.] Welsh. When he heard what had happened, he ran; he ran to the jail over there at Somerville together with the whites who were present. They went into the jail.

Then Mditshwa went there.

"I'm here, Welsh! Come out, I'll go with you to Umthatha."

"No, I'm afraid of you! You must come in!"

"No, come out! I'll go with you! But I won't come in there!"

Then Mditshwa called Silothile and Mngcothane. Silothile's offspring now lives in the place called Noziyongwane, and Mngcothane's progeny lives on Tsolo Mountain. He called those two men, "Go and report at Umthatha. Say that Welsh should be fetched." So they set out.

After a few days, an army of Mpondo arrived, led by these two men. There were also some white men with them, and Mngcothane and Silothile came along with this army. They came to this place which is now Somerville. These men had been told to take care that nothing was done by the Mpondomise to help this magistrate in any way, and so these two men departed and were rewarded by the government. Mngcothane was given a chieftaincy, and Silothile was given a chieftaincy, and then they departed.

Now came the armed might of the white man. Well, there was not even a fight. The Mpondomise were scattered, scattered in this land; the Mpondomise were scattered now. On the day of Khohlombeni, which is over there in Qumbu, the Mpondomise were gathered in great numbers, and the white army came. The army of the white men came there. The armies of the Mpondomise were routed, the Mpondomise were pushed over cliffs, they were surrounded in that marsh of Khohlombeni. Then, in the night, they got up and walked in the water, and broke through. At dawn, the government armies poured fire on that place where the Mpondomise armies had been. When they found that there was no response, they let up. In the morning, they saw that the Mpondomise forces had broken through. So the white man's armies departed.

When the armies of the white man had gone, one fellow said, "My lord, Mhlontlo, Gxumisa is dead."

Gxumisa was that orator who had spoken briefly during Mhlontlo's meeting. He is that man who had spoken at the meeting at the royal residence, he is the man Mhlontlo had said would command the force that would go to Magwayi's place. They told Mhlontlo how Gxumisa had remained behind—that is to say, he was dead.

Mhlontlo covered himself, and was quiet. Then he got up and said, "Mpondomise, today the government has defeated us. So—those of the mountain, to the mountain! Those of the water, to the water! Let us disperse!"

The Mpondomise said, "How can we do that?"

"Wherever we turn, we'll be stabbed if we dare separate from each other!"

"We'll die fighting!"

He said, "No, if you appear before a group of people and they ask, 'Who are you?' you shouldn't say, 'We're Mpondomise.' You should say, 'We're Tikita,' and when you've said that, the people will know you're not combatants. And they'll leave you alone. They'll even pick you up."

There was agreement that, "Well, we've been defeated!"

Mahlangeni got up then—that man who had stabbed Hope, Hamilton Hope. And he said, "Please say, '*Ntsuke-ntsuke*!'"

It was said, "*Ntsuke-ntsuke*!"

He said, "Please say, '*Ntsuke-ntsuke*!'"

It was said, "*Ntsu—*"

He said, "I'll never go anywhere!"

As he said this, he took a gun and put it here, and said, "I'll not go anywhere myself! I'll stay here!"

The nation dispersed then, the people went in all directions.

And Mhlontlo said, "Let's go to Lesotho!"

Mditshwa said, "No, if we depart from here, the quality of Mpondomise, the Mpondomise ethos, will come to an end. We'll become refugees who'll never have any land! As for me, *I* choose to surrender myself. And when I've done that, I'll be arrested. They might even hang me, if they so desire, but they'll leave these people alone to rebuild the land."

After he had said this, insisting that he would not go to Lesotho, that he would hand himself over, he called the Mpondomise together and took a cloth. He tied it to a long stick, and said that this cloth should be carried to Umthatha to signify that he was surrendering himself. When he had said this, he said, "Nokhaka!" Nokhaka was an important aide of his. "Take this stick!"

Nokhaka said, "I'll be shot by the white men! I won't go!"

Then Mditshwa said, "Edward!" Edward was a lay preacher who had come with Bishop Key. "You can speak the white man's language, you take this stick!"

Edward said, "Have I, a Thembu, been wrong to fight for you to the very end of the war that you should now order me to go and die over there?"

There was silence, and when it was quiet an important man whose name was Nomlala shot up. He said, "Mditshwa, be quiet a bit and let us of the Nomlala clan speak. Manqophu!" Manqophu was his son."Thembani!" Thembani was also his son. "The chief here is speaking. What do you say?"

"We have nothing to say."

As they said this, another fellow, Sibhalala of Somhlahlo, whose offspring lives right here now, got up. He rose and took the cloth, and said, "Let's go!" and they left, going to Umthatha.

They were gone for some time, then they returned.

"Well, the army is going to come. If Mditshwa has indeed been pacified, they'll be able to tell when he comes forward to this army. They'll shoot overhead. If he doesn't retaliate, but comes ahead, then it'll be all right."

The army arrived. When it had arrived, when it had come into sight, the Mpondomise stood still. Shots were fired!

The Mpondomise said, "This self-deliverance idea is a sham! We're being shot at just as we think that we're calmly surrendering ourselves."

They fled to the forests.

Those other three men got up then and went forward, they went to the army.

"What's the matter now? Why do you run? We said we'd only shoot over your heads! Where is Mditshwa?"

"Never mind! Come, I'll take you to him!"

Thembani, Sibhalala, and Manqophu went now to where Mditshwa was.

Well, Mditshwa emerged, and he gave himself up. And so he was in the hands of the government. Peace was made.

Now then, concerning Mahlangeni over there—the man who had said he should have been given ammunition belts, guns, bullets, that man who had remained there. Before long, the armies heard him, and they went to the place where he was. An exchange of fire took place there. Mahlangeni was dug in among the rocks, and—well, he shot it out. They tried everything, but they could not discover where he was. Then the soldiers came back and waited for him; they took out their food, and ate. Day after day, they waited. Then one morning, there was a fog. And when the fog had lifted—here he is, plucking maize cobs right there in the army camp! He was picking maize cobs! By the time he was hurrying to his horse, they had seen him. They gave chase, pursuing him to his stronghold. As they approached his hideaway, he looked back and saw Larry riding hard on a gelding, on Gcazimbana, Mhlontlo's gelding that had already been taken as spoils from Mhlontlo.

He said, "Larry! Larry, hurry! You'll hold the seed with your mouth! You'll know that you met Mahlangeni today! You'll surely know all about it!"

He drove the gelding harder.

When Mahlangeni got to his stronghold, he jumped off, and, drawing his gun, said, "Now is the right moment!" As he drew, he was hit by a bullet from Larry's revolver.

He fell, and that was the end of Mahlangeni.

It was the end of Mahlangeni, the one who had stabbed those three white men. That was his finish.[314]

A SECOND VIEW OF THE STORY

The Trial of Mhlontlo

The events of the early eighties when the Basutos [Sotho], Pondos [Mpondo] and Pondomise [Mpondomise] rose in rebellion are brought prominently before us by the trial of Umhlonhlo [Mhlontlo] for the murder of Messrs. Hope, Warren, and Henman at Qumbu in 1880, which will take place at the Eastern Districts Court on Friday next.

Great interest was evinced at the preliminary hearing which took place at Kingwilliamstown on December the 2nd 1903, and succeeding days; when Umhlonhlo the Pondomise chief was brought before Mr. Dick,

Acting R.M., charged with the murder of Mr. Hamilton Hope (Magistrate of Qumbu), and Messrs. Henman and Warren at Qumbu in 1880. The accused appeared in dock neatly dressed in a dark grey suit and white sweater. Throughout the proceedings the accused conducted himself with a quiet dignity. The prosecution was conducted by Mr. R. W. Rose-Innes. Mr. H. Squire Smith, assisted by Mr. Gush, of Umtata [Umthatha], appeared for the defense.

Jantjo Boy, an aged Hottentot [Khoi], said he knew the late Mr. Hope. Witness was working for Messrs. Warren and Henman. He was present when his masters were killed. He could not recollect the date, but it was over 20 years ago. The party consisted of Messrs. Hope, Warren, Henman and Davis, and 6 natives [Africans], including the witness. At Sulenkama, the party found Umhlonhlo and his people. They then outspanned. By Mr. Hope's orders eight oxen were killed and given to Umhlonhlo and his people. After the oxen had been eaten, the natives started a dance and formed a ring. Messrs. Hope, Warren, Henman and Davis, accompanied by Umhlonhlo, went over to the ring where the natives were dancing. Witness understood Kafir [Xhosa], and followed what was being said. Mr. Hope spoke in English, Mr. Davies acting as interpreter. Mr. Hope said, "I am doing the work that I must do for the Government." Umhlonhlo said, "They're your god, I'm not considered." The latter spoke in Kafir in a very loud voice. Mr. Hope again said he must do the Government work, and do it well. A native from Maitshwa then broke into the ring, held up his assegai [spear], and shouted, "Tomorrow will be the right day." The ring then broke up, the natives firing guns, many being armed in this way, the rest with assegais. Mr. Hope and party then returned to their tents. No more oxen were killed that night. Early next morning, Umhlonhlo was walking up and down between the wagons with Mr. Davis. While witness was preparing breakfast a Basuto chief named Tehama arrived with about 30 mounted men, and rode straight to the ring. That night the Pondomise slept on the veldt, their numbers having increased. They again formed a ring, and started dancing and singing, "Our Satan today is out of heaven, he's on the ground." Witness, continuing, said that Messrs. Hope, Henman, Warren, and Davis went towards the ring. He saw Messrs. Hope, Henman, and Warren go into the ring. Mr. Davis and Umhlonhlo standing outside talking. Witness was saddling the horses when he heard shouts of "he he" from the people in the ring. He looked round and saw Mr. Warren being held in the air on the points of assegais. Mr. Warren brought his hand round for his revolver, but before he could reach it his

Asilita Philiswe Khumalo, a Zulu storyteller

hand fell back. Witness then went into the tent with Matanga, who had a gun. Previous to this witness secured the money from the saddlebags and tied it in his handkerchief round his body. They were told by Mr. Davis to off-load the guns from the wagons, Umhlonhlo standing by at the time the guns and ammunition were placed in lots, and Umhlonhlo pointed out the lots each of his captains were to take. Witness saw the bodies of Messrs. Hope, Warren, and Henman, they had been stripped of their clothing. Mr. Hope's beard had been skinned entirely off his face. One of Umhlonhlo's men asked Mr. Davis how far the guns would carry a bullet, Mr. Davis told him explaining the working of the gun.[315]

A THIRD VIEW OF THE STORY

The Murder of Mr. Hope

Three or four days after my return from Matatiele, Mr. Hope, the Magistrate with Umhlontlo [Mhlontlo], informed me by letter that Umhlontlo had volunteered to raise men for my relief while I was besieged, and had proposed that Hope should accompany the force, but having heard of my escape he sent "to congratulate me, his father, for my escape from Basuto [Basotho] treachery." Hope considered this sympathy and congratulation genuine and spontaneous, inasmuch as many of the headmen, apparently without Umhlontlo's knowledge, had sent similar messages of congratulation; but I was doubtful at least of Umhlontlo's sincerity, for I knew that he was one of the chiefs who had given their adhesion to the Basuto proposal in April. Moreover, I well knew his treacherous and unreliable disposition.

A day or two afterwards Hope proposed to take the field with Umhlontlo and his clan against the rebels. I replied that I could neither suggest nor recommend such a course, for the risk to Hope was too great as he might fall by Umhlontlo's treachery. Nevertheless, if he himself wished it, I would not object, for if he succeeded he would detach Umditshwa [Mditshwa] and the Tembu [Thembu] clans from the rebellion, and to accomplish such an object he was justified in incurring serious risks. In writing thus to Hope, I felt that I myself would have incurred serious risks to secure so great an end.

Mr. Hope then immediately took the field and from Sulinkama, his last resting place, he wrote me a most characteristic note, comparing his position to a game of whist when one may be confident of the game, but finds that his opponent holds the ace of trumps. He added that he was sure of success, for, he held the ace of trumps in his hand. He proceeded to say that Umhlontlo had dined with him, and that he was then quietly sleeping beneath the ammunition wagon.

Two hundred rifles with ammunition had been supplied to Hope without my knowledge, and had I known in time I should have objected; but having heard of the receipt, I directed him to send half the supply to Mr. Thomson who had reliable men in whose hands he could have placed the arms, which would have been of incalculable value to him in his subsequent struggle with the rebels; but Hope kept all, and the following morning they fell into Umhlontlo's hands.

Mr. Hope's bright vision was but for one night; the following morning ushered in the darkest tragedy of this dark period. After breakfasting with Hope, Umhlontlo went to muster his men, forming them into a circle and appointing six men who, when Hope and his staff came into the circle, were to stand behind Hope, Warren, and Henman, and at a given signal were to assassinate them from behind. This having been arranged, Umhlontlo went to Hope's tent and told him that all was now ready, and that he was prepared to hand over his people to the Magistrate for his final orders. The two walked arm-in-arm into the fatal circle, the staff following. Calmly and coolly addressing the people, Umhlontlo told them that he had now relinquished them into Mr. Hope's hands, that he would now issue his instructions to them, and they were to obey them. Having said this he took Davis, Mr. Hope's clerk, by the hand, saying he wished to speak to him. This being the appointed signal, the six men stabbed their unsuspecting victims and despatched them. Three Pondos [Mpondo], who had accompanied Umhlontlo, were then directed to proceed to Umqikela [Mqikela] to tell him what they had seen—Umhlontlo adding that Umqikela would now no longer doubt him. The messengers were further entrusted with Hope's gun and horse, which they were directed to take as a present to Ndabankulu, Umqikela's brother. Ten of the Government rifles were subsequently sent as a present to Umqikela. . . .

On the day on which Mr. Hope and his companions were murdered, Stephen Adonis, a Native missionary, laboring among Umhlontlo's people, made his escape and brought the tidings to Mr. Welsh, who at once with his family and that of the Rev. Mr. Stuart and Mrs. Stuart, and the family of Mr. Leary, took refuge in the gaol, a small stone building with an iron roof, the only defensible one on the Residency, the others being roofed with thatch.

In this small space the three families with other Europeans, and three or four Native policemen, were shut up for fourteen days under the most distressing circumstances. I repeatedly endeavored to open communication with Mr. Welsh without effect, and when matters appeared hopeless and the death of the party either by starvation or violence appeared certain, Major Elliot, the Chief Magistrate of Umtata, arranged for their rescue, through Nqwiliso, whose men were accompanied by the Rev. Mr. Morris, Wesleyan missionary with Nqwiliso, and a small band of European volunteers from Umtata, whose names, if I had them, I would gladly record in the report.[316]

A FOURTH VIEW OF THE STORY

The White Men's Bullets

Ngxabane related a legend of *Mhlontlo,* son of Matiwane, the most illustrious of the Mpondomise warrior-kings and the most renowned for his power of magic. According to the legend, when Mhlontlo was being doctored in order to make him immune to witchcraft, he was locked up in a special *phempe* [a temporary shelter] which was then burnt down completely. But lo and behold! *Mhlontlo* emerged unscratched, without a mark on his body. The medicine-men stood amazed and said: "Mhlontlo, you are the first King to go through this ordeal. I have doctored other Kings, but when it came to the burning of the *phempe,* invariably their courage deserted them and they refused to endure the ordeal of fire. Since you have shown such valor and endurance, I say that no bullet will ever have the power to slay you."

"And true enough," Ngxabane went on, "when, during *Honis* [Hope's] *war,* the White soldiers surrounded Mhlontlo in a cave and aimed their guns at him several times, they failed to kill him, for he was guarded by two dogs—though nobody knows whence they came—who caught the White men's bullets and swallowed them."[317]

A FIFTH VIEW OF THE STORY

Hamilton Hope Is Dead!

When the Basuto [Sotho] rebellion broke out, animated by a desire to serve his country, he volunteered to take the field with

Eva Ndlovu, a Ndebele storyteller

Umhlontlo [Mhlontlo] and his men in order to check the rebels, and to support such of the Basutos as desired to remain on the side of Government. For this purpose he went out for a few days, and to all appearance succeeded in what he had undertaken to do. Being desirous of committing Umhlontlo still further to our side, Mr. Hope proposed to go a step further, and take Umhlontlo out against the rebels.

Warnings of treachery came in from all sides. The Chief Magistrate, in telegraphing to Government, used these expressive words, "Hope has heroically gone out with his life in his hand, alone with a treacherous devil."

This message was communicated to Mr. Hope, who was further informed by the Chief Magistrate, that in what he was doing he was incurring a serious risk and danger to himself; but as the move was originally proposed by Umhlontlo himself, and as Mr. Hope had gone into the thing, true to the chivalrous traditions of his family and name, he stood to his purpose. He believed he could perform an important service to his country, and was prepared to incur any risk in accomplishing this end. Mr. Davis, Mr. Hope's clerk, volunteered to accompany his chief in this dangerous duty, also two young men, named Henman and Warren, from the Chief Magistrate's office at Umtata; but when the intended treachery of Umhlontlo came to Mr. Hope's knowledge, he mentioned it to the young men, and advised them to stay at home, saying that he was prepared to meet the risk and danger alone; but, with generous British hearts, which clime and change do not degenerate, they expressed their determination to stand by Mr. Hope at all hazards.

Henman and Warren fell with Hope. Of Davis, it is said that as his father was for many years Umhlontlo's missionary, and, as his brother now occupies the same position, Umhlontlo saved Davis.

Hamilton Hope is dead! These words will be read with a thrill by thousands in the Cape Colony who had the privilege of his acquaintance, and by whom his sterling qualities and upright manly character were known.

Such calm courage and fortitude as Mr. Hope displayed are virtues of the highest kind. A man may storm a battery or lay his body in the breach, animated by enthusiasm or inspired by the stirring cheers of applauding comrades; but to be exposed to danger for days and nights, with shattered health, in rain and cold, and bear constantly before one the idea of treachery without flinching, requires an amount of fortitude which few men possess; and when the history of the present rebellion is recorded, the names of Hope, Warren, and Henman should be exhibited in bold relief; for though they fell by the hands of treacherous assassins, they fell foremost in their country's cause.

"Died Abner as a fool dieth? Thy hands were not bound, nor thy foot put into fetters. As a man falleth before wicked men, so fellest thou. And all the people wept over him."[318]

The Poem in the Story

MHLONTLO MATIWANE INKOSI YAMAMPONDOMISE[319]

Sisibhekeb' esisibhebhe sakulo *Yokazi,*
Esimpondo zizibhebhelele.
Yinjobonde kaMakrolisa.
Ngudada ngesabhokwe kumakhumsha,
Undlebe zoLudidi ngamaholoholo.
Ingubo kaMakhepe yegush' isikelwe kuye yamalingana.
Ngusiswenye sakwaHala esikhwel' ehasheni.
Esithe sakuba senkundleni satheth' indaba.
NguMandondo, uvungam' axel' inja yakhe,
UBholokondlela, uphila kuzenzela.
Lihashe likaMatiwane elingavumi *kubhosolwa.*
Wakhe wath' *uHope* uyalibhosola,
Lamlahla phantsi unanamhla,
Alaziwa apho laya khona.

MHLONTLO MATIWANE THE CHIEF OF THE MPONDOMISE

He is a flapping thing which is thin, broad, and flat of
Yokazi's,
With broad flat horns.
He is a long thing of Makrolisa.
He is floater with a whip among the foreigners,
The ears of Ludidi and others are hollow.
The sheep blanket of Makhepe has been cut on him and
fits him.
He is a bunch of maize cobs of Hala's place that rides a
horse.
Who related news about the court.
He is Mandondo, he roars like his dog,

Bholokondlela, he thrives through doing for himself.
He is the horse of Matiwane that refuses to be brushed,
Hope, on brushing it,
Was thrown down by it up to this day,
Nobody knows where it went.

A Page from a Journal

January 2, 1968

The storyteller leans forward, pipe tobacco smoke curling around her head: "You begin with the remembered image," she said, "Everything builds on that." But then she sinks back into the shadows, against the rounded wall of her rondavel-style home, only the fired surface of the pipe visible in the darkness. "Yes," she says, "the remembered image. But that's not what the story is all about. That's just the material for its construction." She allows her body to fall deeper into the concealing dark. "If I have to find one really crucial aspect of storytelling, the one that has to do with the ultimate meaning of the story, then that's feeling." She considers this, and then bows her body out of the darkness, and the light of the dimming fire in the center of the rondavel again reveals the elongated face, the deep eyes. "Feeling: without that, there's no story. Without feeling, there is only talk." And now, she is clearly considering image and feeling, not yet entirely pleased with her discourse. "No, there's something more, another critical ingredient. That's repetition, the patterning of the images. There is no feeling without rhythm, no message without rhythm. So these are the three things then . . . image, feeling, rhythm." She seems content now, her body easily moving to a rhythm that she clearly hears but it is a silent rhythm, heard only by her.

Every Poem Has a Story . . .

THIS IS THE POEM . . .

Mon coeur est tout joyeux,
Mon coeur s'envole en chantant,
Sous les arbres de la forêt,
Forêt notre demeure et notre mère,
Dans mon filet j'ai pris
Un petit, tout petit oiseau.
Mon coeur est pris dans le filet,
Dans le filet avec l'oiseau.[320]

My heart is very happy,
My heart soars, singing,
Under the trees of the forest,
The forest: our home and our mother,
In my net I have caught
A tiny bird.
My heart is caught in the net,
In the net with the bird.

. . . AND THIS IS THE STORY . . .

A Baka mother in Cameroon has just given birth to a child.

The storyteller never forgets the music.

Notes
Bibliography
Index

Notes

1. “The storyteller,” said Walter Benjamin, “is the figure in which the righteous man encounters himself” (“The Storyteller” in *Illuminations,* 109).

2. Ryunosuke Akutagawa writes of the death of a twenty-six-year-old man, Kanazawa no Takehiko, who is killed by a sword in a forest. Who killed him? There is the testimony of a woodcutter who thinks he was murdered; a traveling Buddhist priest wonders. A policeman thinks the murderer is the notorious robber, Tajomaru. An old woman, the mother of Masago, Kanazawa’s wife, thinks it was Tajomaru, and wonders where her daughter is. Each adds something, a detail, a comment, an observation, to the story of the man’s death and the woman who accompanied him. And there is also Tajomaru’s confession: he fell in love with Masago, he says, and admits killing Kanazawa in a sword fight. But then there is the story of the wife, Masago, who confesses in a temple that she killed her husband because of the loathing he seemed to express towards her after helplessly watching her and Tajomaru have sex. And then, there is the story by the murdered man himself, as told through a medium: he says that he stabbed himself because he was heartbroken. And as he died, someone “drew the small sword softly out of my breast in its invisible hand.” The same story, from a number of vantages, with a different view, a different cast each time it is told. . . . All we have is the story. “Beyond this was only darkness . . . unknown and unknown” (44).

3. From William Faulkner’s Nobel Prize speech, December 10, 1950.

4. Don Hewitt, *Tell Me a Story,* 1.

5. Adewale Maja-Pearce, “Binding the Wounds,” 50.

6. Sallustius, “On the Gods and the World,” 246.

7. Thoreau, *A Week on the Concord,* 400.

8. For a story created by Díä!kwąin, see “The Young Man of the Ancient Race,” in Scheub, *Story,* 195–200.

9. W. H. I. Bleek Collection, Notebook V15, translations by Lucy Lloyd, 5079 to 5109.

10. W. H. I. Bleek Collection, Notebook V15, translations by Lucy Lloyd, 5101 to 5103. “The above is a lament, sung by χāä-ttĭn̈ after the death of his friend, the magician and rainmaker, |nųĭn|kúï-tẹn; who died from the effects of a shot he had received when going about, by night, in the form of a lion. . . . Now that ‘the string is broken,’ the former ‘ringing sound in the sky’ is no longer heard by the

singer, as it had been in the magician's lifetime" (Bleek and Lloyd, *Specimens of Bushman Folklore,* 236–37). This poem is analyzed elsewhere in this book.

11. Journal entries in this book are taken from field notes that I made while conducting three research trips to southern Africa, in 1967–1968, 1972–1973, and 1975–1976, where I worked among the Ndebele, Swati, Xhosa, and Zulu. The notes were usually written down late at night, after I had attended storytelling presentations.

12. In my collection: Tape 4, Section 29 (1S-162), dgt. 1703. "1S" refers to the first research trip that I made in southern Africa. This story can be found at digit 1703, the twenty-ninth section of the fourth tape in that first collection of voice tapes.

13. *amaqaba* (Xhosa)—traditionalists.

14. "*chos'* (Xhosa)—*interj.* used by a mother in the form *makube chosi!* hush! to her child when it cries or is ill or after it sneezes; the phrase seems to have the import of a prayer; *chos' ibekho!* is used when one, whom we wish to see, unexpectedly arrives" (Kropf, *A Kafir-English Dictionary,* 65). "*camagu* (Xhosa)—*Interj.* Be appeased or pacified! be propitious! This is a religious word, though . . . its use is not restricted to religion. 1. It is addressed to one afflicted with severe illness, the affliction being supposed to be sent by his ancestors in displeasure at something done or left undone. . . . 2. It is addressed to an officiating witch doctor. . . . [I]t is used when searching or unpleasant questions are being put to the witch doctor" (55).

15. Later in this same lecture, he develops this: "The aesthetic attitude is an attitude in which we imaginatively contemplate an object, being able in that way to live in it as an embodiment of our feeling" (29–30). And he concludes, "We may conclude then that the aesthetic attitude as far as enjoyable may fairly be described in some such words as these: The pleasant awareness of a feeling embodied in an appearance presented to imagination or imaginative perception; or, more shortly, 'Feeling expressed for expression's sake'" (36–37).

16. The historical materials in this section are derived from Peter Becker, *Hill of Destiny,* 54–55, 68–69, 77, 80–81, 144–49, 164–79, 214–15, 220–24, 233–47, 247–51, 256–57, 262–64; Hugh Ashton, *The Basuto,* 4; D. Fred Ellenberger, *History of the Basuto,* 143–48; G. Tylden, *The Rise of the Basuto,* 106; M. Damane and P. B. Sanders, *Lithoko,* 1–9, 82–83; and N. J. Van Warmelo, *History of Matiwane and the AmaNgwane Tribe,* 6.

17. Thaba Bosiu—another poem in the story: "Thaba Bosiu" (Night Mountain), by S. E. K. Mqhayi: Khaya labeSuthu! / Khaya lethu beSuthu!! / Likhumbulen' ikhaya labeSuthu!!! / Zikhumbulen' iimini zamzuzu,—/ Iminyakan' elikhul' elinama-20,—/ Thina beSuthu besingenaKhaya; / BesiziMpula zikaLujaca! / Sixel' iinyamakazi zasendle,—/ Sityhutyh' amatyholo namahlathi. / Safika eNtaba Busuku, / Silandel' okaMkhatshane; / Indwebi yendod' enethongo, / Salandel' inkwenkwezi yayo,—/ Ethe kanti yeyenyaniso. / Sazuz' ikhefu sazinza; / Sazuz' ubuntu samila; / Baphela bonk' ubunyamakazi. / Sazigxoth' izizw' emva

kwethu; / Saty' amaxhoba saphila. . . . Home of the Sotho! / Our Sotho home! / Remember the days of the Sotho! / Remember the days of that time—/ The great years of the twenties: / We Sotho had no home, / We were the Mpula of Lujaca! / We resembled the game of the open veldt, / Roaming the bush and the forests. / We arrived at Night Mountain, / We followed those sons of Mkhatshane; / The suspicious follower of the man with the weapon / We pursued his star—/ He having said it was that of truth. / We rested and settled; / We gained our manhood, we flourished; / Our great ignorance ended. / We defeated the peoples behind us; / We ate the booty, we thrived. (S. E. Krune Mqhayi, "Thaba Bosiu" in *Inzuzo,* 73–74.) Only the first two verses are quoted here.

18. Z. D. Mangoaela, *Lithoko tsa Marena a Basotho,* 13.

19. 'MaMakhabane—Makhabane's mother.

20. Mofephe was a subject of Posholi who turned against him. See Damane and Sanders, 82 n.5.

21. Makhawula was also known as Silonyana, leader of the Bhaca.

22. Molulela and Lehana were Tlokoa leaders.

23. Vechtkop and Spitzkop, in Afrikaans. Bolokoe was Posholi's mountain fastness.

24. Maluke and Selete were Posholi's sons.

25. Damane and Sanders, *Lithoko,* 38.

26. Lewis Turco, *The Book of Forms,* 4. Turco writes, "Since poetry is the product of the poet who is interested in the vehicle itself, in *language* as the medium for expression, then poetry is 'the *art* of *language*.' Like the other genres, . . . poetry also has four elements, but in this case they are *levels* of language usage, those of *typography, sound, tropes* ('figures of speech'), and *theme*. And there is *fusion* as well—how do all these levels come together to make a poem?"

27. See Mdukiswa Tyabashe, "All the Land of the Mpondomise," in Harold Scheub, *The Tongue Is Fire,* 227–74.

28. A number of people in Tsolo District in the Transkei told me this story about Mdukiswa Tyabashe. For Tyabashe's comments about the creation of oral poetry, see Scheub, *The Tongue Is Fire,* 220–22.

29. The idea of praising a leader for upholding tradition is widespread: "Let us now praise famous men, and our fathers that begat us. . . . Such as did bear rule in their kingdoms, men renowned for their power, giving counsel by their understanding, and declaring prophecies: Leaders of the people by their counsels, and by their knowledge of learning meet for the people, wise and eloquent in their instructions. . . . All these were honored in their generations, and were the glory of their times. There be of them, that have left a name behind them, that their praises might be reported" (Ecclesiasticus, 44: 1, 3, 4, 7–8).

30. Susanne K. Langer, *Feeling and Form,* 208.

31. For the full text of this poem and for comments by Tyabashe on the creation of such poetry see Scheub, *The Tongue Is Fire,* 220–26.

32. This is the meaning of the king's name.

33. John Ciardi, "Introduction," in Ciardi and Williams, *How Does a Poem Mean?* xx.

34. Mark Strand, "On Becoming a Poet," xxiv. He writes, "Good poems . . . have a lyric identity that goes beyond whatever their subject happens to be. They have a voice, and the formation of that voice, the gathering up of imagined sound into utterance, may be the true occasion for their existence. A poem may be the residue of an inner urgency, one through which the self wishes to register itself, write itself into being, and, finally, to charm another self, the reader, into belief. It may also be something equally elusive—the ghost within every experience that wishes it could be seen or felt, acknowledged as a kind of meaning" (xxiii–xxiv).

35. "But only a poem can illustrate how a poem works" (Ciardi and Williams, *How Does a Poem Mean?* 6).

36. Sigmund Freud, *Beyond the Pleasure Principle,* 30.

37. Eavan Boland, "Poetic Form: A Personal Encounter," xxviii. Boland also writes, "Now when I sit down to write a poem I am determined that this voice will be integral to it. That I will hear it in the poem. . . . And it is that voice that now begins to shift the interior of the poem, with its granite weights of custom and diffidence. It is that voice that complies with a life rather than the other way around. Without realizing it, I have come upon one of the shaping formal energies: the relation of the voice to the line" (xxviii–xxix).

38. Freud, *Beyond the Pleasure Principle,* 29.

39. Langer, *Feeling and Form,* 27.

40. John Blacking writes, "The motion of music alone seems to awaken in our bodies all kinds of responses" (*How Musical Is Man?* 52).

41. "The same piece of music may move different people in the same sort of way, but for different reasons" (ibid., 52).

42. Franz Boas, *Primitive Art,* 349.

43. Blacking, *How Musical Is Man?* 73.

44. Joyce Carol Oates, "The Mystery of JonBenét Ramsey," 31.

45. The reference is to the digit number on the relevant voice tape on which the performance appears.

46. In Gatyana District in the Transkei in 1967.

47. From my journal, 1968.

48. Archie Mafeje, "The Role of the Bard in a Contemporary African Community," 195.

49. A. C. Jordan, *Towards an African Literature,* 21.

50. Gerard Paul Lestrade, "Bantu Praise-Poems," 8.

51. Edison M. Bokako, "Bo-Santagane, an Anthology of Tswana Heroic Verse," Appendix A, p. 1.

52. Benedict Wallet Vilakazi, "The Oral and Written Literature in Nguni," 23.

53. R. C. A. Samuelson, *Long Long Ago,* 254.

54. The word for such poetry in Xhosa and Zulu is *izibongo,* in Swati *tibongo,* in Sotho *lithoko,* in Tswana *mabôkô.*

55. Andrew Smith, *The Diary of Dr. Andrew Smith, 1834–1835,* II, 208. Quoted in Isaac Schapera, *Praise-poems of Tswana Chiefs,* 3.

56. David Livingstone, *Missionary Travels and Researches in South Africa,* 165.

57. Schapera, *Praise-poems of Tswana Chiefs,* 2–3.

58. "Zulu, kaNogandaya," in James Stuart, *uBaxolele,* 102, lines 10–12. "iSiguq' esizifulele ngamahlamvu, / Emzileni wezinkomo zikaNxaba; / Sath' ukuvula sadl' abantwana bakaNxaba."

59. "Masopha," in Mangoaela, *Lithoko tsa Morena a Basotho,* 44, line 5. "Khomohali ea moqolopo, khunoana."

60. "Izibongo zikaDingiswayo, kaJobe wakwaMthethwa," in Stuart, *uBaxolele,* 42, lines 4–5. "Izotengana nayiph' enenekazi? / Izotengana noMbangambi woVuma, emaTshobeni."

61. "Izibongo zikaSenzangakhona," in ibid., 58, line 6. "Ilang' eliphume linsizwa."

62. "Sebele," in Schapera, *Praise-poems of Tswana Chiefs,* 139, lines 1–3. "Motšhatšha mogakatsa mala, / more mojewa obotlhoko, / mokgalo obotlhoko." Translation by Schapera.

63. "Griffith," in Mangoaela, *Lithoko tsa Morena a Basotho,* 180, line 3. "Koena, tsosa maqhuba har'a mohlaba."

64. "Cetshwayo," by Nombhonjo Zungu, a sixty-five to seventy-year-old Zulu bard. The performance (2S-733) took place on September 13, 1972, in a home in Yanguya, kwaZulu, before an audience of some fifty Zulu men, women, and children.

65. This poem, "Sobhuza II" (2S-1426), was performed by the Swati bard, Matshopane Mamba, on October 9, 1972, at the royal residence of King Sobhuza II in Entfonjeni, Swaziland, before an audience of ten men, five women, and one child. Mr. Mamba was sixty years old. "Libhungane limlom' inkelekethe / Kade kwasa liyigwiny' imihlambi yamadoda."

66. "Izibongo zikaOfisi Kona, the right hand. He is born of Nobhesi, the daughter of Bikitsha of the Qoco clan," in W. B. Rubusana, *Zemk' Inkomo Magwalandini,* 262–63, lines 1–5. "NguDela, uxhalis' 'izulu ngomoya, / Owaphezulu ab' etsalele phezulu; / Owasezantsi ab' etsalel' ezantsi. / Ovuk' emini akabonanga nto, / Kub' akayibonang' inamb' icombuluka." Compare a poem by Nongenile Masithathu Zenani: "The late-riser has foolishly seen nothing / because he will never see the python uncoil" (Scheub, *The Tongue Is Fire,* 207).

67. "Izibongo zikaSixhonxo Dada, of the Tshawe clan," in Rubusana, *Zemk' Inkomo Magwalandini,* 389, lines 6–7. "Yintsimb' equthu yasemlungwini, / Ethiyel' amachant' emlanjeni."

68. "Kgamanyane," in Schapera, *Praise-poems of Tswana Chiefs,* 71, lines 5–6. "Kemao lentlhapêdi aMasonya, / letlhaba kobô lemoroki." Translation by Schapera.

69. "Izibongo zikaCetshwayo," in James Stuart, *uHlangakula,* 92, lines 8–9. "Uyawukok' umnyateliso, / Iqabi lakwabo elinkone, le zinkabi."

70. "Izibongo zikaMandoyi Qalo," in Rubusana, *Zemk' Inkomo Magwalandini*, 399, line 1. "Ngumbodl' enezixhinga yeyase-Qonce."

71. "Izibongo zikaSonamzi Nazo, born of Nofasi Mbhala; a son of the Khomazi clan," in ibid., 382, line 2. "NguSuzel' ilitye liqhekeke."

72. "Izibongo zikaSeyisi Khotho, the other son of Dyan Khotho," in ibid., 393, line 4. "Ngucikucik' isikhumba senyati de sibe zintambo."

73. "Izibongo zikaNcuka," in ibid., 435, line 8. "Inyamakaz' ezimigcantsi mide."

74. "Izibongo zikaNcuka," in ibid., 435, lines 1–2. "Ingxazangxaza, / Intw' engangemvul' enkulu eyabulal' inkomo."

75. "Izibongo zikaMambi," in ibid., 435, line 6. "Intw' empondo zinamachaphaz' egazi."

76. "Izibongo zikaJiningisi Mangona, umCira," in ibid., 429, lines 1–3. "NguMgungu ixhak' elilubhelu, / Ixhak' elintusi nelilubhelu; / Umhlophekaz' oziziba zibomvu."

77. "Izibongo zikaNcuka," in ibid., 435, lines 11–13. "Nguxhents' enkunkumeni, / Uxhents' ephethe umpu, / Ufun' ukudubul' abantu bentlombe."

78. "Izibongo zikaCofumncono," in ibid., 387, line 4. "Ngumthi ndomile kanti ndiluhlaza."

79. "Izibongo zikaJohn Dlabazana, of the Tshatshu clan who is at Xonxa in Thembuland," in ibid., 401, line 34. "Uthand' ukutya 'ngabuk' atsh' angayi nangasele."

80. "Izibongo zikaPhotyo Nqelanga, the son of Nqhosini, who used to inhabit Zidenge," in ibid., 394, line 1. "Ngufud' olumdaka olubethwa lungafi."

81. "Izibongo zikaMagwaza Memani, son of the Ntakwende clan," in ibid., 402, lines 12–13. "NguSutlan' ompondo zimnyama, / Ujikajik' isicith' esinerorwana phakathi."

82. "Izibongo zikaKhwezi Khotho," in ibid., 393, lines 9–10. "Ngunyos' asaz' apho zilala khona, / Sesiva ngodume lwamahlathi."

83. "Izibongo zikaMhala Ndlambe," in ibid., 269, line 11. "Inkos' iba nkos' ukub' ikhaliphe."

84. "Izibongo zikaTokwe Bhotomani, the chief of the Dange," in ibid., 284, line 9. ". . . unkos' iba nkosi ngankosikazi."

85. "Izibongo zikaMathuthu Gxabhana, son of the Zango clan, staying at Mgwali," in ibid., 387, lines 1–5. "Ngumakrot' aphelile kowakwaNgqika, / Agqitywe luhlang' olumagwangqa / Lwaphesha kolwandle. / Ngusesibanjw' intliziyo ngokaGxabhana, / Ikrot' eliseleyo kowakwaNgqika."

86. "Izibongo of Ngani Bhotomani, born of Nomanto Mxinwa the woman of the Bamba clan," in ibid., 287, line 1. "NguNohamile, intw' emhlan' usigingqi wokuhlal' abelungu."

87. "Izibongo of Phato Chungwa, the chief of the Nxwala who used to live at Bhira," in ibid., 312, lines 1–2. "NguMandoli akavunyw' emlungwini, / Uyakuz' abanjwe nyak' abonwayo."

88. "The Leopard," in S. K. Lekgothoane, "Praises of Animals in Northern Sotho," 192–93, lines 1–9.

89. "The Black Vulture," in D. F. van der Merwe, "Hurutshe Poems," 333, lines 1–2.

90. "The Bicycle," in ibid., 336, lines 3–4.

91. "The Train," in H. J. van Zyl, "Praises in Northern Sotho," 131, lines 1–2.

92. Theodore Roethke, "Meditation at Oyster River," in Theodore Roethke, *The Far Field,* 18.

93. S. E. Krune Mqhayi, *Ityala Lamawele* (The Case of the Twins), 32–35.

94. "Shaka's Poem," part 3, in Stuart, *uBaxoxele,* 85, lines 2–7.

95. "Shaka's Poem," part 4, in James Stuart, *uKulumetule,* 79, lines 13–14.

96. "Shaka's Poem," part 4, in ibid., 78, lines 3–9.

97. "Shaka's Poem," part 3, in Stuart, *uBaxolele,* 84, lines 7–13. My italics.

98. "Letsie I," in Mangoaela, *Lithoko tsa Morena a Basotho,* 32, lines 17–20. My italics.

99. "Dalindyebo Ngangelizwe," by E. Mdolomba, in Rubusana, *Zemk' Inkomo Magwalandini,* 298, lines 34–48. My italics.

100. "Senzangakhona's Poem," part 1, in Stuart, *uBaxolele,* 56, lines 14–21. My italics.

101. "Shaka's Poem," part 4, in Stuart, *uKulumetule,* 79, lines 1–3. My italics.

102. From Mtshophane Mamba's poem, "Snapping at the Water's Foam," in Harold Scheub, *The Tongue Is Fire,* 276.

103. Mangoaela, *Lithoko tsa Morena a Basotho,* 128, part 3, lines 18–24.

104. These comments about the characteristics of the *line* are based on my analyses of those oral poets I studied during my various research trips to southern Africa, and especially based on the poets referred to in this chapter.

105. Grant tells of how, "apart from the clear emphasis on the penultimate syllable of each word, additional emphasis fell periodically on the penultimates of certain words, each of which would be followed by a perceptible pause. Thus the poem was broken up into short phrases, each of which appeared to be uttered with one breath. A magnificent rhythm was in this way apparent to the hearer" (E. W. Grant, "The Izibongo of the Zulu Chiefs," 202).

106. *intonjane* (Xhosa)—the girl's puberty rite of passage.

107. *lobola* (Xhosa)—dowry.

108. From my collection (1S-123).

109. In the W. H. I. Bleek Collection, Notebook VIII, with translations by Lucy Lloyd, 6137 (reverse). See also Bleek and Lloyd, *Specimens of Bushman Folklore,* 234–37. ||kábbo adds this comment: "Famine ["tobacco-hunger" is meant here]—he did not smoke, because a dog had come in the night (and) carried off

from him his pouch. And he arose in the night, he missed his pouch. And then he again lay down, while he did not smoke. And we were early seeking for the pouch. We did not find the pouch" (Bleek and Lloyd, 235, 237 [6138]).

110. W. H. I. Bleek Collection, Notebooks XI and XII-6, edited by Bleek, 9436 and 9436 (reverse).

111. W. H. I. Bleek Collection, Notebook V-15, translations by Lucy Lloyd, 5079–109.

112. W. H. I. Bleek collection, Notebook V-15, translations by Lucy Lloyd, 5101–3. Notes in Bleek and Lloyd: "The above is a lament, sung by χãä-ttĭń after the death of his friend, the magician and rainmaker, |nų̆in|kúĭ-tęn; who died from the effects of a shot he had received when going about, by night, in the form of a lion. . . . Now that 'the string is broken,' the former 'ringing sound in the sky' is no longer heard by the singer, as it had been in the magician's lifetime." See also Bleek and Lloyd, 236–37.

113. In the notebooks, Lloyd toys with another possible translation of "stood open" as "stood empty."

114. The San song: |háń≠kaśs'ō, "The Song of the Springbok Mothers," in Bleek and Lloyd, 234–35. The Tswana poem: Hendrik Molefi, "Isang," in Schapera, *Praise-poems of Tswana Chiefs,* 108 (the poem was recorded in 1931). The Zulu poem: Nombhonjo Zungu, "Shaka," collected by Harold Scheub (2S-733 in the collection; the poem was performed on September 13, 1972, in Yanguya, Zululand).

115. Mangoaela, "Jonathane Molapo," 116–17.

116. Ibid., 117.

117. Stuart, "Izibongo zikaTshaka, II," in *uHlangakula,* 30–31.

118. See Nongenile Masithathu Zenani, "The Necessary Clown."

119. Nongenile Masithathu Zenani, "And So I Grew Up, the Autobiography of Nongenile Masithathu Zenani," 31.

120. Eisenach: Erich Röth-Verlag, 1951, 7. Lizenz-Nummer, 364. Germany. From the Baule of Ivory Coast: Früher spielte man die Laute / zusammen mit der Trommel zum Tanz. / Heute kann nur noch ich sie zu meinen Geschichten spielen. / Ich bin ein junger Mann, meine Laute ist schön, / wegen meiner Laute habe ich keine Pflanzung angelegt, / wegen meiner Laute habe ich jetzt nichts zu essen.

121. See Scheub, *The Tongue Is Fire,* 28, 30.

122. Manyawusa Sodidi and Manto Matshezi, both Xhosa, performed about twenty stories, singly and in tandem, before large and demonstrative audiences on August 23 and 24, 1972.

123. Ernest Sedumeli Moloto. "The Growth and Tendencies of Tswana Poetry," 59–60.

124. Ibid., 94–95.

125. All translations in this section are by me, with the exception of the Zulu "Dinuzulu" poem, the Tswana poems, and the San poems. Conclusions about performance in this chapter are based on performances by some two

hundred oral poets whose poetry I witnessed in performance. Many of my conclusions are based on conversations with and close analyses of performance techniques and the poetic technique of, among others, Mdukiswa Tyabashe and Ashton Ngcama, Xhosa poets; Umhle Biyela and Nombhonjo Zungu, Zulu poets; and Mtshophane Mamba, a Swati poet. The generalizations apply to the techniques of these poets and others.

126. The poem was performed at the Entfonjeni Royal Residence in Swaziland on October 9, 1972, for an audience of Swati people and fellow poets. See Scheub, *The Tongue Is Fire,* 275–78, for the entire text of this poem.

127. From my collection. This poem was performed in 1968, before an audience of some thirty Zulu people in kwaZulu. Ndaba is a forebear of the Zulu king, Shaka.

128. The poem was performed at the royal residence of Diliz' Iintaba Mditshwa on August 12, 1967, with the king in attendance, along with some two hundred Mpondomise people. The Mpondomise people are a Xhosa-speaking people then living in the Transkei. See Scheub, *The Tongue Is Fire,* 223–26, for the entire text of this poem.

129. The poem was performed on August 23, 1972, in Mount Ayliff District in the Transkei, before an audience of seven Xesibe men. The Bhaca, Mpondo, Thembu, and Xesibe are Xhosa-speaking peoples; Nguni is the generic term for the language family comprising the Ndebele, Swati, Xhosa, and Zulu peoples. See Scheub, *The Tongue Is Fire,* 282–86, for the entire text of this poem.

130. Grant, "The Izibongo of the Zulu Chiefs," 201–44.

131. Cleanth Brooks and Robert Penn Warren, *Understanding Poetry,* 16, 20.

132. Jordan, *Towards an African Literature,* 21.

133. Rubusana, *Zemk' Inkomo Magwalandini,* vi.

134. Bokako, "Bo-Santagane, An Anthology of Tswana Heroic Verse," Appendix A, 2.

135. Some oral poems *are* narrative; others (e.g., those of Melikhaya Mbuthuma in Mafeje's article, "The Role of the Bard in a Contemporary African Community") are primarily arguments, frequently with little imagery. The conclusions in this chapter are based on my own experiences as a member of audiences of southern African poets, and on poetry found in such collections as those of Rubusana (Xhosa), Schapera (Tswana), Mangoaela (Sotho); Henry Masilo Ndawo, *Izibongo Zenkosi Zama-Hlubi nezama-Bhaca* (Oral Poetry of Hlubi and Bhaca Chiefs) (Xhosa); C. L. Sibusiso Nyembezi, *Izibongo Zamakhosi* (Oral Poetry of the Kings) (Zulu); in the James Stuart collections: *uBaxolele, uHlangakula, uKulumetule, uThulasizwe,* and *uVusezakithi* (Zulu), and in articles such as those of Grant, Lekgothoane, van der Merwe, van Zyl, Bokako, and Moloto.

136. Stuart, *uThulasizwe* 17; and *uHlangakula,* 30–32.

137. B. W. Vilakazi, "The Conception and Development of Poetry in Zulu," 118.

138. The letter is in the Manuscripts Division, Jagger Library, University of Cape Town Libraries. William Philip Schreiner (1857–1919) was a South African jurist. Olive Emilie Albertina Schreiner (1855–1920) was a South African writer. Her most important book was *The Story of an African Farm.*

139. Senzangakhona ruled over a relatively small clan, fragment of a larger group, called "the people of Zulu." His son, Shaka, grew up with his mother's people of the Langa clan. Shaka became chief of the Zulu people when Senzangakhona died c. 1810.

140. Shaka's cousin, Maphitha, occupied a part of the territory northeast of Nongoma during Shaka's reign. Maphitha's son, Zibhebhu, was an important figure in Zulu history. During the reign of Cetshwayo, the estrangement between the uSuthu (that section of the people loyal to the reigning house) and the Mandlakazi (the followers of Zibhebhu) became acute, and developed into open warfare. An epic of Zulu history is Zibhebhu's descent upon Ulundi, Cetshwayo's royal kraal; the kraal was destroyed, Cetshwayo fled in 1883. The quarrel continued during the reign of Dinuzulu, and the British imposed a settlement when Dinuzulu was removed. But the uSuthu/Mandlakazi split remained.

141. Quoted in C. T. Binns, *Dinuzulu,* 113. J. Y. Gibson remembers the comment this way: "'The House of Tshaka,' the Governor declared (he might perhaps more correctly have said the House of *Zulu*), 'is a thing of the past; like water that is spilt'" (*The Story of the Zulus,* 292). Gibson goes on, "[Dinuzulu] always ridiculed the notion that he had been so presumptuous as to contemplate war against the English queen. He likened what he did to the scratching which a cat might attempt if trodden upon by an elephant" (301).

142. Dinuzulu died the morning of October 18, 1913. His last wish: "Bury me with my fathers at Nobamba." In 1966, his grave was still guarded by OkaHlabane, "the last remaining of his widows" (Binns, *Dinuzulu,* 255).

143. James Stuart, *A History of the Zulu Rebellion,* 14. But R. C. A. Samuelson writes, "It cannot be said with certainty from what root the name 'Dinuzulu' originated, because it has two meanings. A person could say so and so 'ungidinile' meaning that he has satisfied me and made my heart happy therefore; peradventure, he was given that name because it was necessary to be made apparent that the Zulu nation was satisfied and made happy when Dinuzulu was given to them. But 'ukudina' also means to tire the heart until a person throws away that which tires him. Therefore it is not quite clear which is the origin of this name; but the deeds of the Zulu people which fulfilled the troubles of Dinuzulu and ended by wrecking him made this name 'uDinuzulu' mean that the Zulu people became tired of Dinuzulu" (*The King Cetywayo Zulu Dictionary,* xviii–xix). Magema M. Fuze writes that Cetshwayo "produced Dinuzulu whose name means that the Zulus would be made tired and exhausted by him" (*The Black People and Whence They Came,* 90).

144. "There is a conception of poetry which is not fulfilled by pure language and liquid versification, with the simple and so to speak colorless pleasure which they afford, but involves the presence in them of something which moves and

touches in a special and recognizable way. . . . There a new element has stolen in, a tinge of emotion. And I think that to transfuse emotion—not to transmit thought but to set up in the reader's sense a vibration corresponding to what was felt by the writer—is the peculiar function of poetry" (11–12). He goes on, "Poetry is not the thing said but a way of saying it. Can it then be isolated and studied by itself? For the combination of language with its intellectual content, its meaning, is as close a union as can well be imagined. Is there such a thing as pure unmingled poetry, poetry independent of meaning?" (37).

145. Samuelson, *The King Cetywayo Zulu Dictionary,* xix–xxv.

146. Cetshwayo, Zulu king 1872–1879. Exiled in 1879, died 1884.

147. Stephanus Johannes Paulus Kruger (1825–1904). President of the South African Republic, 1883–1900.

148. Nongqayi, a fort to house the Natal Native Police, established by the British in 1883.

149. Nongoma, the seat of the magistracy in the Zululand district of Nongoma.

150. Moshoeshoe (c. 1786–1870), leader of Sotho.

151. Banganomo was the principal kraal of Zibhebhu.

152. Ndunu hill, near Nongoma, was occupied by Zibhebhu's forces. On June 23, 1888, Dinuzulu's army attacked, and Zibhebhu lost the battle. Dinuzulu's army, four thousand in number, marched through the night, and when the sun arose it appeared in full army gear in front of Ndunu hill and Nongoma.

153. The Mandlakazi were a clan headed in 1872 by Zibhebhu.

154. Maphitha was the father of Zibhebhu and head of the Mandlakazi. Maphitha was Shaka's cousin, and occupied a part of the territory northeast of Nongoma during Shaka's reign. He died in 1872.

155. Ndlovu was the son of Madlangala of the Maseko clan.

156. Somfula was a Hlabisa chief, a follower of Zibhebhu.

157. Zibhebhu (c. 1842–1904) was Maphitha's son, and he was related to Zulu King Mpande. He was to become an important figure in Zulu history. During the reign of Cetshwayo, he became the chief of the Mandlakazi (1872). There was bad feeling between Zibhebhu and Cetshwayo. Hamu, Cetshwayo's cousin, defected to the British. He was appointed a chief in 1879. There was an alliance between Hamu and Zibhebhu. Hamu's claim to the kingship received little support, but he nevertheless created problems for Cetshwayo and Dinuzulu, and his defection caused bloodshed.

158. Ziwethu (Siwetu, Ziwedu) was one of Cetshwayo's chief officers, son of Mpande. He was one of Cetshwayo's brothers. Mnyamana was the son of Ngqengelele and one of Cetshwayo's chief officers. He died in 1892.

159. Ceza, a mountain where Dinuzulu constructed his stronghold.

160. Mkhuze River, in the northern part of kwaZulu.

161. In the English translation, Samuelson adds a line, "Which held the men at Sewana's," but he does not provide the Zulu original of this line.

162. Ntini was a Gumbi chief.

163. Nyoni-mhlophe, white bird.

164. Samuelson's translation of this line: "Which was pressing back the cavalry regiment."

165. Below the mountain, Ceza, was the valley of the Sikhwebezi River.

166. Ndaba (1697–1763) was the great-grandfather of the Zulu king, Shaka (c. 1787–1828).

167. The Mahashini plateau, on which Dinuzulu had established a kraal to keep his horses (Gibson, *The Story of the Zulus,* 307).

168. Phunga and Mageba were Zulu kings.

169. Cetshwayo (c. 1826–1884) was the son of King Mpande (1798–1872), Zulu king from 1840 to 1872. Cetshwayo was king of the Zulu from 1872 to 1879.

170. Dlungwana was of the Dlamini clan.

171. Stuart, *A History of the Zulu Rebellion,* 551.

172. Salempore, gossamer material.

173. Stuart observes, "This song is in the form of an enigma. The word 'It' evidently refers to an *impi,* which, when on the march, very much resembles a snake. The object of the song was, no doubt, to promote a spirit of defiance against Europeans" (Stuart, *A History of the Zulu Rebellion,* 117).

174. Stuart comments, "The meaning probably is that Dinuzulu is the last person that will die among Europeans, as his own people are determined to prevent his being taken" (ibid., 116–17).

175. See "Ritual: The Performance of the Story."

176. "He used to tell how, for a long time, he concealed his profanity from her; how one morning, when he thought the door was shut between their bedroom and the bathroom, he was in there dressing and shaving, accompanying these trying things with language intended only for the strictest privacy. . . . Halfway across the room he heard a voice suddenly repeat his last terrific remark. He turned to see her sitting up in bed, regarding him with a look as withering as she could find in her gentle soul. The humor of it struck him.

"'Livy,' he said, 'did it sound like that?'

"'Of course it did,' she said, 'only worse. I wanted you to hear just how it sounded.'

"'Livy,' he said, 'it would pain me to think that when I swear it sounds like that. You got the words right, Livy, but you don't know the tune'" (I, 559).

A concurring comment: "If you want to know who won the debates, ignore the ratings of the commentators. They are only evaluating the words, while the rest of the country is listening to the music" (Richard N. Goodwin, writing of presidential debates in the United States, "Debate Tips from J.F.K.").

And again the words of the Zulu storyteller come to mind: "If I am to tell you what this story means, I must tell it again" (from my field notes, January 26, 1969).

177. Comments in this section are derived from my article, "A Review of African Oral Traditions and Literature."

178. Dickey, *Metaphor as Pure Adventure,* 2.

179. Mark Bryant, *Riddles Ancient and Modern,* 13. Of particular interest here is Andrew Welsh, *Roots of Lyric.* For other general works on the riddle, see Robert A. Georges and Alan Dundes, "Toward a Structural Definition of the Riddle"; Ian Hamnett, "Ambiguity, Classification and Change"; Charles T. Scott, "On Defining the Riddle"; Brian Sutton-Smith, "A Developmental Structural Account of Riddles"; Archer Taylor, "The Riddle" and *English Riddles from Oral Tradition;* and the studies of Elli Köngäs Maranda: "The Logic of Riddles," "Theory and Practice of Riddle Analysis," "A Tree Grows," and "Riddles and Riddling." Works specifically on the African riddle include Derek F. Gowlett, "Common Bantu Riddles" and "A Structural Typology for Bantu Riddles"; Lyndon Harries, "The Riddle in Africa"; and Jeffrey L. Kallen and Carol M. Eastman, "'I Went to Mombasa, There I Met an Old Woman . . .'" See also William Bascom, "Literary Style in Yoruba Riddles"; John Blacking, "The Social Value of Venda Riddles"; James Bynon, "Riddle Telling among the Berbers of Central Morocco"; Lee Haring, "On Knowing the Answer"; Monique J. Layton, "Luba and Finnish Riddles"; John C. Messenger, "Anang Proverb-Riddles." Thomas A. Green and W. J. Pepicello have written a series of articles on the subject: "Wit in Riddling," "The Folk Riddle," "Sight and Spelling Riddles," "The Riddle Process."

180. P-D. Beuchat, "Riddles in Bantu," 140.

181. Archer Taylor concludes, "A true riddle consists of two descriptions of an object, one figurative and one literal, and confuses the hearer who endeavors to identify an object described in conflicting ways" ("The Riddle,"130).

182. Robert Petsch's doctoral dissertation was published as *Neue Beiträge zur Kenntnis des Volksrätsels;* quoted in Robert A. Georges and Alan Dundes, "Toward a Structural Definition of the Riddle," 111.

183. Stanley B. Hadebe, "A Brief Survey of Zulu Riddles," 33. The answer is *"Isibhakabhaka"* ("the sky").

184. Bynon, "Riddle Telling among the Berbers of Central Morocco," 170–71. The answers are needle and thread, pubic hair, a cow.

185. There are some useful collections of African oral lyric poetry, much of it in translation only. See, for example, Willard R. Trask, *The Unwritten Song,* and Leonard Doob, *Ants Will Not Eat Your Fingers.* For a more complete bibliography, see Scheub, *African Oral Narratives, Proverbs, Riddles, Poetry and Song.*

186. Welsh, *Roots of Lyric,* 58.

187. Henri Trilles, *L'Âme du Pygmée d'Afrique,* 228. The poem appears at the end of this book, on page 252.

188. T. Cullen Young, "Some Proverbs of the Tumbuka-Nkamanga Peoples of the Northern Province of Nyasaland," 345. A sampling of proverb research: Erastus Ojo Arewa, "Proverb Usage in a 'Natural' Context and Oral Literary Criticism"; Alan Dundes and Erastus Ojo Arewa, "Proverbs and the Ethnography of Speaking Folklore"; and Peter Seitel, "Proverbs: A Social Use of Metaphor." See also: F. A. de Caro and W. K. McNeil, *American Proverb Literature;* J. L. Fischer and Teigo

Yoshida, "The Nature of Speech According to Japanese Proverbs"; and Robert K. McKnight, "Proverbs of Palau." For a bibliography of collections of African proverbs, see Scheub, *African Oral Narratives, Proverbs, Riddles, Poetry and Song.*

189. Young, "Some Proverbs of the Tumbuka-Nkamanga Peoples of the Northern Province of Nyasaland," 344.

190. M. Mary Senior, "Some Mende Proverbs," 205.

191. For a listing of collections of oral stories from Africa, see Scheub, *African Oral Narratives, Proverbs, Riddles, Poetry and Song.*

192. The performer was a Hlubi woman, about fifty years old. The performance (1S-1910) took place on November 11, 1967, at 6 P.M., in a home in Nyaniso, Matatiele District, the Transkei. The audience consisted of five Hlubi women. Scheub, *The Xhosa Ntsomi,* 272–81.

193. See Nongenile Masithathu Zenani, *The World and the Word.*

194. The performance (1S-706) took place on September 19, 1967, in Mrs. Zenani's home in Nkanga Location, Gatyana District, the Transkei. The audience consisted of about ten men and women.

195. The performer was a Hlubi woman, about fifty years old. The performance (1S-2010) took place on November 14, 1967, in a home in Nyaniso, Matatiele District, the Transkei. In the audience were twenty women, six teenagers, and fifteen children. Scheub, *The Xhosa Ntsomi,* 280–85.

196. W. B. Rubusana uses that as a title for his collection of Xhosa heroic poems: *Zemk' Inkomo Magwalandini.*

197. Henry Callaway, *Nursery Tales, Traditions, and Histories of the Zulus,* 221–37. Callaway notes, "The meaning of *Ubongopa* is not known. *Uma-'gadhlela* is the name of Ubongopa's father. It is compounded of *Uma* and *gadhlela,* to strike against with the head, as rams in fighting. The full form would be *Uma-e-gadhlela;* it is a name implying, When he strikes with the head, *he conquers*" (221).

198. Hayden White writes, "But real events should not speak, should not tell themselves. Real events should simply be; they can perfectly well serve as the referents of a discourse, can be spoken about, but they should not pose as the subjects of a narrative." He argues, "What we wish to call mythic narrative is under no obligation to keep the two orders of events, real and imaginary, distinct from one another. Narrative becomes a problem only when we wish to give to real events the form of story. It is because real events do not offer themselves as stories that their narrativization is so difficult" (*The Content of the Form,* 3–4).

199. See Scheub, *Story,* 24–29.

200. "What really happens is that the story-maker proves a successful subcreator. He makes a Mythic World which your mind can enter. Inside it, he relates what is 'true'; it accords with the laws of that world. You therefore believe it, while you are, as it were, inside. The moment disbelief arises, the spell is broken; the magic, or rather art, has failed. You are then out in the Primary World again, looking at the little abortive Mythic World from outside" (J. R. R. Tolkien, *Tree and Leaf,* 36).

201. The mythic image becomes significant when it is brought into a relationship with a real-life character. If one sees them as a part of a seamless whole, the mythic image as the ghostly double of the real-life character, then our understanding of that real character and his transformation experience deepens. Two fantasy characters may come to represent a real-life character, as significant parts of that character as he goes through his transformation. Fantasy is present even if the images themselves are not fantastic. We can conceive of two opposing fantasy or mythic characters as embodiments of the changes that the central character is experiencing; other characters in the story support, comment on, and develop that essential mythic-real relationship. If we can experience the fantasy or mythic character as the embodiment of the realistic character, then we begin to understand the poetic and metaphorical ties between reality and fantasy.

202. The patterns link the two worlds: the connection might be between two sides of a character, with other patterns emphasizing identity, and the patterned movement is between those two identities; the connection might be between two fantasy worlds, on the one hand, and the central character's real world, on the other, emphasizing insight, rebirth, identity, and within these two fantasy worlds the real character and fantasy are patterned into a single character; or the connection might be between two worlds, that of a death-dealer and that of a life-giver, with the essential patterned movement having to do with the central character's movement between those worlds; or the connection might be a mysterious one, between two worlds, that of the mythic world and that of the real world, a world that is perhaps blemished: those realms of fantasy—the mythic imagery—and reality are joined in the end.

203. Peter Høeg, *Smilla's Sense of Snow,* 366.

204. Arnold van Gennep, *The Rites of Passage,* 189–90 (*Les Rites de Passage,* 271–72).

205. Barbara Myerhoff, "Rites of Passage," 112.

206. William Frost, "Shakespeare's Rituals and the Opening of *King Lear,*" 578–79. Frost writes, "I should like to extend the term 'ritual' here to include any speech or situation which will be felt by participants or spectators to be predictable in important respects. In this sense ritual would include not only marriages and funerals . . .; not only prayers, curses, and invocations . . .; not only coronation processions and depositions; not only banquets, dances, masques . . .; but also ceremonial arrivals and departures . . .; trial scenes . . .; obituary announcements and their reception . . . ; the swearing of oaths . . ." (577–78).

207. The trickster is aggressive, selfish, amoral. He creates a world of illusion, imposing his own sense of order on the real world. An agent of chaos, he disrupts harmony; when he establishes harmony, it is according to his own whim, his own sense of order. Trickster combines horror and glee: his is the comedy of the grotesque. He has no place that he can call home; he is an outsider. In his amoral actions, the trickster represents a liminal state, embodying that period of betwixt and between that all humans experience as they move from one state

to another. He may appear tame, but in the next instant he shows that he is not. In the trickster, all is change, transformation. He represents enormous untamed energy that is in the process of being controlled, funneled. He is always reinventing the world, testing boundaries, relearning the possibilities. He is our id, unvarnished, untempered.

208. *Icheya,* a game that involves the drawing of lots. See Kropf, *A Kafir–English Dictionary,* 60; Theal, *Kaffir Folklore,* 221–22.

209. Theal parenthetical comment: "A fabulous monster."

210. George McCall Theal, *Kaffir Folklore,* 78–88.

211. Edouard Jacottet, *The Treasury of Ba-Suto Lore,* I, 208–15. Note by Jacottet: "In this tale the name of Sekholomi is not given, but the other versions show well that he is meant. His name means *the talker.* This is rather strange, as in one of the Ba-Suto versions (cf. my *Contes pop. des Bassoutos,* p. 262) which has, undoubtedly, kept here a more original form, as also in one of the Kaffir tales and in the Ronga version, the boy is mute and only begins to talk when hunting the birds. Another proof that in the original tradition he was considered mute is that in one of the Ba-Suto versions he is named *Semumu,* the mute, though strange to say, in that very version he is not said to be mute" (208–9). For other versions of stories having to do with the pursuit of birds, see "Usikulumi kahlokohloko," in Callaway, *Nursery Tales, Traditions, and Histories of the Zulus,* 41–47; Jeremiah Mali, "The Story of Umshalishali and Umlomo'sibucu" (Zulu); "The Magic Flight" (Zulu) in Alice Werner, *Myths and Legends of the Bantu,* 184–86; "Sikhalomi and the Bird with the Beautiful Plumage" (Sotho), in Phyllis Savory, *Basuto Fireside Tales,* 11–17.

212. The performer was Sarah Dlamini, a Swati woman, thirty-five to forty years old. The performance (2S-1312) took place in her home in Mliba in Manzini District, Swaziland. The date was October 6, 1972; the time, about 10 A.M. The audience consisted of five women and three children. For other stories having to do with the struggle with the water monster see "A Sister Seeks a Fabulous Monster" (Xhosa), in Scheub, *The Xhosa Ntsomi,* 374–81; "Manzabilayo" (Zulu), in Stuart, *uThulasizwe,* 25–31; "Ugungqu-kubantwana" (Zulu), by Lydia umkaSethemba, in Callaway, *Nursery Tales, Traditions, and Histories of the Zulus,* 164–78; "Semumu le Semumunyane" (Sotho), in Edouard Jacottet, *Litsomo tsa Basotho,* II, 36–40; "The Nyamatsane" (Sotho), in Jacottet, *The Treasury of Ba-Suto Lore,* 2–17; "Kgolodikane" (Sotho), edited by Mrs. S. H. Edwards; "Kammapa and Litaolane" (Sotho), in Eugene Casalis, *The Basutos,* 347–49; "Nabulela" (Zulu), in Phyllis Savory, *Zulu Fireside Tales,* 47–52.

213. Jacottet, *The Treasury of Ba-Suto Lore,* 200–209.

214. Stuart, *uThulasizwe,* 25–31.

215. "The Magician's Daughter." This performance (1S-2050) took place on November 16, 1967, at about 9 A.M., in a home in Bubesi Location, Matatiele District, the Transkei. The narrative was performed by a Hlubi woman, about

forty years old. Her audience consisted of fifteen children, fifteen women, and about fifteen teenaged boys and girls. It was a highly rhythmic performance, with much body movement and gesturing to develop the images, vivid use of body and vocal dramatics in the evocation of Dolosikuhlumba's evil activities. She was a very engaging performer, close to the members of the audience. As she calmly developed her story, she was constantly seeking the participation of the members of the audience, anxious to keep all of them totally involved in her images. For other stories having to do with the quest to Mangangedolo's place, see "Zembeni" (Zulu), in Callaway, *Nursery Tales, Traditions, and Histories of the Zulus,* 47–52; another version of "Zembeni" can be found in the same volume, 53–54; "Mabejana" (Zulu), in Stuart, *uThulasizwe,* 37–43.

216. The story (1S-618) was performed on September 13, 1967, at about 2:30 P.M., outside, in the kraal of Nontsomi Langa, in Mboxo (Nkanga) Location, Gatyana District, the Transkei. Nontsomi Langa, a Gcaleka woman, about fifty-five years old, was the performer. In the audience were twenty women, six or seven men, fifteen teenagers, and thirty children, all Gcaleka. For another version of a story that combines the quest for the water monster and the journey to Mangangedolo's place, see "Sikuluma" (Xhosa), in William Kehale Kaye, "Kafir Legends and History," 117–31.

217. "Sikuluma" (Xhosa), in Kaye, "Kafir Legends and History," 117–31.

218. Jacottet, *The Treasury of Ba-Suto Lore,* 214–21.

219. "Sikouloumé," in Henri Alexandre Junod, *Les BaRonga,* 284–303.

220. The performer was Nongenile Masithathu Zenani, a Xhosa woman, about fifty-five years old. The performance (1S-656) took place on September 15, 1967, in Mrs. Zenani's home in Nkanga, Transkei, South Africa. In the audience were five women and fifteen children. Collected and translated by Harold Scheub. Another version of this story, combining the pursuit of birds, the water monster, and Mangangedolo's place, performed by Nongenile Masithathu Zenani on August 2, 1972 (2S-16), can be found in Richard M. Dorson, *African Folklore,* 525–61. See also "The Story of Sikhulume," also a Xhosa version of the tale, in Theal, *Kaffir Folklore,* 78–88.

221. "The muse in charge of fantasy wears good, sensible shoes. No foam-born Aphrodite, she vaguely resembles my old piano teacher, who was keen on metronomes" (Lloyd Alexander, "The Flat-Heeled Muse," 242). At the same time, fantasy has its own seditious intent: Rosemary Jackson observes that fantasy is a "violation of dominant assumptions" and it therefore "threatens to subvert (overturn, upset, undermine) rules and conventions taken to be normative." It disturbs, Jackson writes, "'rules' of artistic representation and literature's reproduction of the 'real'" (*Fantasy,* 14). And things can become complex: "Fantastic narratives," she writes, "confound elements of both the marvelous and the mimetic. They assert that what they are telling is real—relying upon all the conventions of realistic fiction to do so—and then they proceed to break that assumption of realism by

introducing what—within those terms—is manifestly unreal" (34). As Tolkien observed, "The human mind is capable of forming mental images of things not actually present" (*Tree and Leaf,* 43).

222. From my field notes, October 15, 1975.

223. James Sibree, Jr., "Malagasy Folk-Tales," 161–66.

224. John Roscoe, *The Baganda,* 136, 460–64.

225. "That willing suspension of disbelief for the moment, which constitutes poetic faith." Samuel Taylor Coleridge, *Biographia Literaria,* II, 6 (chapter 14).

226. Mircea Eliade, *Myth and Reality,* 5–6.

227. Marcel Griaule and Germaine Dieterlen, *Le renard pâle.*

228. For Gulu, see Harry Johnston, *The Uganda Protectorate,* II, 700–705. For Mantis, see Dorothea F. Bleek, ed., *The Mantis and His Friends,* 5–9, 30–40. For Winnebago, see Paul Radin, "The Winnebago Trickster Cycle," in *The Trickster,* 3–60.

229. Mark Schorer, *William Blake,* 25. He writes, "Myths are the instruments by which we continually struggle to make our experience intelligible to ourselves. . . . A mythology is a more or less articulated body of such images, a pantheon. Without such images, experience is chaotic, fragmentary and merely phenomenal. It is the chaos of experience that creates them, and they are intended to rectify it" (25–26).

230. Henry A. Murray, "The Possible Nature of a 'Mythology' to Come," 344. The myth, he writes, is "a story which is manifestly about one or more extraordinary persons or preternatural psychic beings (e.g. god, whale, Frankenstein) or about a group or society as a unit, earnestly and wholly engaged in a series of important, critical endeavors (matters of physical, social, or spiritual vitality or death)—not about trivial people involved in inconsequential interactions."

231. Robert Ellwood, *The Politics of Myth,* 174. Ellwood asks, "What about the myth of myth itself? Whether there was ever such a thing as living primordial myth in the sense the mythologists envisioned it may be questioned. . . . 'Official' myths like these are inevitably reconstructions from snatches of folklore and legend, artistically put together with an eye for drama and meaning. But the real mythic images of a society, those that are so fresh they are not yet recognized as 'myth' or 'scripture,' are fragmentary, imagistic rather than verbal, emergent, capable of forming many different stories at once" (174–75). He goes on, "Moreover myth, unlike much later 'civilized' literature, has one peculiar characteristic: it deals almost entirely in generic, 'archetypal' categories, reducing individuals (and races or peoples) to types and roles, stereotyping them as Hero or Trickster, as Good or Evil. To be sure, mythology teaches us that abstractions are not the solutions to problems, but merely their distancing, and that the real truth is in story. This should mean that one must also avoid the pseudoabstraction of story that is merely stereotyping didacticism, as myth can be when it is no more than archetypal" (177–78).

232. Wole Soyinka, *Myth, Literature and the African World,* 86.

233. John B. Vickery, *Myths and Texts,* 148. He adds, "Yet another striking feature is the centrality of the notion of story to myth and fiction alike. In effect, these suggest that the underlying and perhaps ultimate issues here are those of the nature of the tale and tale telling activity together with the problematic and even enigmatic question of the name of the teller, that is to say, the conceptual identity of the narrator."

234. Frederick Clarke Prescott, *Poetry and Myth,* 67.

235. G. S. Kirk, *The Nature of Greek Myths,* 226.

236. George Santayana, *The Life of Reason,* IV, 42, 43.

237. Updike, *Writers at Work, The Paris Review Interviews,* 443.

238. Some of these images are sometimes referred to as motifs. See Stith Thompson, *Motif-index of Folk-literature* and *The Folktale.* See also Antti Aarne, *The Types of the Folktale.* This is Thompson's definition of a motif: "the smallest element in a tale having the power to persist in tradition. In order to have this power it must have something unusual and striking about it" (*The Folktale,* 415–16). Motifs include images of animals, fantasy and real; images of magic, including transformation; images of the dead, of marvelous creatures and activities, of ogres, of supernatural and superhuman tests involving identity, recognition, tests of cleverness; images of the acquisition and possession of wisdom; deceptions; chance and fate. See also Alan Dundes, *Cinderella;* Jack Zipes, *The Trials and Tribulations of Little Red Riding Hood;* Rosemary Jackson, *Fantasy.*

239. "Ma'aruf the Cobbler and His Wife," in *The Book of the Thousand Nights and a Night,* edited and translated by Richard F. Burton, X, 1–50.

240. *zim* (*izim* or *izimu;* pl. *amazim* or *amazimu*) (Xhosa)—fantasy swallowing monster. *imbulu* (pl. *iimbulu*) (Xhosa)—a fantasy creature that can take human shape.

241. Gabriel García Márquez, *Writers at Work, The Paris Review Interviews,* 325.

242. Leonard Bernstein, *The Unanswered Question,* 8.

243. Aaron Copland, *What to Listen for in Music,* 26. Copland goes on, "It is their combined effect—the seemingly inextricable web of sound that they form—with which listeners are concerned for the most part."

244. James Lincoln Collier, *Practical Music Theory,* 6.

245. Susanne K. Langer, *Feeling and Form,* 28.

246. See Vladimir Propp, *Morphology of the Folktale.*

247. Collier, *Practical Music Theory,* 80.

248. Leon Dallin, *Listeners Guide to Musical Understanding,* 83, 84.

249. Copland, *What to Listen for in Music,* 40. "To do that," he goes on, "the melodic line will generally be long and flowing, with low and high points of interest and a climactic moment usually near the end."

250. Propp, *Morphology of the Folktale.* See also Joseph Campbell, *The Hero with a Thousand Faces;* Jan De Vries, *Heroic Song and Heroic Legend;* FitzRoy Richard Somerset Raglan, *The Hero.*

251. Langer, *Feeling and Form,* 27.

252. Robert Jourdain, *Music, the Brain, and Ecstasy,* 80.

253. Charles R. Hoffer, *The Understanding of Music,* 33.

254. Hoffer writes, "Melody refers to pitches sounded one after another in a logical, meaningful series. It is an organized group of pitches strung out sequentially to form a satisfying musical entity" (ibid., 30–31).

255. Ibid., 31. Hoffer adds, "Such a melody is often called a *theme,* to indicate its place as a central musical idea for the piece."

256. Copland, *What to Listen for in Music,* 40.

257. Ibid., 39.

258. Ibid., 40.

259. Ibid., 47–48. "Always remember," Copland writes, "that in listening to a piece of music you must hang on to the melodic line. It may disappear momentarily, withdrawn by the composer, in order to make its presence more powerfully felt when it reappears. But reappear it surely will, for it is impossible, except by rarest exception, to imagine a music, old or new, conservative or modern, without melody."

260. Hoffer, *The Understanding of Music,* 34.

261. Jourdain, *Music, the Brain, and Ecstasy,* 81. He explains, "A melody's notes form a pattern of varying durations with some notes made more prominent by accentuation. This pattern is extremely important to our understanding of melody."

262. Hoffer, *The Understanding of Music,* 42–43. "It is rhythm," notes Collier, "that fills music with life" (*Practical Music Theory,* 105).

263. Jourdain, *Music, the Brain, and Ecstasy,* 123.

264. Hoffer, *The Understanding of Music,* 44. He notes, "Metrical patterns in music hark back to the metrical patterns used in poetry." Dallin writes, "*Meter* is defined as systematically arranged and measured rhythm, rhythmic structure as concerned with the division into measures consisting of a uniform number of beats or time units. Rhythm and meter are slightly different but closely related aspects of the same element. In musical parlance, meter refers to the basic, underlying pulse—the fixed pattern of strong and weak beats to which one responds physically . . . Rhythm, properly, means the organized interplay of varied note values, including durations both longer and shorter than the beat" (*Listeners Guide to Musical Understanding,* 70).

265. Jourdain, *Music, the Brain, and Ecstasy,* 124. He writes, "Fittingly, psychologists call this grouping activity *chunking,*" and notes, "Chunking is often hierarchical, with small chunks grouped into larger chunks, and so on, until large musical objects are formed. We comprehend the smallest chunks more or less instantly. But the largest chunks do not come together until a long sequence of events is complete. Comprehension remains tentative until everything suddenly snaps into place. . . . Rhythmic markers simplify our perception of such hierarchies, and thereby make them possible" (125).

266. Plato, *The Republic,* 153 (Bk. III, 401a).

267. Hoffer, *The Understanding of Music,* 35. He notes, "In music there is almost always an element of the horizontal (the progression of music in point of time) and the vertical (the effect of sounds at any particular instant). The difference between harmony and counterpoint, therefore, lies in the degree of emphasis given to each dimension" (39).

268. John Blacking, *How Musical Is Man?* 54.

269. From my field notes, October 15, 1975. These notes were taken after lengthy discussions with storytellers and their audiences about the use of repetition in storytelling.

270. Judith Lynne Hanna, *To Dance Is Human,* 25.

271. Ibid., 28–29.

272. Olive Schreiner, in a letter to Katie, her sister, in early 1878, written in Ratel Hoek, South Africa. From S. C. Cronwright-Schreiner, *The Letters of Olive Schreiner,* 4.

273. Lu Chi, quoted in Archibald MacLeisch, *Poetry and Experience,* 17. See also Scheub, *The Tongue Is Fire,* 53.

274. Bernard Bosanquet, *Three Lectures on Aesthetic,* 13.

275. "The aesthetic attitude is that in which we have a feeling which is so embodied in an object that it will stand still to be looked at, and, in principle, to be looked at by everybody" (ibid., 6).

276. Susanne K. Langer, *Mind,* I, 111.

277. Kinzie argues, "When one thing represents another thing with which it is not usually associated—which is what occurs in many instances of metaphor—the original object is invested with a quality invisible before the comparison provided it. When not outlandish . . . the unexpected but apt comparison provides a quality of evocative abstraction, of unspoken thought, and of nuanced feeling" (175). She sees metaphor as a "transfer of meaning in which one thing is explained by being changed either into another thing or into an emotion or idea." The tenor of a metaphor, she writes, is the "originating scene, situation, object, or state" (435–36). The vehicle is the "part of trope that is transferred from another realm of discourse in order to give clarification of the tenor, or which acts as the literal ground from which the figurative idea emerges"(479).

278. Burke states, "A metaphor tells us something about one character considered from the point of view of another character. And to consider A from the point of view of B is, of course, to use B as a *perspective* upon A" (503–4).

279. Colin Murray Turbayne writes of Max Black: "An effective metaphor, he says, acts as a *screen* through which we look at the world; or it *filters* the facts, suppressing some and emphasizing others. It 'brings forward aspects that might not be seen at all through another medium.' . . . A good metaphor produces thereby 'shifts in attitudes'" (*The Myth of Metaphor,* 21). He quotes from Black's "Metaphor," 287–88.

280. Wheelwright writes, "The transmutative process that is involved may be described as *semantic motion;* the idea of which is implicit in the very word 'metaphor,' since the motion (*phora*) that the word connotes is a semantic

motion—the double imaginative act of outreaching and combining that essentially marks the metaphoric process. The outreaching and the combining, which are the two main elements of metaphoric activity, appear most effectively in combination" (71–72).

281. Paz argues, "Immersed in the movement of language, a continuous verbal coming and going, the poet chooses certain words—or is chosen by them. By combining them, he constructs his poem: a verbal object made of irreplaceable and immovable signs" (195).

282. Kittay writes, "The metaphor was itself instrumental in having identified a *something* to be named. The metaphor therefore provides us with a way of learning something new about the world, or about how the world may be perceived and understood. Where metaphor is used when a 'proper' name exists, Aristotle indicated yet another cognitive feature: it is a means of remarking on a previously unrecognized similarity. . . . Aristotle, believing similarity to be the basis of metaphorical transference, and granting to the perception of similarity an important cognitive role, saw in metaphor a conceptual tool of much power" (2–3).

283. Boruah argues, "It is the interaction between an evaluative belief and the imagination that suffices to generate an emotional response to a fictional character or event. The alleged paradox disappears when it is realized that we can form an evaluative belief about a character or event without at the same time having an existential belief about the character or event. A fictional depiction of a life or situation is as much the object of some evaluative belief as a description of an analogous actual life or situation: the same evaluative paradigm is applicable in both cases. As a genuine, first-order belief, the evaluative belief is a causally potent factor in the evocation of an emotion. Whereas in the real-life case this potency is actualized when the evaluative belief is appropriately united with the imagination" (125).

284. This section builds on the comments made in the earlier section, "The Riddle in the Story: Propensity for Metaphor."

285. Michael J. Arlen, *Passage to Ararat,* 57–58.

286. James W. Fernandez, "Reflections on Looking into Mirrors," 27.

287. Richard Edward Dennett, *At the Back of the Black Man's Mind,* 30, 50–51. He wrote of "Lu Muéno or Mirror. It is 'Xina' (a thing forbidden) to throw the light reflected from a mirror upon a person, and when the light passes across the face of an individual he cries out: 'Leave me alone. I have *ndudu* medicine in my body.' It is not a crime, but more of the nature of an insult, to throw this light upon a person. Bits of looking-glass are to be found fixed in trees, and in the eyes and stomach of many fetishes. The light thus thrown is called *'ntenia lu muéno'*" (84). For stories incorporating this concept of mirroring, see "The Twin Brothers," a Fiote story from the Democratic Republic of Congo (Richard Edward Dennett, *Notes on the Folklore of the Fjort [French Congo],* 60–64), and "The Magic Mirror," a Sena story from Mozambique (Andrew Lang, *The Orange Fairy Book,* 16–23).

288. John Ciardi and Miller Williams, *How Does a Poem Mean?* 668. Ciardi continues, "No matter how serious the overt message of a poem, the unparaphraseable and undiminishable life of the poem lies in the way it performs itself through the difficulties it imposes upon itself" (669–70). He argues, "The performance of a true poem is endless in being not a meaning but an act of existence" (674).

289. Ibid., 864.

290. Dickey argues that metaphor "is a way of causing the items of the real world to act upon each other, to recombine, to suffer and learn from the mysterious value systems, or value-making systems, of the individual, both in his socially conditioned and in his inmost, wild, and untutored mind. It is a way of putting the world together according to rules which one never fully understands, but which are as powerfully compelling as anything in the whole human makeup" (from *Metaphor as Pure Adventure*). This was a lecture delivered at the Library of Congress on December 4, 1967.

291. "Story is the foundation of all entertainment. You must have a good story—otherwise, it's just masturbation" (George Costanza, *Seinfeld*). Yet, generally writers of popular situation comedy television stories in the final half of the twentieth century, while they had two or perhaps three stories moving simultaneously in a given script, seldom made the metaphorical connections between them.

292. "In figurative language, a familiar thing is linked to an unknown thing, as a key, to unlock the mystery, or some part of the mystery, of the thing that is unknown" (Mary Oliver, *A Poetry Handbook,* 99).

293. Lawrence Zillman noted, "For poetic purposes the vivid metaphor can be a most effective part of the poem only when it is fresh and carefully devised to bring out the desired shade of emphasis" (*The Art and Craft of Poetry,* 112). George Santayana stated, "Yet if the myth was originally accepted it could not be for this falsity plainly written on its face; it was accepted because it was understood, because it was seen to express reality in an eloquent metaphor" (*The Life of Reason,* 41).

294. Janet Martin Soskice writes, "As a working definition of metaphor, we shall say that *metaphor is that figure of speech whereby we speak about one thing in terms which are seen to be suggestive of another*" (*Metaphor and Religious Language,* 15).

295. Colin Murray Turbayne develops Aristotle's argument: "Metaphor is the application of the name of a thing to something else, working either (a) from genus to species, or (b) from species to genus, or (c) from species to species, or (d) by proportion [analogy]." Turbayne writes, "Wide as Aristotle's definition is I make it wider. Without stretching his meaning unduly, I interpret his singular 'name' to mean either a proper name, a common name, or a description expressible as a phrase, a sentence, or even a book. In which case, a more adequate presentation of the defining feature of metaphor I am now considering is made by Gilbert Ryle [*The Concept of Mind* (London: Hutchinson's University Library,

1949) 8]. Metaphor consists in 'the presentation of the facts of one category in the idioms appropriate to another'" (*The Myth of Metaphor,* 12).

296. This is I. A. Richards' position: "In the simplest formulation, when we use a metaphor we have two thoughts of different things active together and supported by a single word, or phrase, whose meaning is a result of their interaction." He goes on, "A first step is to introduce two technical terms to assist us in distinguishing from one another what Dr. Johnson called the two ideas that any metaphor, at its simplest, gives us. Let me call them the tenor and the vehicle. . . . We need the word 'metaphor' for the whole double unit, and to use it sometimes for one of the two components in separation from the other is as injudicious as that other trick by which we use 'the meaning' here sometimes for the work that the whole double unit does and sometimes for the other component—the tenor, as I am calling it—the underlying idea or principle subject which the vehicle or figure means" (*The Philosophy of Rhetoric,* 93). Seymour Chatman writes, "A metaphor is an expression in which a word or phrase and the concept represented stand figuratively for another word or phrase and *its* concept. Remember that 'figuratively' is the opposite of 'literally': the comparison holds only in the world of the imagination. The word or phrase doing the 'standing for' is often called the 'vehicle'; the word or phrase being 'stood for' is called the 'tenor'" (*An Introduction to the Language of Poetry,* 45).

297. Sigmund Freud, *Beyond the Pleasure Principle,* 30. "Nor can children have their *pleasurable* experiences repeated often enough, and they are inexorable in their insistence that the repetition shall be an identical one. This character trait disappears later on. If a joke is heard for a second time it produces almost no effect; a theatrical production never creates so great an impression the second time as the first; indeed, it is hardly possible to persuade an adult who has very much enjoyed reading a book to re-read it immediately. Novelty is always the condition of enjoyment" (29).

298. John Hollander, *Rhyme's Reason,* 33.

299. Freud, *Beyond the Pleasure Principle,* 29.

300. Koestler, *The Act of Creation,* 312. He writes, "Without the message, the rhythm is of course meaningless, in poetry as in science. A monotonous rhythm, for instance, can be either sleepy-making or exciting, according to the message which it carries. . . . Unlike the beat of the tom-tom, or the rattle of the carriage wheels, a strophe of verse does not consist in a simple repetitive rhythm, but in complex patterns of short and long, stressed and light syllables, further complicated by super-imposed patterns of assonance or rhyme. As music has evolved a long way from the simple, repetitive figures of monochords and drums, so the various metric forms in poetry contain their substructure of rhythmic pulsation in an *implied,* and no longer in an explicit form" (313–14).

301. Paul Klee, *The Thinking Eye,* 169.

302. Seymour Chatman, *An Introduction to the Language of Poetry,* 87. He writes, "The events can be any physical occurrence capable of impinging upon

any sense: rhythm is not only auditory . . . but also visual . . . or even tactile. . . . It is not enough to say that meter is a species of rhythm; it is, more exactly, a species of a certain kind of rhythm, namely 'grouped rhythm.' . . . It is possible for the events in rhythm to be precisely equal in all respects of their composition and for all time intervals to be precisely equal. A virtually perfect clock or metronome. . . . This we shall call 'simple' rhythm. On the other hand, some rhythms exhibit not only recurrence, but patterned recurrence. That is, events and time intervals are not equal. . . . One event . . . makes a stronger impression on our ears than the other, which phenomenon we shall call 'prominence'" (87–89).

303. Alfred Corn, *The Poem's Heartbeat,* 5–6. "Both poetry and music use accents to divide passing time into measurable units. . . . Music appeals to the ear through the play of varying pitch, through its rhythm" (3).

304. Mircea Eliade, *Images and Symbols,* 25. Eliade states, "The history of a symbolism . . . is the best introduction to what is called the philosophy of culture. Images, archetypes and symbols are variously lived and valued; and the product of these multiple realizations of them is largely constitutive of the different 'cultural styles' of life" (172).

305. I. A. Richards, *Principles of Literary Criticism,* 139. He argues, "As with rhythm so with meter, we must not think of it as in the words themselves or in the thumping of the drum. It is not *in* the stimulation, it is in our response. Meter adds to all the variously fated expectancies which make up rhythm a definite temporal pattern and its effort is not due to our perceiving a pattern in something outside us, but to our becoming patterned ourselves. With every beat of the meter a tide of anticipation in us turns and swings, setting up as it does so extraordinarily extensive sympathetic reverberations" (139–40).

306. "*'Figures of speech' (imagery)* or *tropes* are word pictures; they are to be found on the *sensory level* of poetry, and they are intended to evoke the senses of taste, touch, sight, smell, hearing, together with the inner 'sense' of feelings. There are four basic kinds of tropes: *descriptions, similes, metaphors,* and *rhetorical tropes*" (Lewis Turco, *The Book of Forms,* 55).

307. Gilbert Ryle, *The Concept of Mind,* 83–84.

308. *hayi ke* (Xhosa)—(a) a decided negative, No! . . . (b) At the commencement of a sentence, it is a strong affirmative. . . ." (Kropf, *A Kafir–English Dictionary,* 147).

309. Olive Schreiner, in a letter to the Rev. J. T. Lloyd, Matjisfontein, October 29, 1892. *The Letters of Olive Schreiner,* edited by S. C. Cronwright-Schreiner.

310. From a letter written by Olive Schreiner to her brother, W. P. Schreiner, dated 1918. Ibid.

311. "Mi alma es una orquestra oculta; no sé qué instrumentos tañe o rechina, cuerdas y harpas, timbales y tambores, dentro de mí. Sólo me conozco como sinfonía." Pessoa, *Selección de textos y análisis de su persamiento,* 23.

312. Rubusana, *Zemk' Inkomo Magwalandini,* 346.

313. Hamilton Hope, magistrate at Quthing, 1877–1878, then with Mhlontlo at Qumbu, was murdered in 1880.

314. From Mdukiswa Tyabashe, "All the Land of the Mpondomise," in Scheub, *The Tongue Is Fire,* 262–68.

315. From the *Cape Mercury,* reprinted in *Grahamstown Journal,* May 12, 1904, an account of the preliminary examination of Mhlontlo.

316. From a lecture by Charles Brownlee to the St. Andrew's Literary Society, King William's Town, May 16, 1887, printed in the *Christian Express* in two parts in April and May, 1889. Brownlee, who died in 1890, was the African administrator and the Cape's first Secretary for Native Affairs. This account is taken from the lecture, titled "A Chapter on the Basuto War," reprinted in Charles Pacalt Brownlee, *Reminiscences of Kafir Life and History, and Other Papers,* 190–221. Relevant passages used here are from pages 213–15, 217, 219–21.

317. A. C. Jordan, *The Wrath of the Ancestors,* 9–10.

318. Charles Brownlee: "a notice I sent to the *[Kaffrarian Watchman]* announcing the death of Hope" (219–21). The final quote is from 2 Samuel, 33–34.

319. Rubusana, *Zemk' Inkomo Magwalandini,* 347.

320. Henri Trilles, *L'âme du Pygmée d'Afrique,* 228. "La jeune mère doit s'abstenir de crier pendant la parturition. Bien plus, elle doit chanter un chant joyeux. Je transcrivis un jour celui-ci après la naissance d'un petit Négrille" (227–28).

Bibliography

Aarne, Antti. *The Types of the Folktale: A Classification and Bibliography.* Translated and enlarged by Stith Thompson. Helsinki: Suomalainen Tiedeakatemia, 1928.

Akutagawa, Ryunosuke. "In a Grove." *Rashomon and Other Stories.* Translated by Takashi Kojima. New York: Liveright, 1952. 19–33.

Akutagawa, Ryunosuke. "Rashomon." *Rashomon and Other Stories.* Translated by Takashi Kojima. New York: Liveright, 1952. 34–44.

Alexander, Lloyd. "The Flat-Heeled Muse." In *Horn Book Reflections: On Children's Books and Reading,* edited by Elinor Whitney Field, 242–247. Boston: Horn Book, 1969.

Alston, William P. "Emotion and Feeling." In *The Encyclopedia of Philosophy,* edited by Paul Edwards, 479–86. New York: Macmillan and Free Press, 1967.

Arewa, Erastus Ojo. "Proverb Usage in a 'Natural' Context and Oral Literary Criticism." *Journal of American Folklore* 38 (1970): 430–37.

Aristotle. *The "Art" of Rhetoric.* Translated by John Henry Freese. London: William Heinemann, 1926.

Aristotle. *Poetics.* Translated by Gerald F. Else. Ann Arbor: University of Michigan Press, 1973.

Arlen, Michael J. *Passage to Ararat.* New York: Farrar, Straus and Giroux, 1975.

Ashton, Hugh. *The Basuto.* London: Oxford University Press, 1952.

Attridge, Derek. *Poetic Rhythm.* Cambridge: Cambridge University Press, 1995.

Auden, W. H. *The Dyer's Hand and Other Essays.* New York: Random House, 1962.

Austin, John Langshaw. *How to Do Things with Words.* Cambridge: Harvard University Press, 1962.

Bascom, William. "Literary Style in Yoruba Riddles." *Journal of American Folklore* 62 (1949): 1–16.

Becker, Peter. *Hill of Destiny: The Life and Times of Moshesh Founder of the Basotho.* London: Longmans, 1969.

Bekker-Nielson, Hans, et al. *Oral Tradition Literary Tradition; A Symposium.* Odense: Odense University Press, 1977.

Bell, Catherine. *Ritual Theory, Ritual Practice.* New York: Oxford University Press, 1992.

Benham, Marion S. *Henry Callaway.* London: Macmillan, 1896.

Benjamin, Walter. *Illuminations*. Translated by Harry Zohn. Glasgow: William Collins Sons, 1973.

Benson, L. "The Literary Character of Anglo-Saxon Formulaic Poetry." *PMLA* 81 (1966): 334–41.

Bernstein, Leonard. *The Unanswered Question: Six Talks at Harvard*. Cambridge: Harvard University Press, 1976.

Bettelheim, Bruno. *The Uses of Enchantment: The Meaning and Importance of Fairy Tales*. New York: Knopf, 1976.

Beuchat, P-D. "Riddles in Bantu." *African Studies* 16 (1957): 133–49.

Binns, C. T. *Dinuzulu: The Death of the House of Shaka*. London: Longmans, Green, 1968.

Black, Max. "Metaphor." *Proceedings of the Aristotelian Society* 65 (1954–1955): 273–94.

Black, Max. *Models and Metaphors: Studies in Language and Philosophy*. Ithaca, N.Y.: Cornell University Press, 1962.

Blacking, John. *How Musical Is Man?* Seattle: University of Washington Press, 1973.

Blacking, John. "The Social Value of Venda Riddles." *African Studies* 20 (1961): 1–32.

Bleek, Dorothea F., ed. *The Mantis and His Friends*. Cape Town: T. Maskew Miller, [1923].

Bleek, W. H. I. Collection. University of Cape Town Library, Manuscripts Division.

Bleek, W. H. I., and Lucy C. Lloyd. *Specimens of Bushman Folklore*. London: G. Allen, 1911.

Boas, Franz. *Primitive Art*. 1927. Reprint, New York: Dover, 1955.

Bodunrin, A. "Leopold Sedar Senghor." *African Statesman* 3, no. 1 (1968): 16–23.

Bokako, Edison M. "Bo-Santagane, An Anthology of Tswana Heroic Verse." Unpublished manuscript prepared under the direction of Professor Z. K. Matthews (Kimberley, 1938). In the collections of Gerard Paul Lestrade and Z. K. Matthews, University of Cape Town Library, Manuscripts Division.

Boland, Eavan. "Poetic Form: A Personal Encounter." In *The Making of a Poem*, edited by Mark Strand and Eavan Boland, xxv–xxix. New York: W. W. Norton, 2000.

Boruah, Bijoy H. *Fiction and Emotion: A Study in Aesthetics and the Philosophy of Mind*. Oxford: Clarendon Press, 1988.

Bosanquet, Bernard. *Three Lectures on Aesthetic*. London: Macmillan, 1915.

Brooks, Cleanth, and Robert Penn Warren. *Understanding Poetry*. New York: Holt, Rinehart and Winston, 1938.

Brown, E. K. *Rhythm in the Novel*. 1950. Reprint, Lincoln: University of Nebraska Press, 1978.

Brownlee, Charles Pacalt. *Reminiscences of Kafir Life and History, and Other Papers*. Lovedale: Lovedale Press, 1896.

Bryant, Mark. *Riddles Ancient and Modern*. New York: Peter Bedrick, 1984.

Budd, Malcolm. *Music and the Emotions: The Philosophical Theories*. London: Routledge and Kegan Paul, 1985.

Budd, Malcolm. "Understanding Music." *Proceedings of the Aristotelian Society* 59 (1985): 233–48.

Bullough, Edward. "'Psychical Distance' as a Factor in Art and as an Aesthetic Principle." *British Journal of Psychology* 5, no. 2 (1912): 87–118.

Burke, Kenneth. *A Grammar of Motives*. New York: Prentice-Hall, 1945.

Burke, Kenneth. *The Philosophy of Literary Form*. 3rd ed. 1941. Reprint, Berkeley: University of California Press, 1973.

Burton, Richard F., ed. and trans. *The Book of the Thousand Nights and a Night: A Plain and Literal Translation of The Arabian Nights Entertainments*. 10 vols. London: The Burton Club, 1885–1886.

Busoni, Ferruccio. *Entwurf einer neuen Aesthetik der Tonkunst*. Frankfurt a. M.: Insel Verlag, 1974.

Bynon, James. "Riddle Telling among the Berbers of Central Morocco." *African Language Studies* 7 (1966): 80–104; 8 (1967): 168–97.

Callaway, Henry. *Nursery Tales, Traditions, and Histories of the Zulus*. Springvale, Natal: John A. Blair, 1868.

Campbell, Joseph. *The Hero with a Thousand Faces*. Princeton: Princeton University Press, 1949.

Casalis, Eugene. *The Basutos; or, Twenty-three Years in South Africa*. London: James Nisbet, 1861. Originally published as *Les Bassoutos; ou, Vingt-trois années de sejour et d'observations au sud de l'Afrique* (Paris: C. Meyrueis, 1859).

Cassirer, Ernst. *An Essay on Man*. New Haven: Yale University Press, 1962.

Cendrars, Blaise. *The African Saga*. Translated by Margery Bianco. New York: Payson and Clarke, 1927.

Chatman, Seymour. *An Introduction to the Language of Poetry*. Boston: Houghton Mifflin, 1968.

Ciardi, John, and Miller Williams. *How Does a Poem Mean?* 2nd ed. Boston: Houghton Mifflin, 1975.

Coleridge, Samuel Taylor. *Biographia Literaria; or Biographical Sketches of My Literary Life and Opinions*. 2 vols. London: Rest Fenner, 1817.

Collier, James Lincoln. *Practical Music Theory: How Music Is Put Together from Bach to Rock*. New York: W. W. Norton, 1970.

Collingwood, R. G. *The Principles of Art*. Oxford: Clarendon Press, 1938.

Cooke, Deryck. *The Language of Music*. London: Oxford University Press, 1959.

Cope, Trevor, ed. *Izibongo: Zulu Praise Poems*. Oxford: Clarendon Press, 1968.

Copland, Aaron. *What to Listen for in Music*. 1939. Reprint, New York: Mentor, 1953.

Corn, Alfred. *The Poem's Heartbeat: A Manual of Prosody*. Ashland, Ore.: Story Line Press, 1998.

Courtney, Richard. *Drama and Feeling: An Aesthetic Theory*. Montreal: McGill-Queen's University Press, 1995.

Cronwright-Schreiner, S. C. *The Letters of Olive Schreiner, 1876–1920*. London: T. Fisher Unwin, 1924.

Curschmann, M. "Oral Poetry in Mediaeval English, French, and German Literature: Some Notes on Recent Research." *Speculum* 42 (1967): 36–52.

Dallin, Leon. *Listeners Guide to Musical Understanding*. Dubuque: William C. Brown, 1968.

Damane, M., and P. B. Sanders. *Lithoko: Sotho Praise-poems*. Oxford: Clarendon Press, 1974.

Damasio, Antonio R. *The Feeling of What Happens: Body and Emotion in the Making of Consciousness*. New York: Harcourt Brace, 1999.

Dammann, R. M. J. "Emotion and Fiction." *British Journal of Aesthetics* 32, no. 1 (1992): 13–20.

Danto, Arthur. *The Transfiguration of the Commonplace*. Cambridge: Harvard University Press, 1981.

Davidson, Donald. "What Metaphors Mean." *Critical Inquiry* 5 (1978): 31–47.

Davies, Stephen. "The Expression of Emotion in Music." *Mind* 89 (1980): 67–86.

Davies, Stephen. *Musical Meaning and Expression*. Ithaca, N.Y.: Cornell University Press, 1994.

Davies, Stephen. "The Rationality of Aesthetic Responses." *British Journal of Aesthetics* 23, no. 1 (1983): 38–47.

de Caro, F. A., and W. K. McNeil. *American Proverb Literature: A Bibliography*. Bloomington: Folklore Forum, 1970.

Delafosse, Maurice. *Essai de manuel de la langue agni*. Paris: Libraire africaine et coloniale, 1900.

Dennett, R. E. *At the Back of the Black Man's Mind, or Notes on the Kingly Office in West Africa*. London: Macmillan, 1906.

Dennett, Richard Edward. *Notes on the Folklore of the Fjort (French Congo)*. London: David Nutt, for the Folk-lore Society, 1898.

De Vries, Jan. *Heroic Song and Heroic Legend*. Translated by B. J. Timmer. London: Oxford University Press, 1963.

Dickey, James. *Metaphor as Pure Adventure*. Washington, D.C.: Library of Congress, 1968.

Dixon, John W., Jr. "The Metaphoric Transformation, An Essay on the Psychology of the Imagination." *Sociological Analysis* 34, no. 1 (1973): 56–74.

Djebar, Assia. *Fantasia: An Algerian Cavalcade*. Translated by Dorothy S. Blair. Portsmouth, N.H.: Heinemann, 1993. Originally published as *L'amour, la fantasia* (Paris: Éditions Jean-Claude Lattès, 1985).

Doob, Leonard, ed. *Ants Will Not Eat Your Fingers*. New York: Walker, 1972.

Dorson, Richard M., ed. *African Folklore*. Garden City, N.Y.: Anchor Books, 1972.

Dryden, John. "Song for St. Cecilia's Day." *The Poems of John Dryden*. Edited by James Kinsley. Vol. 2, 538–39. Oxford: Clarendon Press, 1958.

Dundes, Alan. *Cinderella: A Folklore Casebook*. New York: Routledge, 1993.

Dundes, Alan, and Erastus Ojo Arewa. "Proverbs and the Ethnography of Speaking Folklore." *American Anthropologist* 66 (1964): 70–85.

Edwards, Mrs. S. H., ed. "Kgolodikane." *Folk-Lore Journal* 1, no. 5 (1879), 110–17.

Eliade, Mircea. *Images and Symbols: Studies in Religious Symbolism.* Translated by Philip Mairet. 1952. Reprint, Princeton: Princeton University Press, 1991.

Eliade, Mircea. *Myth and Reality.* Translated by Willard R. Trask. 1963. Reprint, New York: Harper and Row, 1968.

Eliade, Mircea. *Rites and Symbols of Initiation: The Mysteries of Birth and Rebirth.* Translated by Willard R. Trask. 1958. Reprint, New York: Harper and Row, 1965.

Ellenberger, D. Fred. *History of the Basuto, Ancient and Modern.* London: Caxton, 1912.

Ellwood, Robert. *The Politics of Myth: A Study of C. G. Jung, Mircea Eliade, and Joseph Campbell.* Albany: State University of New York Press, 1999.

Fernandez, James W. "Reflections on Looking into Mirrors." *Semiotica* 30, no. 1/2 (1980): 27–39.

Fischer, J. L., and Teigo Yoshida. "The Nature of Speech According to Japanese Proverbs." *Journal of American Folklore* 81 (1968): 34–43.

Forster, E. M. *Aspects of the Novel.* New York: Harcourt Brace and World, 1927.

Fraisse, Paul. "The Emotions." In *Motivation, Emotion and Personality.* Vol. 5 of *Experimental Psychology, Its Scope and Method,* 102–91. Edited by Paul Fraisse and Jean Piaget, and translated by Madame Alain Spillmann. London: Routledge and Kegan Paul, 1968. Originally published as *Motivation, emotion et personnalité,* vol. 5 of *Traité de psychologie expérimentale* (Paris: Presses Universitaires de France, 1963).

Freud, Sigmund. *Beyond the Pleasure Principle.* Translated by James Strachey. New York: Liveright, 1950.

Frost, William. "Shakespeare's Rituals and the Opening of *King Lear.*" *The Hudson Review* 10, no. 4 (1957–1958): 577–85.

Fussell, Paul. *Poetic Meter and Poetic Form.* Rev. ed. New York: McGraw-Hill, 1979.

Fuze, Magema M. *The Black People and Whence They Came.* Translated by H. C. Lugg. Pietermaritzburg: University of Natal Press, and Durban: Killie Campbell Africana Library, 1979. Originally published as *Abantu Abamnyama Lapa Bavela Ngakona* (Pietermaritzburg: City Printing Works, 1922).

Gandz, Salomon. *The Dawn of Literature: Prolegomena to a History of Unwritten Literature. Osiris* 7 (1939): 261–522.

Gass, William H. *Fiction and the Figures of Life.* Boston: Nonpareil Books, 1980.

Gatz, Felix M. *Musik-äesthetik in ihren Hauptrichtungen.* Stuttgart: F. Enke, 1929.

Geertz, Clifford. *The Interpretation of Cultures.* New York: Basic Books, 1973.

Georges, Robert A., and Alan Dundes. "Toward a Structural Definition of the Riddle." *Journal of American Folklore* 76 (1963): 111–18.

Gibson, J. Y. *The Story of the Zulus.* London: Longmans, Green, 1911.

Gombrich, E. H., J. Hochberg, and Max Black. *Art, Perception, and Reality*. Baltimore: Johns Hopkins University Press, 1972.

Goodwin, Richard N. "Debate Tips from J.F.K." *New York Times,* September 30, 2000, A27.

Gowlett, Derek F. "Common Bantu Riddles." *African Studies* 34 (1975): 79–145.

Gowlett, Derek F. "A Structural Typology for Bantu Riddles." *African Studies* 38 (1979): 47–65.

Grant, E. W. "The Izibongo of the Zulu Chiefs." *Bantu Studies* 3, no. 3 (1929): 201–44.

Graves, Robert. *Poetic Unreason and Other Studies*. New York: Biblo and Tannen, 1968.

Green, O. H. "Emotions and Belief." *Studies in the Philosophy of Mind* 6 (1972): 24–40.

Green, Thomas A., and W. J. Pepicello. "The Folk Riddle: A Redefinition of Terms." *Western Folklore* 38 (1979): 3–20.

Green, Thomas A., and W. J. Pepicello. "The Riddle Process." *Journal of American Folklore* 97 (1984): 189–203.

Green, Thomas A., and W. J. Pepicello. "Sight and Spelling Riddles." *Journal of American Folklore* 93 (1980): 23–34.

Green, Thomas A., and W. J. Pepicello. "Wit in Riddling: A Linguistic Perspective." *Genre* 11 (1978): 1–13.

Griaule, Marcel, and Germaine Dieterlen. *Le renard pâle*. Paris: Institut d'ethnologie, 1965.

Guiart, Jean. "Multiple Levels of Meaning in Myth." Translated by John Freeman. In *Mythology,* edited by Pierre Maranda, 111–26. Harmondsworth: Penguin, 1972.

Guthrie, Jerry L. "Self-deception and Emotional Response to Fiction." *British Journal of Aesthetics* 21, no. 1 (1981): 65–75.

Hadebe, Stanley B. "A Brief Survey of Zulu Riddles." *Limi* 4 (1968): 27–37.

Hall, Donald. *The Pleasures of Poetry*. New York: Harper and Row, 1971.

Hall, Donald. *Poetry: The Unsayable Said.* Port Townsend, Wash.: Copper Canyon Press, 1993.

Hamnett, Ian. "Ambiguity, Classification and Change: The Function of Riddles." *Man* 2 (1967): 379–92.

Hanna, Judith Lynne. *To Dance Is Human: A Theory of Nonverbal Communication.* Austin: University of Texas Press, 1979.

Hanslick, Eduard. *Musical Criticisms, 1946–99.* Translated and edited by Henry Pleasants. Rev. ed. Harmondsworth: Penguin, 1963.

Hanslick, Eduard. *On the Musically Beautiful: A Contribution towards the Revisions of the Aesthetics of Music.* Translated and edited by Geoffrey Payzant. Indianapolis: Hackett, 1986. Originally published as *Vom Musikalisch-Schöen: ein Beitrag zur Revision der Aesthetik der Tonkunst* (Leipzig: J. A. Barth, 1881).

Haring, Lee. "On Knowing the Answer." *Journal of American Folklore* 87 (1974): 197–207.

Harries, Lyndon. "The Riddle in Africa." *Journal of American Folklore* 84 (1971): 377–93.

Hartshorne, Charles. *The Philosophy and Psychology of Sensation*. Chicago: University of Chicago Press, 1934.

Hewitt, Don. *Tell Me a Story: Fifty Years and 60 Minutes in Television*. New York: PublicAffairs, 2001.

Himmelheber, Hans. *Aura Poku; Mythen, Tiergeschichten und Sagen Sprichwörter, Fabeln und Rátsel*. Eisenach: Erich Röth-Verlag, 1951.

Hindemith, Paul. *A Composer's World: Horizons and Limitations*. Cambridge: Harvard University Press, 1952.

Høeg, Peter. *Smilla's Sense of Snow*. Translated by Tiina Nunnally. New York: Farrar Straus and Giroux, 1993.

Hoffer, Charles R. *The Understanding of Music*. Belmont, Calif.: Wadsworth, 1967.

Hollander, John. *Rhyme's Reason*. New Haven: Yale University Press, 1989.

Housman, A. E. *The Name and Nature of Poetry: The Leslie Stephen Lecture Delivered at Cambridge 9 May 1933*. Cambridge: Cambridge University Press, 1933.

Jackson, Rosemary. *Fantasy: The Literature of Subversion*. London: Methuen, 1981.

Jacottet, Edouard. *Litsomo tsa Basotho*. 2 vols. 1911. Reprint, Morija: Sesuto Book Depot, 1941.

Jacottet, Edouard. "Semumu et Semumunyane." *Revue des Traditions Populaires* 3 (1888): 654–62.

Jacottet, Edouard. *The Treasury of Ba-Suto Lore*. Morija: Sesuto Book Depot, 1908.

James, William. "What Is an Emotion?" *Mind* 9 (1884): 188–205.

Jinarajadasa, Curuppumullage. *Art and the Emotions*. Kila, Mont.: Kessinger Publishing Co., n.d. Reprint, London: Theosophical Publishing House, n.d.

Johnston, Harry. *The Uganda Protectorate*. 2 vols. London: Hutchinson, 1904.

Jordan, A. C. *Towards an African Literature: The Emergence of Literary Form in Xhosa*. Berkeley: University of California Press, 1973.

Jordan, A. C. *The Wrath of the Ancestors*. Translated by A. C. Jordan and Priscilla P. Jordan. Lovedale: Lovedale Press, 1980.

Jourdain, Robert. *Music, the Brain, and Ecstasy: How Music Captures Our Imagination*. New York: William Morrow, 1997.

Joyce, James. *Ulysses*. New York: Random House, 1934.

Joyce, James. *Ulysses*. A critical and synoptic edition prepared by Hans Walter Gabler. New York: Garland, 1984.

Junod, Henri Alexandre. *Les BaRonga; étude ethnographique sur les indigénes de la baie de Delagoa*. Attinger: Neuchâtel, 1898.

Kallen, Jeffrey L., and Carol M Eastman. "'I Went to Mombasa, There I Met an Old Woman . . .': Structure and Meaning in Swahili Riddles." *Journal of American Folklore* 92 (1979): 418–44.

Kaye, William Kehale. "Kafir Legends and History." Manuscript 172c, pp. 117–31. Manuscript Division, University of Cape Town Library.

Keller, Hans. "Closer Towards a Theory of Music." *Listener* (February 18, 1971): 218–19.

Keller, Hans. "Towards a Theory of Music." *Listener* (June 11, 1970): 795–96.

Kinzie, Mary. *A Poet's Guide to Poetry*. Chicago: University of Chicago Press, 1999.

Kirk, G. S. *Myth: Its Meaning and Function in Ancient and Other Cultures*. Cambridge: Cambridge University Press, 1970.

Kirk, G. S. *The Nature of Greek Myths*. Harmondsworth: Penguin Books, 1974.

Kittay, Eva Feder. *Metaphor: Its Cognitive Force and Linguistic Structure*. Oxford: Clarendon Press, 1987.

Klee, Paul. *The Thinking Eye*. Vol. 1 of *Notebooks*. Translated by Ralph Manheim. Edited by Jürg Spiller. New York: Wittenborn Art Books, 1961.

Knight, G. Wilson. *The Wheel of Fire*. London: Methuen, 1949.

Koestler, Arthur. *The Act of Creation*. New York: Dell, 1967.

Köngäs Maranga, Elli. "The Logic of Riddles." In *Structural Analysis of Oral Tradition,* edited by Pierre Maranda and Elli Köngäs Maranda, 189–232. Philadelphia: University of Pennsylvania Press, 1971.

Köngäs Maranda, Elli. "Riddles and Riddling: An Introduction." *Journal of American Folklore* 89 (1976): 127–37.

Köngäs Maranda, Elli. "Theory and Practice of Riddle Analysis." *Journal of American Folklore* 84 (1971): 51–61.

Köngäs Maranda, Elli. "A Tree Grows: Transformations of a Riddle Metaphor." In *Structural Models in Folklore and Transformational Essays,* 116–39. The Hague: Mouton, 1971.

Kropf, Albert. *A Kafir–English Dictionary*. Edited by Robert Godfrey. Lovedale: Lovedale Mission Press, 1915.

Lahr, John. "The Forest and the Trees." *New Yorker,* April 12, 1993, 105–7.

Lakoff, George. "The Contemporary Theory of Metaphor." In *Metaphor and Thought,* 2nd ed., edited by Andrew Ortony, 202–51. Cambridge: Cambridge University Press, 1993.

Lamula, Petros. *Isabelo sikaZulu*. Pietermaritzburg: Lincroft Books, 1963.

Lang, Andrew. *The Orange Fairy Book*. New York: Longmans, Green, 1906.

Langer, Susanne K. *Feeling and Form: A Theory of Art*. New York: Charles Scribner's Sons, 1953.

Langer, Susanne K. *Mind: An Essay on Human Feeling*. 3 vols. Baltimore: Johns Hopkins University Press, 1967.

Layton, Monique J. "Luba and Finnish Riddles: A Double Analysis." *Journal of American Folklore* 89 (1976): 239–48.

Leighton, Stephen R. "Feelings and Emotion." *Review of Metaphysics* 38 (December 1984): 303–20.

Lekgothoane, S. K. "Praises of Animals in Northern Sotho." *Bantu Studies* 12 (1938): 189–213.

Lessing, Gotthold Ephraim. *Laocoön; Nathan the Wise; Minna von Barnhelm.* New York: Dent, 1930.

Lestrade, Gerard Paul. "Bantu Praise-Poems." *The Critic* 4, no. 1 (October 1935): 1–10.

Livingstone, David. *Missionary Travels and Researches in South Africa.* London: Murray, 1857.

MacLeisch, Archibald. *Poetry and Experience.* Baltimore: Penguin Books, 1964.

Mafeje, Archie. "The Role of the Bard in a Contemporary African Community." *Journal of African Languages* 6, no. 3 (1967): 193–223.

Maja-Pearce, Adewale. "Binding the Wounds." *Index on Censorship* 5 (1996): 50.

Mali, Jeremiah. "The Story of Umshalishali and Umlomo'sibucu." Edited by W. Ireland. *Folk-Lore Journal* 2, no. 1 (January 1880): 6–11.

Mangoaela, Z. D. *Lithoko tsa Morena a Basotho.* Morija: Sesuto Book Depot, 1921.

Márquez, Gabriel García. Interview by Peter H. Stone. In *Writers at Work: The "Paris Review" Interviews,* edited by George Plimpton. 6th ser., 313–39. New York: Viking Press, 1984.

Matravers, Derek. *Art and Emotion.* Oxford: Clarendon Press, 1998.

Matsebula, J. S. M. *Isakhiwo zamaSwazi.* Johannesburg: Afrikaanse Pers Boekhandel, 1952.

McKnight, Robert K. "Proverbs of Palau." *Journal of American Folklore* 81 (1968): 3–33.

Messenger, John C. "Anang Proverb-Riddles." *Journal of American Folklore* 73 (1960): 225–35.

Meyer, Leonard B. *Emotion and Meaning in Music.* Chicago: University of Chicago Press, 1956.

Moloto, Ernest Sedumeli. "The Growth and Tendencies of Tswana Poetry." D. Litt. and Phil. diss., University of South Africa, Pretoria, 1970.

Moore, Sally F., and Barbara G Myerhoff. *Secular Ritual.* Assen: Van Gorcum, 1977.

Morris, Donald R. *The Washing of the Spears.* London: Jonathan Cape, 1966.

Morris, H. F. *The Heroic Recitations of the Bahima of Ankole.* Oxford: Clarendon Press, 1964.

Morrow, Lance. "It takes time to sort the spin from the truth." TIME.com. June 5, 2000. <http://www.cnn.com/2000/US/06/05/morrow6_5.a.tm/index.html>.

Mqhayi, S. E. Krune. *Inzuzo.* Johannesburg: Witwatersrand University Press, 1957.

Mqhayi, S. E. Krune. *Ityala Lamawele* (The Case of the Twins). Lovedale: Lovedale Press, 1931.

Murray, Gilbert. *Five Stages of Greek Religion.* New York: Columbia University Press, 1925.

Murray, Henry A., ed. *Myth and Mythmaking.* Boston: Beacon Press, 1960.

Murray, Henry A. "The Possible Nature of a 'Mythology' to Come." In *Myth and Mythmaking,* edited by Henry A. Murray, 300–353. Boston: Beacon Press, 1960.

Myerhoff, Barbara. "Rites of Passage: Process and Paradox." In *Celebration, Studies in Festivity and Ritual,* edited by Victor Turner, 109–35. Washington, D.C.: Smithsonian Institute Press, 1982.

Ndawo, Henry Masilo. *Izibongo Zenkosi Zama-Hlubi nezama-Bhaca* (Oral Poetry of Hlubi and Bhaca Chiefs). Mariannhill: Mariannhill Mission Press, 1928.

Nketia, J. K. Kwabena. "The Musical Heritage of Africa." *Daedalus* 103, no. 2 (1974), 151–61.

Novitz, David. "Fiction, Imagination and Emotion." *Journal of Aesthetics and Art Criticism* 38 (1980): 279–88.

Nyembezi, C. L. Sibusiso. "The Historical Background to the Izibongo of the Zulu Military Age." *African Studies* 7, nos. 2–3 (1948): 110–25; 7, no. 4 (1948): 157–74.

Nyembezi, C. L. Sibusiso. *Izibongo Zamakhosi* (Oral Poetry of the Kings). Pietermaritzburg: Shuter and Shooter, 1958.

Oates, Joyce Carol. "The Mystery of JonBénet Ramsey." *New York Review of Books* 46, no. 11 (June 24, 1999): 31–32, 34–37.

Oliver, Mary. *A Poetry Handbook.* New York: Harcourt Brace, 1994.

Ortony, Andrew, ed. *Metaphor and Thought.* 2nd ed. Cambridge: Cambridge University Press, 1993.

Paine, Albert Bigelow. *Mark Twain, a Biography: The Personal and Literary Life of Samuel Langhorne Clemens.* New York: Harper and Brothers, 1912.

Paz, Octavio. *Convergences: Essays in Art and Literature.* Translated by Helen Lane. New York: Harcourt Brace Jovanovich, 1987.

Paz, Octavio. "Literature and Literalness." In *Convergences: Essays in Art and Literature,* translated by Helen Lane, 184–200. New York: Harcourt Brace Jovanovich, 1987.

Paz, Octavio. "The Verbal Contract." In *Convergences: Essays in Art and Literature,* translated by Helen Lane, 143–71. New York: Harcourt Brace Jovanovich, 1987.

Pessoa, Fernando. *Selección de textos y análisis de su persamiento, Anthropos, Revista de documentación científica de la cultura.* Barcelona: Anthropos, 1987.

Petsch, Robert. *Neue Beiträge zur Kenntnis des Volksrätsels.* Berlin: Mayer and Müller, 1899.

Pinsky, Robert. *The Sounds of Poetry.* New York: Farrar, Straus and Giroux, 1998.

Plato. *The Republic.* Translated by Alexander Kerr. Chicago: Charles H. Kerr, 1918.

Pope, Alexander. "An Essay on Criticism [1711]." In *Literary Criticism of Alexander Pope,* edited by Bertrand A. Goldgar, 3–22. Lincoln: University of Nebraska Press, 1965.

Prescott, Frederick Clarke. *Poetry and Myth.* New York: Macmillan, 1927.

Propp, Vladimir. *Morphology of the Folktale.* 2nd ed. Edited by Svatava Pirkova-Jakobson. Translated by Laurence Scott. Austin: University of Texas Press, 1968.

Propp, Vladimir. "Transformations in Fairy Tales." Translated by Petra Morrison. In *Mythology,* edited by Pierre Maranda, 139–50. Harmondsworth: Penguin, 1972.

Radin, Paul. *The Trickster: A Study in American Indian Mythology.* New York: Philosophical Library, 1956.

Raglan, FitzRoy Richard Somerset. *The Hero: A Study in Tradition, Myth, and Drama.* New York: Oxford University Press, 1937.

Rao, V. Narayana. "Problems of Terminology in Poetics." Paper presented at the conference, "In Search of Terminology," Central Institute of Indian Languages, Mysore, 1982.

Rappaport, Roy A. *Ecology, Meaning and Religion.* Richmond, Calif.: Atlantic Books, 1979.

Richards, I. A. *The Philosophy of Rhetoric.* 1936. Reprint, New York: Oxford University Press, 1965.

Richards, I. A. *Principles of Literary Criticism.* New York: Harcourt Brace, 1925.

Ricoeur, Paul. *The Rule of Metaphor.* Translated by Robert Czerny, et al. Toronto: University of Toronto Press, 1977. Originally published as *La métaphore vive* (Paris: Éditions du Seuil, 1975).

Roberts, Brian. *The Zulu Kings.* 1974. Reprint, London: Sphere Books, 1977.

Roberts, Robert C. "What Emotions Is: A Sketch." *Philosophical Review* 97 (April 1988): 183–209.

Roethke, Theodore. *The Far Field.* Garden City, N.Y.: Doubleday, 1964.

Roscoe, John. *The Baganda: An Account of Their Native Customs and Beliefs.* London: Macmillan, 1911.

Rubusana, W. B. *Zemk' Inkomo Magwalandini.* London: Butler and Tanner, 1911.

Ryle, Gilbert. *The Concept of Mind.* London: Hutchinson, 1949.

Sallustius. "On the Gods and the World." In *Five Stages of Greek Religion,* by Gilbert Murray, 214–67. New York: Columbia University Press, 1925.

Samuelson, Robert Charles Azariah. *The King Cetywayo Zulu Dictionary.* Durban: Commercial Printing, 1923.

Samuelson, Robert Charles Azariah. *Long Long Ago.* Durban: Knox, 1929.

Santayana, George. *The Life of Reason.* Vol. 4. New York: Charles Scribner's Sons, 1936.

Savory, Phyllis. *Basuto Fireside Tales.* Cape Town: Howard Timmins, 1962.

Savory, Phyllis. *Zulu Fireside Tales.* Cape Town: Howard Timmins, 1964.

Schapera, Isaac. *Praise-poems of Tswana Chiefs.* Oxford: Clarendon Press, 1965.

Schechner, Richard. "From Ritual to Theatre and Back." In *Ritual, Play, and Performance: Readings in the Social Sciences/Theatre,* edited by Richard Schechner and Mady Schuman, 196–222. New York: Seabury Press, 1976.

Scheub, Harold. *African Oral Narratives, Proverbs, Riddles, Poetry and Song: An Annotated Bibliography.* Boston: G. K. Hall, 1977.

Scheub, Harold. *A Dictionary of African Mythology: The Mythmaker as Storyteller.* New York: Oxford University Press, 2000.

Scheub, Harold. "A Review of African Oral Traditions and Literature." *African Studies Review* 28, no. 2/3 (1985): 1–72.
Scheub, Harold. *Story*. Madison: University of Wisconsin Press, 1998.
Scheub, Harold. *The Tongue Is Fire*. Madison: University of Wisconsin Press, 1996.
Scheub, Harold. "Translation of Oral Narrative-performance to the Written Word." *Yearbook of Comparative and General Literature* 20 (1971): 28–36.
Scheub, Harold. *The Xhosa Ntsomi*. Oxford: Clarendon Press, 1975.
Schorer, Mark. *William Blake: The Politics of Vision*. New York: Vintage Books, 1959.
Schreiner, Olive. *The Story of an African Farm*. London: Chapman and Hall, 1883.
Scott, Charles T. "On Defining the Riddle: The Problem of a Structural Unit." *Genre* 2 (1969): 129–42.
Scruton, Roger. *The Aesthetics of Music*. Oxford: Clarendon Press, 1997.
Scruton, Roger. *The Aesthetic Understanding*. London: Methuen, 1983.
Searle, John R. *Speech Acts: An Essay in the Philosophy of Language*. Cambridge: Cambridge University Press, 1970.
Seitel, Peter. "Proverbs: A Social Use of Metaphor." *Genre* 2 (1969): 143–61.
Senghor, Léopold Sédar. "Comme les lamantins vont boire a la source." In *Liberté I, Négritude et humanism*, 218–27. Paris: Éditions du Seuil, 1964.
Senior, M. Mary. "Some Mende Proverbs." *Africa* 17 (1947): 205.
Shepherd, R. H. W. *Bantu Literature and Life*. Lovedale: Lovedale Press, 1955.
Sibree, James, Jr. "Malagasy Folk-Tales." *Folk-Lore Journal* 2 (1884): 161–66.
Sittard-Hamburg, Josef. "Die Musik im Lichte der Illusions-ästhetik." *Die Musik* 10 (1903): 243–52.
Smith, Andrew. *The Diary of Dr. Andrew Smith, 1934–1835*. Edited by P. R. Kirby. 2 vols. Cape Town: Van Riebeeck Society, 1940.
Soga, J. Henderson. *The South-eastern Bantu*. Johannesburg: Witwatersrand University Press, 1930.
Solomon, Robert C. "The Philosophy of Emotions." In *Handbook of Emotions*, edited by Michael Lewis and Jeannette M. Haviland, 3–15. New York: Guilford, 1993.
Soskice, Janet Martin. *Metaphor and Religious Language*. Oxford: Clarendon Press, 1985.
Soyinka, Wole. *Myth, Literature and the African World*. Cambridge: Cambridge University Press, 1976.
Stevens, Wallace. *Collected Poetry and Prose*. Edited by Frank Kermode and Joan Richardson. New York: Library of America, 1997.
Stevens, Wallace. "Peter Quince at the Clavier." In *Harmonium*, 153–57. New York: Alfred A. Knopf, 1947.
Storr, Anthony. *Music and the Mind*. New York: Free Press, 1992.
Strand, Mark. "On Becoming a Poet." In *The Making of a Poem*, edited by Mark Strand and Eavan Boland, xxii–xxiv. New York: W. W. Norton and Co., 2000.

Stuart, James. *A History of the Zulu Rebellion, 1906, and of Dinuzulu's Arrest, Trial and Expatriation*. London: Macmillan, 1913.

Stuart, James. *uBaxolele*. London: Longmans, Green, 1924.

Stuart, James. *uHlangakula*. London: Longmans, Green, 1924.

Stuart, James. *uKulumetule*. London: Longmans, Green, 1925.

Stuart, James. *uThulasizwe*. London: Longmans, Green, 1934.

Stuart, James. *uVusezakithi*. London: Longmans, Green, 1926.

Sullivan, Lawrence E. "Sound and Senses: Toward a Hermeneutics of Performance." *History of Religions* 26, no. 1 (August 1986): 1–33.

Sutton-Smith, Brian. "A Developmental Structural Account of Riddles." In *Speech Play: Research and Resources for the Study of Linguistic Creativity*, edited by Barbara Kirschenblatt-Gimblett, 111–19. Philadelphia: University of Pennsylvania Press, 1976.

Tambiah, S. J. "A Performative Approach to Ritual." *Proceedings of the British Academy* 65 (1979): 113–69.

Taylor, Archer. *English Riddles from Oral Tradition*. Berkeley: University of California Press, 1951.

Taylor, Archer. "The Riddle." *California Folklore Quarterly* 2 (1943): 129–47.

Thalberg, Irving. "Emotion and Thought." *American Philosophical Quarterly* 1, no. 1 (January 1964): 45–55.

Theal, George McCall. *Kaffir Folklore: A Selection from the Traditional Tales Current among the People Living on the Eastern Border of the Cape Colony*. London: S. Sonnenschein, Le Bas and Lowrey, 1886.

Thompson, Stith. *The Folktale*. New York: Rinehart and Winston, 1946.

Thompson, Stith. *Motif-index of Folk-literature: A Classification of Narrative Elements in Folk-tales, Ballads, Myths, Fables, Mediaeval Romances, Exempla, Fabliaux, Jest-books, and Local Legend*. Helsinki: Suomalainen Tiedeakatemia, 1932–1936. Revised editon, Bloomington: Indiana University Press, 1955–1958.

Thoreau, Henry David. *A Week on the Concord and Merrimack Rivers; Walden, or, Life in the Woods; The Maine Woods; Cape Cod*. New York: Library of America, 1985.

Tolkien, J. R. R. *Tree and Leaf*. London: George Allen and Unwin, 1964.

Trask, Willard R., ed. *The Unwritten Song*. Vol. 1. New York: Macmillan, 1966.

"Trial of Umhlonhlo." *Grahamstown Journal*, May 12, 17, 19, 1904.

Trilles, Henri. *L'âme du Pygmée d'Afrique*. Paris: Éditions du Cerf, 1945.

Turbayne, Colin Murray. *The Myth of Metaphor*. New Haven: Yale University Press, 1962.

Turco, Lewis. *The Book of Forms: A Handbook of Poetics*. 3rd ed. Hanover: University Press of New England, 2000.

Tyabashe, Mdukiswa. "All the Land of the Mpondomise." In *The Tongue Is Fire*, by Harold Scheub, 227–74. Madison: University of Wisconsin Press, 1996.

Tylden, G. *The Rise of the Basuto*. Cape Town: Juta, 1950.

Updike, John. Interview by Charles Thomas Samuels. In *Writers at Work: The "Paris Review" Interviews,* edited by George Plimpton. 4th ser., 425–54. New York: Viking Press, 1976.

Van der Merwe, D. F. "Hurutshe Poems." *Bantu Studies* 15 (1941): 307–37.

Van Gennep, Arnold. *The Rites of Passage.* Translated by Monika B. Vizedom and Gabrielle L. Caffee. Chicago: University of Chicago Press, 1960. Originally published as *Les rites de passage* (Paris: Émile Nourry, 1909).

Van Warmelo, N. J. *History of Matiwane and the AmaNgwane Tribe, as Told by Msebenzi to His Kinsman Albert Hlongwane.* Pretoria: Government Printer, 1938.

Van Zyl, H. J. "Praises in Northern Sotho." *Bantu Studies* 15 (1941): 119–56.

Vickery, John B. *Myths and Texts: Strategies of Incorporation and Displacement.* Baton Rouge: Louisiana State University Press, 1983.

Vilakazi, Benedict Wallet. "The Conception and Development of Poetry in Zulu." *Bantu Studies* 12 (1938): 105–34.

Vilakazi, Benedict Wallet. "The Oral and Written Literature in Nguni." D. Litt. diss., University of the Witwatersrand, Johannesburg, 1945.

Von Lange, Konrad. *Das wesen der kunst; grundzüge einer realistischen kunstlehre.* Berlin: G. Grote, 1901.

Welsh, Andrew. *Roots of Lyric; Primitive Poetry and Modern Poetics.* Princeton: Princeton University Press, 1978.

Werner, Alice. *Myths and Legends of the Bantu.* London: George G. Harrap, 1933.

Westermann, Diedrich. *Grammatik der Ewe-Sprache.* Berlin: D. Reimer, 1907.

Wheelwright, Philip. *Metaphor and Reality.* Bloomington: Indiana University Press, 1962.

White, Hayden. *The Content of the Form: Narrative Discourse and Historical Representation.* Baltimore: Johns Hopkins Press, 1987.

White, Roger M. *The Structure of Metaphor: The Way the Language of Metaphor Works.* Oxford: Blackwell, 1996.

Whitman, Walt. *Leaves of Grass* (1891–92). *Complete Poetry and Collected Prose.* Edited by Justin Kaplan. New York: Library of America, 1982.

Wordsworth, William. Preface to *Lyrical Ballads* (1800 edition). In *The Prose Works of William Wordsworth,* edited by W. J. B. Owen and Jane Worthington Smyser. Oxford: Clarendon Press, 1974.

Young, T. Cullen. "Some Proverbs of the Tumbuka-Nkamanga Peoples of the Northern Province of Nyasaland." *Africa* 4 (1931): 344–45.

Zenani, Nongenile Masithathu. "And So I Grew Up, The Autobiography of Nongenile Masithathu Zenani." In *Life Histories of African Women,* edited by Patricia W. Romero, 7–46. London: The Ashfield Press, 1988.

Zenani, Nongenile Masithathu. "The Necessary Clown." In *The Tongue Is Fire,* by Harold Scheub, 61–77. Madison: University of Wisconsin Press, 1996.

Zenani, Nongenile Masithathu. *The World and the Word.* Edited by Harold Scheub. Madison: University of Wisconsin Press, 1992.

Zillman, Lawrence John. *The Art and Craft of Poetry*. New York: Macmillan, 1966.

Zipes, Jack. *The Trials and Tribulations of Little Red Riding Hood*. New York: Routledge, 1993.

Zuckerkandl, Victor. *Sound and Symbol: Music and the External World*. Translated by Willard R. Trask. Princeton: Princeton University Press, 1956.

Index